9.20

D1369578

Second Edition Understanding and Guiding Young Children

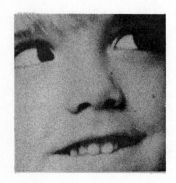

Understanding and Guiding

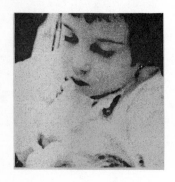

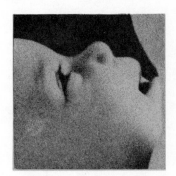

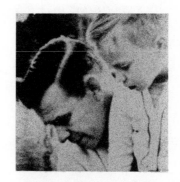
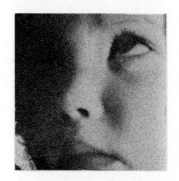

Young Children

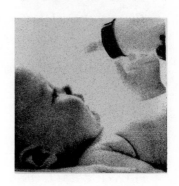

KATHERINE READ BAKER

Former Head, Department of Family Life
and Home Administration
Oregon State University

XENIA F. FANE

Assistant Director of Home Economics
New York City Public Schools

PRENTICE-HALL, INC., ENGLEWOOD CLIFFS, NEW JERSEY

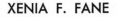

RELATED PRENTICE-HALL BOOKS

BUILDING YOUR LIFE, by Judson T. Landis and Mary G. Landis

EXPLORING HOME AND FAMILY LIVING, by Henrietta Fleck and
Louise Fernandez

FOOD AND YOUR FUTURE, by Ruth Bennett White

LIVING WITH YOUR FAMILY, by Henrietta Fleck, Louise Fernandez,
and Elizabeth Munves

PERSONAL ADJUSTMENT, MARRIAGE, AND FAMILY LIVING,
by Judson T. Landis and Mary G. Landis

YOU AND YOUR FOOD, by Ruth Bennett White

Front matter and chapter opening design by Gary Schuermann.

PRENTICE-HALL INTERNATIONAL, INC., London
PRENTICE-HALL OF AUSTRALIA, PTY. LTD., Sydney
PRENTICE-HALL OF CANADA, LTD., Toronto
PRENTICE-HALL OF INDIA PRIVATE LTD., New Delhi
PRENTICE-HALL OF JAPAN, INC., Tokyo

Preface

This second edition of *Understanding and Guiding Young Children* includes a complete new chapter, together with updated material in the text and an abundance of new photographs. The lists of reference works have been brought up to date as well. All of these changes are designed to make the book more interesting and even more effective as a teaching tool.

This book is written for students interested in understanding more about personality development. It is intended for those who take seriously their responsibility of preparing themselves for the profession of parenthood and is suitable for men and women, boys and girls.

The examples used and the points emphasized are in areas of behavior of special concern to teen-agers, such as the effort to be independent; the need to feel valued; the problems of jealousy and rivalry; and problems with authority and with managing strong feelings, especially anger and aggressiveness. Understanding more about such problems in young children may help teen-agers to understand their own similar problems.

This book stresses child understanding rather than child care. It approaches child understanding through self-understanding. It presents lasting principles, generalizations, and concepts rather than minute techniques which may become outmoded. The generalizations give the bases for decision making so that students can face new situations as they arise. In this way the early understanding which this book gives in the field of child development may be the basis for intelligent actions in the years ahead.

Presentation of the broad viewpoint of child development, as opposed to emphasis on the minutiae of child care, extends to a view of outside-the-family influences on personality development. In Chapter 10 both school and community influences are analyzed and applied to the growth of the individual, with emphasis on the role of the individual as a citizen as well as a family member. The new chapter, "Children Are Members of Families," rounds out the picture by showing how children learn the fundamental values of family life, and how their experiences with siblings and other children help them develop into responsible adults.

This book may be used as a basic text for child development or child care courses. It may also be useful for adult education courses. Stress on the universality of underlying principles helps students of all backgrounds to identify with the contents. It gives them the feeling that the book applies to them as well as to others.

The style of writing is informal and conversational. The artistic use of color and illustrations likewise contributes to the ease of use. More than 300 photographs of children, including various ethnic and cultural groups, are used throughout the book. The illustrations follow the content of the book so closely that even the slowest reader can get the ideas of the text from the pictures and captions.

Ample teaching aids are provided. These include a large variety of student activities and exercises and supplementary readings. The accompanying *Teachers Guide* will help the teacher adapt the subject matter for use in various teaching situations.

The authors wish to express their appreciation to Morey L. Appell, Stout State University, Wisconsin; Clara H. Lloyd, North Texas. State University; and James L. Hymes, Jr., University of Maryland, for their helpful suggestions in the preparation of the manuscript.

KATHERINE READ BAKER
XENIA F. FANE

Contents

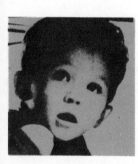

1
WHAT ARE CHILDREN LIKE?

Think of children you know. Children need to be understood. Why children differ. Why people change. Accepting children as they are. Activities. References.

Opening photograph by Burk Uzzle from Magnum

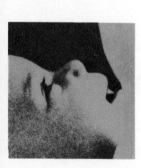

2
LET'S TALK ABOUT BABIES

Making plans for a baby. At birth. Growing in the first year. Activities. References.

Opening photograph courtesy of Gerber Products Company

3
CHILDREN WHO ARE ONE AND TWO YEARS OLD

What are toddlers like? Attitudes and developmental tasks. Taking care of a toddler. Growing intellectually. What we know about toddlers. Activities. References.

Opening photograph courtesy of Dial Soap

7
DISCIPLINE AND SPOILING

Being spoiled. Mutual regulation. Being satisfied or unsatisfied. Building any new relationship. Helping spoiled children. Firmness. Discipline with love. What is good discipline? Activities. References.

Opening photograph courtesy of Prudential Insurance Company of America

8
STUMBLING BLOCKS IN GROWING

Feelings of jealousy and rivalry. Feelings of anger and resentment. We have feelings, too. The problem of authority. Activities. References.

Opening photograph courtesy of the Equitable Life Assurance Society of the United States

9
HANDICAPS AND CRISES

An only child. Adopted children. A child with only one parent. Children whose mothers work outside the home. The neglected child. A child acutely ill. A blind child. A mentally retarded child. Common problems. Activities. References.

Opening photograph by Hella Hammid from Rapho-Guillumette

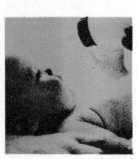

Second Edition Understanding and Guiding Young Children

What Are Children Like?

Each of us was once a child. Many of us, probably most of us, are around young children at one time or another. They are fascinating to know and to know about. When they are newborn, they may *seem* to be very much alike; yet each will grow to be a distinct person, just as each of us is. By the time a child starts to school, he is unlike anyone else and is very different from himself as a newborn. In spite of these differences, there are some things that every child needs, and there are some things we should know about children to help them grow up to be happy, well-adjusted adults.

This chapter introduces us to our study of children. We shall look for answers to such questions as:

1. What are children like?
2. Where do differences among children come from?
3. Why and how do children change?
4. How do we learn about children?

What do you yourself want to learn about children? List some questions you have about children. Check this list at the end of the course and see what answers you have found to these questions.

THINK OF CHILDREN YOU KNOW

Think of the children you know. They may be children you see on your way to school in the morning, or in the grocery store, or on the bus. They may be children in your neighborhood or perhaps your own brothers and sisters.

They are all different. They may be round and plump or skinny and tall. They may cry a lot and often look unhappy. They may smile a lot and have sunny dispositions that make you feel like playing with them. They may be quiet or they may be active. They may be naughty much of the time and difficult to take care of, or they may be easy to manage and fun to be with. Even the same child is different at different times.

In other words, children are people just as the rest of us are. They have feelings. They grow and change. They want to be understood. Each one is a little different from anyone else. He is *himself,* just as each one of us is.

Children like to explore and to discover things. Making sounds is fun.

Gerber Products Company

Play is hard work, and children get tired.

Things children do. When we watch children, we can see that they love to explore and to *discover* things. They discover things that may happen to water—how it splashes, how it spills, or how it disappears in sand. They are fascinated by funny things like a fly buzzing against a window pane. They *work hard* lining up a row of stones or filling a pan with dirt or carrying all their blocks from one place to another.

They like to *watch* cars go by or people on the street or to *listen* to the sound of a spoon banged on the table. It's an exciting world for them because so much is new and unexpected. They *get tired*, and they may fall asleep wherever they are, in the most uncomfortable-looking positions. Or, they may climb up into someone's arms and settle down for a *rest*.

They *become frightened* easily by such things as sudden, loud noises or by

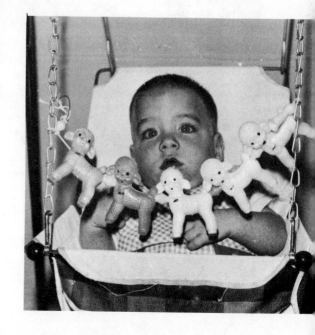

The world is a fascinating place to a young child, but sometimes it is overwhelming.

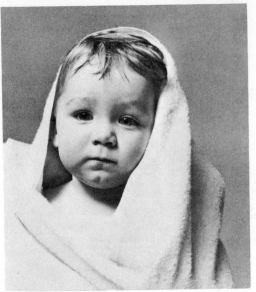

Johnson and Johnson

Quaker Oats Company—Corn Goods

Every child is himself and different from everyone else.

Some children smile a lot.

Some children are serious.

UNICEF Photo—Thailand

James A. Say

Some children are outgoing.

Some children are shy.

Even the same child is different at different times.

being separated from the person taking care of them. They often *need help* in feeling safe or in actually being safe. They do not understand clearly what is dangerous and what isn't. They are often afraid of the wrong things! They *get angry* easily when they can't have what they want. They *find it hard to wait* for things and to be patient.

They are children, and things look different to children than to people who have lived a few years longer.

How we react to children.   Every child is different and we may find ourselves acting differently toward each one. For example, Jane and Mary are both three years old but they are different.

Jane stands quietly watching a group of children playing on the sidewalk. She is thin with blonde, straight hair and a wistful expression. The other children are not paying any attention to her. If you speak to her, she hangs her head and may put her finger in her mouth. She doesn't answer you.

Mary comes running to the group. She picks up a toy lying nearby and plumps herself down in the midst of the children. She chatters away, paying little attention to the fact that no one seems to be listening to her. She looks up and calls "Hi" to you as you pass.

Would you act differently toward Jane and Mary if you were taking care of them? You probably would. Most people would.

You can hardly act the same toward a child who hangs her head and doesn't speak as you do toward a child who calls out a friendly "Hi." Children make other people behave differently toward them because of what they themselves do. Like everyone else, Jane and Mary, by their different ways of feeling and acting, make a different place for themselves in the world of people. In a sense each is building her own world.

Jane may feel, "No one wants me," when she is with people. When Mary is with people, she may feel, "Here are some people to play with. What fun!" Most people will act in a friendly way toward Mary. She builds that kind of world for herself as she says "Hi" and begins to play as though she expected people to like her and want to play with her. Jane is building a different world for herself. Most

O. J. Wikse   The Soap and Detergent Association

What a child does helps determine how we respond to him.

people will go on about their business and forget her. A few people may feel sorry for her and try to help her and perhaps tell her what she should do.

Because people act differently toward them, these children may go on becoming more "fixed" in their ways of acting. Mary may become more sure that people are friendly. Jane may become more sure that no one wants her or that others only try to boss her.

How did these children get started feeling and acting this way? *Can* they change? *Should* they change? What can we do about helping children become satisfied and happy, liking themselves and other people?

These are things we want to understand. We study children so that we can find some answers to questions such as these.

CHILDREN NEED TO BE UNDERSTOOD

We all want to be understood. We all know how many times we are misunderstood. We know this from our own experience. It happens often to children, too.

Watch a small child whose mother has just swept up the litter of sticks and stones on the walk. He weeps because for him it was a city with carefully laid out roads. She has ruined it. He does not understand that his mother is only trying to get things clean because company is coming. She is too busy to listen to what he is trying to tell her. He cries hopelessly. It isn't easy to be little!

Another mother calls her four-year-old daughter, "Come here this minute." By the time the child comes, the mother is talking on the telephone—a long conversation. The child waits and she may be wondering why she had to leave her play. She may wonder, "What's the matter with me when people don't pay any attention to me? Do they think that what I do is of no importance? Why do they interfere so often?"

Children are frequently misunderstood.

Sometimes it is hard to figure out what grown-ups expect.

Ayerst Laboratories, New York

UNICEF Photo by Mallica Vajrathon—Philippines

UNICEF Photo by Prathana Konsupto—Thailand

We really cannot be sure what a child is like until we have watched him carefully over a period of time.

It is often hard to feel valued and important when one is a little child. It is easy to get confused about what is expected. These kinds of things go on happening to us even when we are older, but then we are aware of some of the reasons, at least. A small child doesn't have the advantages of our experience. He needs understanding from us.

Observing children carefully. To understand children we must learn to look at them as they really are, *to observe closely and with care* and not just glance at them and say thoughtlessly, "I know what that child is like."

We really cannot be sure what a child is like until we watch him carefully over a period of time. And then there will still be a lot we do not know.

Do you think anyone could understand all about you even if this person had watched you for one whole day? You can act in so many different ways under different circumstances. It is sometimes hard to tell just what the real "you" is.

Certainly you are lots of things! So is the child! The one advantage we have in learning what he is like is that he doesn't hide as much as an older person often does. He really lets us know how he feels. And this is a good thing because he can't put his feelings into words. He has to show us through the way he behaves, the way he yells when he is hurt, or hits out when he is angry, or wiggles with joy when he is pleased. If we learn to watch closely, we can begin to learn to understand his behavior and some of its meanings.

We must train ourselves to observe details and not be content to describe in a general way what we think is happening. Maybe one bit of behavior is like something we saw another child do and we jump to the conclusion that one child is like the other child, but this is not true. Every child is unique, different from any other.

Understanding what you observe.   What we expect to see may interfere with our seeing what is there. All of us tend to have "images" in our mind of children and their behavior. We think of them as "cute" or "naughty" or "noisy" or something else. What we see

Is he naughty? Is he lonely? Is he discovering something? Your "image" of him may influence what you see.

James A. Say

when we look at them will often depend on what these "images" are or what we expect to see unless we are observing each individual child carefully. What we expect to see may interfere with our seeing what actually is happening. It may prevent our understanding the child's behavior.

Let us look at some of the ways children behave. Here is a child who fusses when he doesn't get what he wants. Is he "spoiled"? Another child cries hard when he falls. Is he a "crybaby"? Still another child grabs a toy from the child near him. Is he "selfish"? Another child calls you "stupid." What does he really mean when he says this?

It may be that a particular child is "spoiled" or a "crybaby," but it also may be your "image" of what children are like. You may be missing some important details. What looks like the same behavior in a general way may really be quite different in two different children or even in the same child at two different times.

For example, the child we might have labeled "selfish" may live in a neighborhood where there are a lot of children and most of them are older than he. They take things from him and he learns to grab to get what he wants when he plays with others. To him this is play and he thinks nothing of it. He doesn't get upset when someone grabs what he has. He expects to grab to get what he wants. He may smile in a friendly way as he grabs. He often gives something to another child. He isn't really "selfish." He is just behaving as he has learned to behave.

The child who cries hard over a small bump may be a child who is feeling lonesome and afraid. Perhaps his mother is away and has left him with an aunt who doesn't care about children. He wants his mother and does not understand why she has left him. He tries to be brave but when he trips and falls, all his miserable feelings of loneliness spill out and he sobs brokenheartedly. He is not a "cry baby" but only a child facing more problems than he can bear comfortably at the moment.

If you are going to do something for this child, it will make a difference whether you are responding to a real situation or to the "image" in your mind.

Lanvin Parfums

She may not be a crybaby but simply a child facing more problems at the moment than she can comfortably bear.

A child behaves as he does because of reasons, such as being hungry, being tired, being anxious or unhappy, being confused or not understanding what is expected of him. He may live under circumstances which produce patterns of behavior, as with the child who grabbed. He may also behave as he does because this behavior belongs with his age and stage of development. Being two or three or four makes a difference in behavior. Being two means having very little idea about property rights, for one thing. A two-year-old is likely to take any toy that attracts him. When he is four, he is likely to have discovered that one toy may be his and another may belong to his playmate. Labeling two-year-old behavior as "selfish" may interfere with our understanding of what the child is really like because of our "image" of selfish people. It may interfere with our giving him the kind of guidance he needs. Observe what actually happens without labeling or judging the behavior. It takes careful observation to discover what he is really telling us by his behavior. We are wise not to pass judgment or speak in general terms about what he is like.

It takes practice to learn to observe what actually happens. Only when we learn to observe with careful attention to details can we discover what children are really thinking and feeling and what they need from us. It makes a big difference to the child whether you respond to the real child or to your "image" of him. We know we react differently if we think of a child as "naughty" rather than as someone who is scared, or if we think of a child as a "cry baby" rather than as a lonely, bewildered little boy. Avoid making snap judgments about children—or anyone.

WHY CHILDREN DIFFER

We began by saying that children are people just as we are and that they need to be understood and respected. We pointed out that each child is different. We know that we react to these differences. We find some children easier to like than others.

You have probably wondered why people are so different. Where do these differences come from?

Children, like all of us, are different because of what they start out with and because of what happens to them along the way. We are all different because of what we inherit from our parents and because of our environments or the experiences we have from birth on. What do we mean by heredity and environment?

We start with heredity. As you probably know, each individual grows from the union of two cells, an ovum and a sperm. Both the ovum and the sperm contain chromosomes. These chromosomes

**Heredity and environment together make each
of us different from anyone else.**

are like rows of beads on a string and in the beads are genes. The
genes are carriers of inherited characteristics such as whether we
are a boy or a girl or have blue eyes or curly hair or react quickly
to stimuli. Incidentally, the gene which determines the sex of the
child comes from the father's chromosomes.

Conception takes place when the sperm cell from the male pene-
trates the ovum, or egg cell, in the female and fertilizes it. The fertilized egg divides. In the process of division, the two sets of chromosomes pair off and divide, too. One cell becomes two, then four, then
eight, then sixteen, and so on. Nine months later, when the infant
is born, there are millions of cells and they have become very spe-
cialized—some making stomach muscles or eyes or some other special
part of the body, all from the union of the sperm and the ovum at
the moment called conception. All that is inherited is present in the
genes in that first fertilized egg.

Combinations of genes in the ova and sperm are not apt to be exactly the same, so that no two children are exactly alike, not even identical twins. Identical twins come from one fertilized ovum.

Environment plays a part. We still have many things to learn about what genes contain, but we know that they play a part in determining what a person will be like as he grows. You notice the words, "play a part" rather than just "determine" what a person is like. For example, we know size is inherited. A gene determines how tall a person *can* become, but how tall he actually does grow will depend also on what he eats, perhaps on an illness he had and the age he was when he was ill, or the climate he lives in. In other words, the environment plays a part along with the genes in setting the limits of possibility. Probably we seldom develop to the full extent of our capacity. Even though we are limited by what we inherit, we have plenty of room for change through improving our environment.

No two children are exactly alike, not even identical twins.

Baldwin Piano and Organ Company   Gerber Products Company

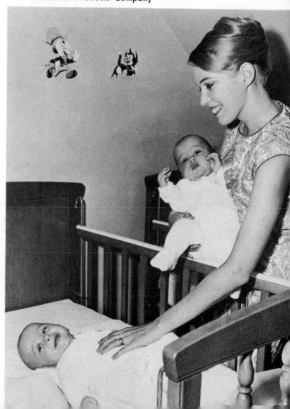

Chinese Information Service

A child learns to speak English or Eskimo or Chinese depending on the language spoken to him.

The Japanese people, for example, are shorter in height than Americans. But Japanese children born and raised in this country tend to be taller than those born and raised in Japan. The diet is different here. You can see how environment makes a difference even though inheritance determines the limits of growth.

There is an almost infinite variety to the ways that people may develop in different environments. A child learns to speak English or Eskimo or Russian depending on the country in which he happens to be reared. He is friendly or unfriendly depending on what kind of people he lives with and what kind of expectations they have for him. He is alert and interested in learning or fails to learn depending on the kinds of opportunities he has had to learn—all these things within the limits set by his individual inheritance.

Many things that people sometimes think are inherited are the result of environment. You may hear someone say, "He got that bad temper from his uncle," or "She inherited her clumsiness from me," or "Her lisp came from my mother." These are not true statements. There is no gene that carries "bad temper" or "clumsiness" or "a lisp." Living with a person with these characteristics means that the child may imitate these things. He follows the example of the adult in having a temper or a lisp or in being clumsy.

Another reason for the child's characteristic behavior patterns may be that the parent had this "image" of the child. The child may have dark hair and features like his uncle. When he gets mad, as everyone does at times, the mother may decide, "Here is a temper just like my brother's," and the child continues to act as she expects him to act. Her "image" helps produce the behavior.

We have seen how we can create a world for ourselves by expecting people to act toward us in certain ways. Parents also may expect a child to behave in a certain way until he does. Then they blame it on heredity! Only general constitutional characteristics such as speed of reaction or sensitivity to sound or light are inherited. These characteristics are the basic building blocks from which the individual personality is fashioned by experiences which the environment provides.

How a child handles misfortunes depends on attitudes learned in the family. Some parents expect their girls to cry but teach their boys to be strong, silent men.

Armour and Company

Janet Mirer

A child's success in learning depends on the opportunities he has and on the limits set by his individual inheritance.

Parents are part of the environment, too. Children inherit from their parents, but parents also provide the most important part of the environment in the child's first years of life. The people who care for the child influence him most and these people are usually the parents. A mother and father who are happy together and who can talk freely together about the things that upset them, little things and big things, create a favorable climate for growing. The care these parents give really nourishes the child. Whether the parents are rich or poor, have a big house or a small one, can give the child many material advantages or few, matters much less in his growth than does this matter of the personal relationship between the parents themselves. If they accept and respect each other, they create an environment in which the child is comfortable. He can be himself and grow in his own way just as his parents are growing in their own ways.

Family values and the respect accorded human relationships are reflected in the management of the tasks of homemaking. Wise management of time and energy as well as money are part of a favorable environment. A mother who finds time to enjoy her baby is building better relationships than is the mother whose time is filled with household routines. The years when children are young are crowded, busy years at best for both fathers and mothers. It takes good management and a sense of values to get the most from these years for parents and children. When this is successful, these years will be happy ones to be treasured throughout life.

WHY PEOPLE CHANGE

Differences in inheritance and differences in environment make each of us a *unique* individual. There never was anyone just like you or just like the child you see playing next door.

We can do nothing to change what a person has inherited as far as we know, but we can do a lot to change the environment in which the person develops and in this way change the kind of person he may become. It is worthwhile understanding more about how these changes take place if we are concerned about children and about helping their personality growth.

People change, first of all, because of the strong impulse to grow and change which is present in all living things. It is one of the strongest forces there is. Have you ever noticed a tiny plant pushing its way between two heavy rocks or a morning-glory vine coming up through an asphalt driveway? Human beings, too, have strong impulses to grow, in spite of obstacles. Children grow without anyone's

Parents who accept and respect each other create an environment in which a child is comfortable.

Clairol, Inc.

A mother who finds time to enjoy her baby is building better relationships than is the mother whose time is filled with household routines.

American Gas Association

pushing them. In fact, they often do better if they are not interfered with too much. We may need to learn not to be obstacles to their growth.

Another reason people change is that someone *cares* for them and about them. The child who, because of unfavorable circumstances, has developed a bad temper, can change if he feels someone cares and wants to see him become different. He changes because he loves and wants to please the person who loves him. If he loves and feels loved, he can change his pattern of behavior into one which is more acceptable to the person he loves. He is not likely to change because he is nagged or scolded or threatened. He changes because someone cares. *Loving makes the difference.* The people who fail to change are those who have lost their capacity to love or to feel close to other people or at least have had this capacity impaired or damaged by unfavorable circumstances. We know that most people can and do change.

Children will grow without anyone's pushing them.

Lawry's Foods, Inc.

ACCEPTING CHILDREN AS THEY ARE

We help children most when we accept them as they are. We all need to feel that we are loved for what we are. This feeling gives each of us the courage to grow and improve. We are likely to want to change at our own rate and in our own way. It makes us uncomfortable or even unsure of ourselves to be pushed. Being pushed often makes it harder to change. Children feel the same way. Each child has different qualities or characteristics. Each one wants to be accepted and liked for what he is. Each needs to be helped to grow in his own way and at his own rate.

If we keep trying to change the way a child acts by saying, "Don't do that, silly" or "That isn't the right way, stupid," he loses confidence in himself, or rather he fails to develop self-confidence.

The child who feels loved develops a healthy, self-reliant personality.

A child wants to please a person who loves him and whom he loves.

Clairol, Inc.

American Gas Association

James A. Say

A child needs to be helped to grow in his own way and at his own rate.

A child needs to feel that she is a person of worth—wanted and needed.

UNICEF Photo by Nagata—Guatemala

A child needs to feel that he is a person of worth. He changes more readily when he feels that we like him and are not always pushing him to be different. We are part of his environment. As we care for him, we want to build an atmosphere in which he grows easily and confidently.

There is a difference between accepting behavior and approving of it. Accepting means being aware and giving understanding, while approval means liking what is there. We should accept children as they are and then give our approval to the behavior we like and to their efforts to change in desirable directions.

TO DO AND DISCUSS   ACTIVITIES

1. What are some of the words you think of in describing children? Write these words down and compare them with what the others in the class have written. What kinds of "images" do members of the class seem to have of children? Where do you think these images came from (one child, many individuals, hearsay, etc.)? Combine some of the students' impressions and construct a "normal" child.

2. Watch a group of three or more preschool children for fifteen minutes while they are playing. List the kinds of behavior you see, such as sharing, quarreling, or playing alone.
   What did the children do that you liked?
   What did they do that you disliked?
   What kinds of behavior would you like to change or improve?
     Why? How?

3. List ten experiences a child might have and suggest how each might affect his personality.

4. Observe a parent with her child. (They may be neighbors, relatives, or people for whom you baby-sit.) In what ways is the child like the parent (coloring, body type, friendliness, quietness, temperament, etc.)? Do you think these characteristics are inherited or learned? Compare your observations and conclusions with those of your classmates.

5. Try to bring to class several pictures of yourself as a young child, for use in a class exhibit. For each picture, prepare a brief statement which would help the viewer to understand the child in the picture..

TO THINK AND WRITE ABOUT

1. Think of something that happened to you when you were young, before you started school. Describe it as completely as you can. What did it seem like to you then? What do you think it might have seemed like to the adults you lived with? How do you think the same type of experience would affect you now?

2. Spend an hour quietly observing your own younger brother or sister or another young child. List the child's changes in activities and moods. What do you think contributed to these changes?

3. List some of the expectations your parents have for you. Be prepared to compare your list with those of your classmates. How have your parents' expectations influenced your behavior? Do you ever feel that they expect too much (or not enough) of you? Why do different parents expect different things of their children?

4. (a) Do you think some of the people you know should change their behavior? Why? Do some people appear to *want* to change their behavior more than do others? (b) How have you changed recently? What do you think caused the change? How would you go about getting a young child to change his behavior?

REFERENCES   PAMPHLETS AND PAPERBACKS

Behavior: The Unspoken Language of Children
New York: Child Study Association of America, 1963

Cohen, Dorothy, and Virginia Stern
Observing and Recording the Behavior of Young Children (pages 1-5)
New York: Bureau of Publications, Teachers College, Columbia University, 1958

English, O. Spurgeon, and Constance Foster
A Guide to Successful Fatherhood
Chicago: Science Research Associates, Inc., 1954

Hymes, James L.
A Healthy Personality for Your Child
Children's Bureau Publication No. 337
U. S. Department of Health, Education, and Welfare

Menninger, William C.
Self-Understanding—A First Step in Understanding Children
Chicago: Science Research Associates, Inc., 1951

Murphy, Lois B.
Colin—A Normal Child
New York: Basic Books, Inc., 1967

Mussen, Paul
The Psychological Development of the Child
Englewood Cliffs, New Jersey: Prentice-Hall, Inc., 1963

Olson, Willard, and John Lewellen
How Children Grow and Develop (page 35)
Chicago: Science Research Associates, Inc., 1953

Spock, Benjamin
Baby and Child Care, Revised Edition
New York: Pocket Books, Inc.

Wolf, Anna W. M., and Margaret Dawson
What Makes a Good Home
New York: Child Study Association of America, 1956

BOOKS

Almy, Millie
Ways of Studying Children
New York: Teachers College, Columbia University, 1959

Frank, Mary, and Lawrence Frank
How to Help Your Child in School (Chapter 2, "How a Young Child
    Grows and Learns")
New York: Viking Press, Inc., 1950

Read, Katherine H.
*The Nursery School: A Human Relationships Laboratory, Fourth Edi-
    tion* (Chapter 1)
Philadelphia: W. B. Saunders Company, 1966

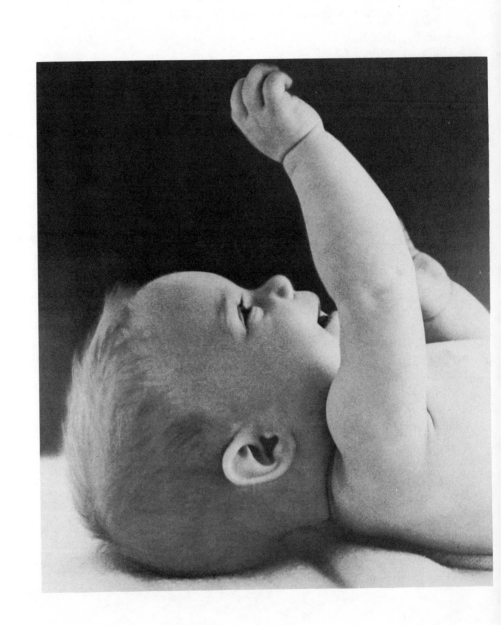

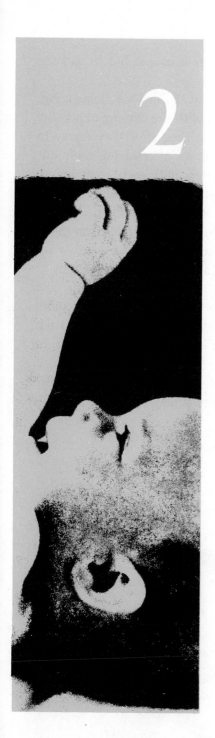

Let's Talk About Babies

The newborn is a very helpless, dependent being. He has a tremendous amount of learning to do before he can become at all independent. Yet he learns very early how to let us know that he needs something. It is up to us to be able to tell what he needs. He also finds ways to tell us when his needs have been met. During his first year he becomes increasingly able to function as an independent person rather than a helpless being.

We shall look at the ways children grow and change, and try to find out what they may need from us if they are to be healthy. We shall start from the beginning, with babies. We shall learn some things about planning for a baby, preparing to become a parent, prenatal care, characteristics of the infant, crying, feeding and weaning, sucking—including thumbsucking, maturation, motor development, social development, and play.

27

MAKING PLANS FOR A BABY

One of the most important decisions a couple has to make is the decision about adding to the family.

Babies take time, energy, and money. Babies are demanding. Parents must make changes in their lives with the coming of a baby. Most men and women need to take some time after they marry to share experiences together, to discover ways of resolving their differences and to talk over important matters with each other before they are ready to become parents. They need time to enjoy one another, too, and to find satisfactions as a couple before they are ready to meet comfortably the demands a baby inevitably makes on them.

For the husband and wife who have taken time to grow together, the coming of a baby usually adds richness and depth to their lives as they go on learning and growing through their new relationship with the baby. They come to respect each other more as they both shoulder their added responsibilities and see each other in new roles. A baby is fortunate if he comes into a home where his parents are truly ready for him.

Not every couple will decide to take the step of adding a baby to the family. A husband and wife together may choose to find ful-

Babies take time, energy, and money—but are worth it!

Gerber Products Company

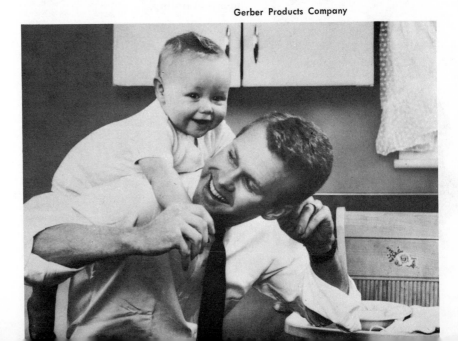

Most of us look forward to the role of a parent with all of its joys as well as the trials it brings.

fillment in other ways than through children. For a woman today there are many ways of living a satisfying, productive life—through professional work, through community services, or through personally creative activity which also enriches the lives of others.

Most people will probably choose to have children if they are able. There is a strong maternal or paternal urge in us which we fulfill most readily in the way that is most direct, that is by having a baby, caring for him, and guiding his growth. Most people look forward to the role of a parent with all its joys as well as the trials it brings. Babies are wonderful.

Another decision a couple must make is about the number of children and the spacing of these children. There are many factors to consider in making this decision. Some of the factors are the money that is likely to be available (higher standards of living mean that many wives must hold jobs outside the home), their expectations for each child (a college education costs money but is important for many jobs today), their health and the circumstances of their jobs (such as the necessity of moving frequently), and their own goals in living (what they themselves want after their children are grown). Religious beliefs or the teaching of the church to which the couple belongs is another factor which will influence the number and spacing of children.

These factors are individual matters for families, but there are some general factors, too. The world is becoming more and more crowded. It takes more careful planning by both the parent and the community to give young children good learning and growing experiences under crowded conditions. It takes more supervision. The world no longer needs more people to get the necessary work done because machines have replaced people in doing many tasks. The world needs people with a much higher level of education and understanding and capacity to assume complex and difficult responsibilities. Parents and communities today must give more thought than formerly to providing well for children under these changing conditions.

Think of all the responsibilities that lie ahead for these new parents.

Metropolitan Life

Preparing to become a parent.   Babies are born. But birth is not the beginning of development. Important things have been happening to them through the nine months that they have been growing inside the protection of the mother's body. They have done the most rapid growing they will ever do. Growth slows down after birth.

The mother cares for the infant by caring for herself during the nine months of pregnancy. Good prenatal care means checking with the doctor each month and, in the last month, checking with him every two weeks or oftener. He advises her about what she may need to do to improve her physical health. He checks the position of the fetus in the uterus and makes plans for the delivery. He listens to the heartbeat which can be heard from around the fourth month.

It is not possible to tell the sex of the baby until birth, but the mother will know whether it is an active baby or a quiet one. She will begin to feel its movements around the fifth month. These movements get stronger and more frequent as the fetus grows.

During the prenatal period the father-to-be plays an important part through the support he gives to the expectant mother. He can help protect her from getting overtired. He can encourage her to follow a good health regime. Most of all he can give her the extra love she may need to carry her through the changes, both physical and emotional, which she faces, and he can share with her some of the miracle of growth before birth as the fetus becomes active.

Prenatal care.   During the prenatal period the mother needs extra milk, a full quart a day at least, to provide calcium for the baby's fast-growing teeth and bones. His first teeth are already formed at birth even though it will be months before they come through the gums. If the mother does not get enough calcium, her teeth will suffer. People used to think that mothers had to expect cavities or the loss of a tooth during pregnancy, but now we know better. We know that mothers just need to get enough calcium in the food they eat so that they can supply both their own needs and those of the baby.

A mother does not need many more calories. She will have plenty of weight to carry with the growing baby, so she will avoid fattening foods such as sweets and rich, starchy foods high in calories. She will eat plenty of fruits and vegetables and plenty of protein foods. Diet is important during pregnancy for the health of both the baby and the mother.

In addition to watching her diet, the mother will be sure to get enough rest. She should rest whenever she feels tired.

Usually a woman feels very well during a pregnancy, except possibly in the first two or three months when so many changes are taking place. She is less likely to catch cold or be sick than at other times. Her immunity to disease tends to be greater. A certain number of women feel sick (nauseated) in the morning during these first weeks, but this can often be controlled by eating a cracker. In any event she should follow the doctor's suggestions. Many women do not have this "morning sickness."

If a woman has an adequate diet and good prenatal care, both physical and emotional, she is probably ready to enjoy the baby when it is born at the end of the nine months.

AT BIRTH

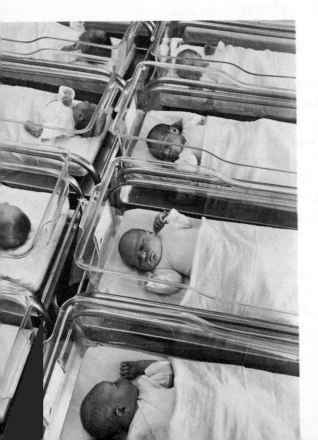

The majority of babies born in the United States are born in hospitals. It is easier for the doctor to give the care there that may be needed. The mother usually stays in the hospital for four or five days. The part of the hospital reserved for mothers and newborn babies is called the maternity ward.

Some hospitals today are making provisions for the mother and baby to be in a room together. The baby's crib or bassinet

Most of the babies born in the United States are born in hospitals.

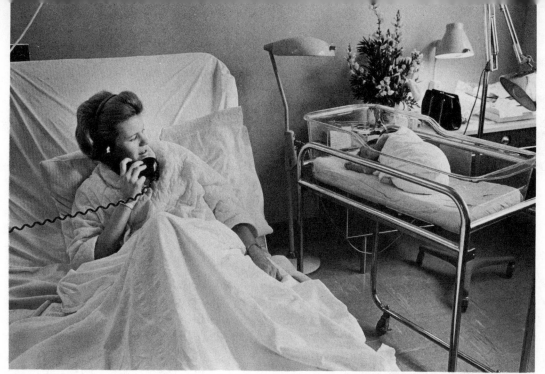

"Rooming-in" at the hospital gives the mother a chance to get acquainted with her baby and begin to care for and enjoy him from the time he is born.

is beside the mother's bed. This arrangement is called "rooming-in." "Rooming-in" gives the mother a better chance to get acquainted with her baby and enjoy him from the beginning. When she wishes she can care for him herself with the help of the nurse. She can nurse him when he is hungry rather than having him wait until the nurse is ready to bring him to her from the hospital nursery. When she takes him home, she knows what he is like and what he is likely to need. Hospitals which have this arrangement do not allow any visitors except the father. But it means that fathers, too, can get acquainted with their babies, not just look at them through a nursery window.

Fathers need to be considered for they face big changes with the birth of the baby. The mother is wrapped up in caring for the baby and in gaining her strength. It is easy for a father to feel "left out" unless he, too, can share in some way in enjoying and caring

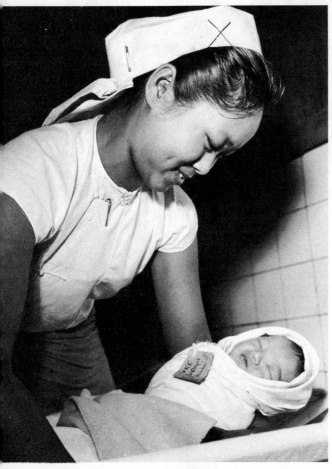

UNICEF Photo by Jack Ling—Burma

Have you ever seen a newborn baby?

for the baby. He needs some attention, too. The couple must be considerate of each other as the family goes through the process of finding a new balance in their relationship and their satisfactions.

Some things to observe about a new baby. Have you ever seen a newborn baby or at least a baby less than a month old?

If you have, you know that he may be red and wrinkled and old looking. His head may be rather out of shape and he may be without much of a chin. He may have hair or he may be almost bald, for babies are different from the first day of birth. We are often surprised at the way they look. They are so tiny and funny looking. But we are also surprised at how fast they change. The wrinkles fill out and the head changes shape and the baby begins to look more human before a month has passed.

THINGS TO NOTICE ABOUT A NEWBORN BABY

1. His *head* is large in proportion to the size of his body. It is about ¼ of his total length. When he is full-grown, it will be only about ⅛ of his total length. His face is relatively smaller and his braincase is relatively larger than it will be later.

2. His *features* are different, a little nose and not much chin compared to what he will have later. His eyes are blue. The eyes may or may not be blue later.

3. His *arms* are longer than his legs at birth. His *legs* will grow and become longer than his arms when he is full-grown.

4. His *fingers* are short, too, but his hands will not change much in shape until he is in his teens.

5. His *toes* fan out, almost like fingers, instead of curling up as they will do later when the bottom of his foot is touched.

6. At birth only about 25% of his total weight comes from *muscle*. More than 40% of it will be muscle when he is grown! His ligaments are not firmly attached which makes his bones seem flexible. We can see why we must support a baby's large head when we hold him, for his muscles have not the strength to do it yet.

7. His *central nervous system* makes up about 15% of his weight at birth but it will make up only 3% of his weight at maturity. No wonder he gets tired from any excitement!

8. He grows plumper very rapidly if he is healthy. He will usually *weigh* between 6-9 pounds when he is born and gain from

How does this newborn baby compare with the description given here?

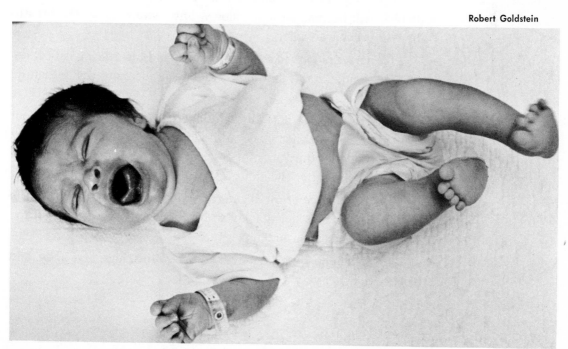

10-15 pounds in the first year. A baby weighing less than 5½ pounds at birth is considered "premature" and must have special care.

9. He is around 20 inches long at birth and will grow about 9-10 inches in the first year. Growth in *length* is less dependent on environmental factors than is gain in weight, although environment plays a part.

10. The *bones* of the infant are not very hard yet. All of his bone growth will not be complete until he is in his twenties. In the skull, for example, he has soft spots called "fontanels" which are covered with a membrane. One can easily see the soft spot at the top of the infant's head, especially if he has very little hair. The spots are filled in by bone by the 18th month. His head needs to be carefully protected at first.

11. The infant has no *teeth* in sight! But all 20 baby teeth are there in the gums, ready to start erupting when he is around six or more months old.

12. He *breathes* in a rapid, somewhat irregular way. He makes funny noises as he breathes. He has difficulty at first in managing to breathe and suck at the same time. He often has the hiccoughs. He sneezes easily. During the first year his *heart* will grow rapidly and its beat will become stronger, slower and more regular. His breathing will become steadier.

13. His *ears* look like grown-up ears and his hearing is well developed. Some infants startle at sudden sounds more easily than do others.

14. His *eyes* are not fully developed at birth. He looks without seeing much in the first weeks and will not really focus on an object until around the third month. Binocular vision is not usually fully developed until after the child is six years old.

15. His *temperature regulating mechanism* is still poor. He chills easily or gets hot quickly so he must be covered, but not too much. He needs an even temperature.

16. When he *cries,* he moves all over, arms, legs, and body, and his face may get very red.

During the first month. The infant under a month old is called a neonate or newborn infant. In the first month the infant sleeps most of the time if he is a healthy baby, waking to be fed and then sleeping again. He has a big adjustment to make after birth. Life has changed for him. He is on his own. At first, even breathing is a new experience and does not go smoothly. Listen to the funny noises a baby makes when he is nursing or taking the bottle as he tries to regulate breathing and swallowing—quite a feat for him! He learns quickly, but it does take practice.

There is no question of "spoiling" a baby in the first month. The important thing is to help him find that the world he has just entered is a place where he can be satisfied, a good place where he will be cared for and his needs will be met. It usually helps if the mother tries to follow the baby's rhythm, feeding him when he seems to indicate he is hungry. The acute hunger pangs he feels are hard to bear. He needs to be protected against acute discomfort if possible. He needs to feel that the world is a comfortable, inviting place. His mother's job is to stay close to him in the first weeks and learn what he is like and what he needs.

A good mother grows to understand her particular infant—whether he takes his time nursing, dozing and then rousing for more feeding, or whether he sucks strongly, vigorously gulping the milk, and then falls sound asleep. Each baby has a somewhat different schedule and he usually develops in a more contented way if the mother fits what she does for him into the rhythm of his wants during these first weeks.

In most babies, the hunger pangs come every three or four hours, but not like clockwork. In the first weeks, the intervals are often shorter. The baby may want frequent feedings in the afternoon and fewer in the early morning hours. Some infants occasionally sleep for six hours or more. Some settle down to a regular schedule fairly soon and some take quite awhile. Schedules change, too, as the baby grows.

Only gradually do babies learn to regulate themselves so they can fit comfortably into a schedule which suits the whole family. This may take several months. If a mother does not have too many

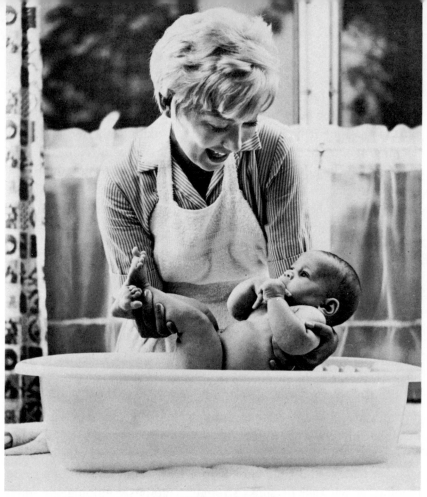

Winthrop Laboratories

A good mother grows to understand her particular infant.

other duties, she can let her baby take his time fitting into the world and becoming a person.

It is a matter of *mutual regulation*. At first the mother fits herself to the baby. As she comes to know him and he comes to feel safe and sure of her and of her willingness to give him what he wants, she asks him to do a little more waiting for her. He is better able to wait to be fed now that he has an idea that food will come eventually. He is not as distressed that it is not there the minute he feels hunger pangs. He is likely to stop crying when he hears his mother's footsteps.

We have mentioned that we build up a picture of ourselves from the responses of other people to us. It is true for the baby, too, and it will be easier for him to get a stable, trustworthy idea of himself and of the world around him if he is cared for by just a few people. At first he needs his mother who can adjust herself to him, with his father helping when he is home and perhaps a third person relieving the mother and sharing in his care.

We think now that an infant who is taken care of by a succession of different people during the first year of life is not likely to be as healthy in terms of physical, social, and emotional well-being as the infant who has had the same people taking most of the care of him.

In these first months he finds it easier to build his concept of the kind of person he is or can become when only a few people are responding to him. Later his experiences with people can be extended without confusing him or making him feel bewildered and

During his first months a baby thrives better if he is usually taken care of by the same people rather than by a number of different people.

Winthrop Laboratories

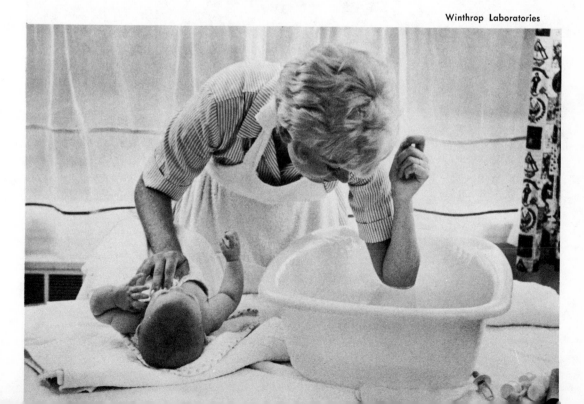

less sure of himself. Too many people caring for the infant in the beginning may slow the process of his gaining a sense of having a separate, individual self. It may make it more difficult for him to develop depth in his later personal relationships. We may ask ourselves how important the capacity for intimate relationships may be or the sense of being a separate individual. We may not know the answers to such questions, but at least we should be aware of possible ways in which circumstances influence personality growth. Growth is a very complex process. Understanding it is not simple.

A baby is fortunate when his early experiences include relationships with children as well as adults. He needs to discover himself in relationships with other children, and in this way extend his ideas about himself as a person and the range of relationships which are possible. Brothers and sisters are a help to a baby for they see him as a very special person in the family.

A baby is fortunate when his early experiences include relationships with children who see him as a very special person.

A. Tafler

Watch a six-month-old child and you will notice that he is likely to respond with special interest and delight to the approach of another child.

Many states have laws which prohibit the care of infants in institutions such as "baby homes" or orphanages. These laws state that a baby whose parents cannot care for him must be placed in a family home. Studies done in institutions have shown that babies cared for in groups by a series of people are more likely to get sick and are less likely to have good relations with people later on in life. Babies need close personal relationships.

The baby's foundations for liking people are laid as the mother and father care for the infant in these first months, put his needs first, feed him when he is hungry, pick him up and cuddle him when he seems to ask for it, and let him rest undisturbed when he is sleepy.

A baby thrives better in a family than in an institution.

Gerber Products Company

The foundations for liking people are laid as the mother and father care for the infant.

Gerber Products Company

They keep him warm and clean and satisfied. They enjoy him. With this kind of care he grows in a healthy way.

GROWING IN THE FIRST YEAR

In the first year the baby grows rapidly in a variety of ways. He takes important steps in mastering the process of communicating, in adapting to his environment and its demands, and in gaining control over his own body.

Crying.   The first thing that a baby does is cry! The birth cry is the first breath he takes. It gets air into his lungs and starts him breathing after he is born. Crying exercises the lungs and all babies do some crying. In the first weeks the cry changes and gets stronger and more individual. A mother soon comes to know her baby's cry.

All babies do some crying and some of them do a lot in the first two or three months. It seems to be a part of the readjusting that

During the first year, the doctor checks baby's progress about once a month.

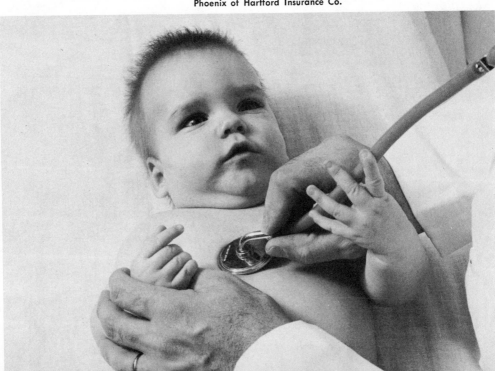

follows birth when the infant's nervous system and digestive system are not completely in working order. He is getting used to eating, sleeping and living in a strange new world. We try to make it as easy as we can for him. A pacifier may help or being held and rocked or perhaps another feeding. But fussing and crying are part of growing and exercising. Babies differ in the amounts they do.

In the first three or four months of life some babies do quite a lot of crying with colic. Colic doesn't seem to have much to do with what the baby eats or how healthy he is. It just seems to be another case of individual difference. Some babies' intestinal tracts are more sensitive and they have a more difficult time making the adjustment to life on their own. They have more gas pains. In time the colic disappears.

Were you one of those babies who had colic? Find out from your parents. If you were, they spent a lot of time with you for a while!

A baby with colic may wake up crying shortly after being fed. Holding him over your shoulder and patting him gently may help. Rocking him and singing may distract him from his discomfort. Some babies love the motion of riding in a car. The worst part of colic, from the standpoint of parents, is that it often comes in the evening or at night and both baby and parents lose sleep over it. A mother needs plenty of extra daytime rest during this period.

Babies have their reasons for crying. Babies cry for reasons other than colic pains. Of course, the main reason they cry is because they are hungry. We can feed them and take care of this kind of crying.

Some babies enjoy riding in a car.

Kantwet Baby Products

UNICEF Photo—Tanzania

Some babies need comforting.

But they may cry when they aren't hungry. They may want some comforting. Some babies are especially fussy when they are teething. They do a lot more crying just before a tooth appears.

They may cry, too, when things aren't going right with the important people in their lives. If his mother is tired or cross and unhappy about something, a baby is often fussy and may do a lot of crying. A baby doesn't understand these things in the same way that we do, but he is very sensitive to the feelings of the people who care for him. A mother communicates her feelings to him by the tone of her voice and the way she touches him. He is miserable if he feels something is wrong with her. Unhappiness in the whole family may make a baby irritable and fussy.

It is important to be calm and rested when one is caring for a little baby. Angry feelings, anxious feelings, feelings of dislike are communicated to the infant and disturb him. Some babies are more sensitive than others and find these things harder to bear, but all babies are influenced by how the people around them feel. If a baby of six months or older does a lot of crying for no reason that we can tell, maybe he is miserable because of trouble in his family.

The most seriously disturbed babies, however, may be those who do almost no crying. Of course there are happy, contented babies who do very little crying, but sometimes babies who do not cry very much are just not protesting or voicing their unhappiness. They may have given up asking for help. Babies without families, in institutions, frequently do almost no crying. They have found that no one cares. This is very serious and they will not grow and develop as they should. They are not healthy.

What *seems* like a lot of crying in an infant, of course, may only be the response of a vigorous, vocally active infant. Some babies exercise their lungs a lot more than others. They may really be quite content. Here again we accept the differences that exist among individual babies. Some babies are active, vigorous, and vocal. Others are quiet, less vigorous, and do less vocalizing. We need to get acquainted with them as individuals before we can be sure about the meaning of any particular bit of behavior. It is worthwhile making sure that nothing is really bothering a baby if he does a lot of crying. Crying is a baby's way of expressing himself when something seems wrong to him.

A baby can usually sense it when his special people are unhappy. He may become irritable.

J. Stefl

Simmons Company

Crying is a baby's way of expressing himself when something seems wrong.

If we care for a baby, we must be comfortable about listening to some crying. He will sometimes cry and protest a thing like going to sleep. It will not hurt him to cry! If we know he is all right, we do not need to be disturbed by his exercising his lungs for a few minutes.

Vocalizing. During the second half of the first year the baby is likely to do a lot of "talking" or vocalizing. The contented sounds he makes as he plays—his grunts, his cooing—have become real consonant and vowel sounds. He makes all the sounds he will use later in speaking, and even a few which do not appear in the English language. Some babies give the muscles of speech plenty of practice during their first year. The pleased response of their parents may encourage these babies to learn to talk early. They seem to listen to themselves with real pleasure. They may be babies who are especially responsive to sounds. They enjoy listening to singing or to sounds of different pitch. Since language is an important form of communication, it is a help to enjoy using it and to achieve some mastery over it early.

All babies gain from being with people who talk to them in soft, pleasant tones, giving them plenty of chance to hear speech. They gain, too, from feeling content, from having new and interesting experiences which are not overwhelming but make them want to "talk," and from being sure there is someone who cares enough to listen with pleasure. Speech flourishes under these conditions, although individual differences remain in patterns and amounts of vocalization.

One sometimes meets a child whose vocalizing does not develop into intelligible speech sounds. One suspects a hearing loss here or

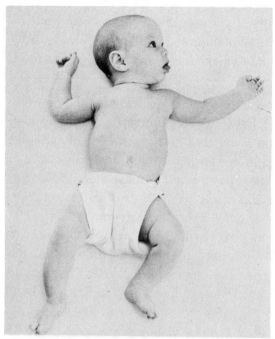

Mead Johnson Laboratories

Before a baby talks he does a lot of vocalizing and experimenting with sounds.

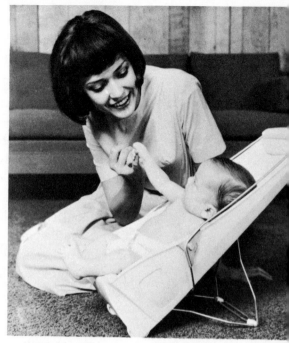

Infanseat Company

The pleased response of a parent may encourage a child to talk early.

perhaps some degree of mental retardation or an emotional disturbance. These possibilities should be checked.

Feeding the baby.   Because he needs not only the food, but also some cuddling, a mother will usually hold a baby even if he is getting his milk from a bottle. This body contact is almost as important as the food. It helps the baby feel safe and content. At first this contact with the feelings of comfort and security it gives comes best at feeding time. The baby gets his very first ideas about his world and about how his life will be from the feelings he has while he is being fed. The person who is feeding him is most important in establishing those feelings. The baby's world must include people!

Arrange to visit a family, if you can, and watch a baby while he is nursing or taking a bottle. Watch how the mother holds the baby to make him comfortable and to make it easy for him to get the food.

It is usually more satisfactory to nurse a baby for the first few months than to depend on bottle feedings. Breast milk is designed for infants. The baby who is nursing gets more contact with his mother and probably feels more satisfied by it. The mother who is nursing a baby, however, must pay attention to her diet, drinking at least a quart of milk a day and eating plenty of fruit and vegetables, meat, poultry, or fish once or twice a day, taking some vitamin D.

A mother may wish to give the baby an occasional bottle to make weaning easier. He gets used to something other than the breast before weaning starts. She changes from breast feeding to bottle feeding if she finds she does not have enough breast milk or

That baby who is nursing probably feels additional satisfaction from contact with his mother.

A mother may wish to give the baby an occasional bottle to make weaning easier.

Evenflo

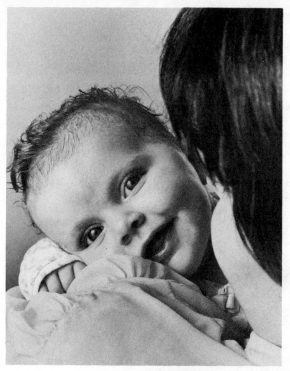

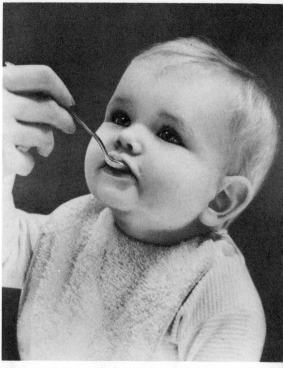

After the baby is fed he will need to be "bubbled" to get out any air he may have swallowed.

By the time a baby is three or four months old, he begins to eat solid food.

for other reasons such as having to return to outside work. Some mothers may continue to nurse their babies for eight or nine months and then change to a cup rather than a bottle.

After a baby has had a feeding and, with some babies, during the feeding, he will need to be "bubbled" or "burped" by holding him over your shoulder and patting him gently to get out any air bubbles which may give him a stomachache and prevent his sleeping comfortably.

In addition to milk, an infant is usually given vitamin D. He may also have strained orange juice beginning in the first month. By the time he is three or four months old, he will have some solid foods such as cereal and perhaps strained fruit. He may also be eating some egg yolk. Pureed (mashed) vegetables will be added followed by meat. With canned foods available for infant feeding, a mother's job of preparing food is much easier than it used to be.

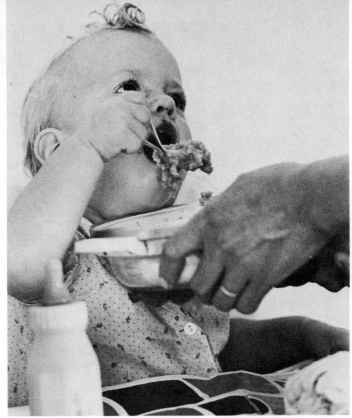

Commercially prepared baby food makes life
easier for a busy mother.

Babies will like some foods more than others. A wise mother
adjusts to the baby's preference but keeps offering him other foods
to help get him accustomed to them. Some babies do better if they
are given their solid foods first, while others like some milk first and
then their solid food. A mother will discover what works best with
her individual baby. She will never force him to eat what he seems
to dislike, or force him to eat more than he wants at any one time.

As they progress in development, babies usually enjoy playing
with their food. It is one way to find out what food is like. It is often
a step in learning to enjoy it. They will try using their fingers to get
food into their mouth along with the spoon. It helps if parents can
feel comfortable about the "messiness" that is part of eating for most
young children. Babies feel better about themselves and eating goes
more smoothly.

Many babies by the end of the first year have a special blanket or object which seems to be associated with sleep and makes it easier for them to settle down. Babies as well as older children often like the security of having familiar things around them and going through the same routines at bedtime.

A baby is fortunate if his bedtime routine includes some time with his father. A father needs to spend time caring for his baby if they are to become really acquainted. Fathers who know their children through caring for them can follow and enjoy the developmental changes taking place. A baby responds well to a change of

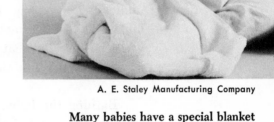

A. E. Staley Manufacturing Company

Many babies have a special blanket which makes it easier for them to settle down.

The baby begins to discover the difference between the male person and the female person.

Gerber Products Company

53

person at the end of the day and to quiet play with his father. He learns to know and feel safe and secure with his father as well as with his mother. He begins to discover the differences between the male person and the female person. A mother is also helped if the father shares in the baby's care. It gives her a rest and it also helps her in the process of beginning to let the baby grow away from his dependence on her. The mother may need to give encouragement to the father in taking over a routine such as play before bedtime or undressing or perhaps the bathing. When the father does this, it is important that the mother accept the father's way of doing things with the baby so that the two may be comfortable together and really enjoy the time they spend together.

Bathing the baby. Some babies have skin that is easily irritated by the acid in urine. Parents of such a baby must use special care to see that he is completely dry when his diapers are changed and the diapers are thoroughly rinsed. He may need to be rubbed with some kind of ointment. Each baby is a bit different in what he needs.

In the first months the baby may feel apprehensive at being bathed. The older baby will enjoy his bath.

Winthrop Laboratories

Gerber Products Company

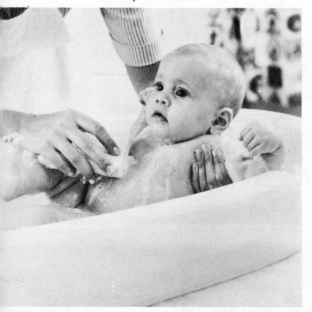

In the first months the infant will often cry when he is being given a bath. He gets tired. He may not enjoy being disturbed this way at first. Later he will enjoy his bath. Bath time may become the most fascinating part of the day. He splashes with his arms and kicks. Before the end of the first year, he is exploring many aspects of water and its wonderful properties.

Elimination.   Each baby will have his own pattern of elimination. He may have several bowel movements a day or he may have a movement only every two or three days. The stools of breast fed and bottle fed babies will be different in color and texture, too. Stools of a baby change after he begins eating solid foods, and his patterns of eliminating will change then.

"Toilet training," as it is called, is not usually undertaken in the first year, so it will be discussed in a later chapter. We just accept the necessity of washing diapers every day or two when there is a baby in the house!

Clothing.   Clothes for babies today are a simple matter. The baby will wear a diaper, a shirt, and a short wrapper of some kind. In colder weather a gown with a drawstring bottom may be worn. The clothes are usually of cotton material which is soft and easily washed. The popular cotton knits require no ironing.

The big item of laundry is the diapers. Soiled ones should be rinsed in the toilet and then put to soak in a diaper pail until washing time. Hot water and soap and plenty of rinsing will keep the diapers clean and soft. People used to think that diapers had to be boiled, but with the hot water possible in an automatic washing machine boiling is not considered necessary today.

Disposable diapers are useful when one is traveling or even away from home for a day. One does not need to carry wet or soiled diapers. Some communities have satisfactory diaper services. These services supply diapers with pickup and delivery service as required. Using the diaper service may be a help to the family, especially at times when the mother is ill or has extra responsibilities or when laundry facilities are not adequate. Disposable diapers or diaper

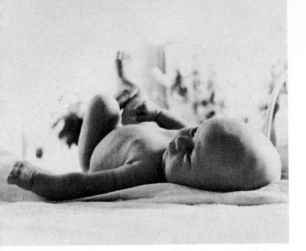

Winthrop Laboratories

At about six months the baby can sit erect, but his posture will be better if he is allowed to exercise his muscles while on his back or stomach.

By about six months the baby can turn over, but some babies do it earlier and some later.

Mead Johnson Laboratories

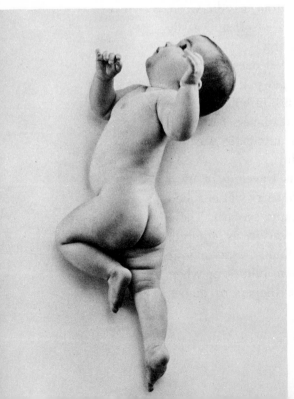

service may seem expensive but may be a wise use of money under some circumstances.

Learning motor control. In the beginning the infant makes many random, uncoordinated movements. He wiggles all over when he is excited. He shakes with rage and his arms and legs wave. As the weeks pass, his movements gradually become less diffuse and less undifferentiated. Instead of merely being random they become more direct and purposeful. He turns his head toward the door when he is expecting his bottle. He waves his arms. He is gaining control over his body movements. Control proceeds in an orderly way. He gains some control over arm movements, then hand and still later fingers. He gains control over head movements before he can control his leg movement. He can turn his head early. When he is held, his head needs support for it wobbles at first, but gradually he holds it up more firmly and turns it in the direction he wishes. Much later he draws his legs up under him and raises himself off the floor or pushes himself forward, scooting over the floor.

A baby not only has to learn what belongs to his body but also has to learn to control his body. Watch a three- or four-month-old baby playing with his hands and fingers. He gets them in front of his face and moves them around, fascinated by what they do. He may stick a finger into his mouth. It gives him a different feeling from sticking a toy into his mouth. He's finding out more about what is the "me" and the "not me" in the world.

We support his head carefully when we pick him up, even at three months. But by this time he will raise his head when he is held over a shoulder, and by the time he is four to six months old he can lift his head and chest when he is placed on his stomach. His head and body control are good enough by six months so that he will be comfortable sitting with support. But his posture will be better later if he does not do much sitting while his bones are still soft. He is better off lying on his stomach raising his head and strengthening his back muscles while he watches things.

By six or seven months he can turn over. He should *never* be left on a bed without sides even when he is only three or four months old. By six or eight months, too, he may be attempting to crawl or creep.

By six or eight months a baby may be beginning to crawl or creep.

Mead Johnson Laboratories

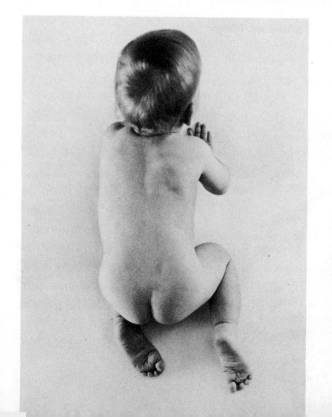
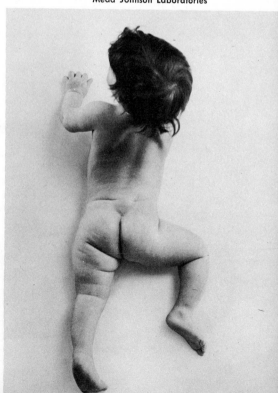

By the time he is eight months old he can usually sit upright for a time without fatigue. He may soon pull himself to a standing position and take steps with support.

The stretching and kicking and waving of his arms which he has been doing are exercises in preparation for standing and walking. Most children are walking by fifteen months. Then they are on their way! They are entering the toddler stage!

Learning to grasp objects is an important milestone in the baby's development. His fingers will fascinate him for a long time. He began observing them at three or four months. At six or eight months he begins to use them. Watch him work to acquire skill in picking up an object. It is like the process that you go through in learning to play tennis or basketball. It takes lots and lots of practice to control the muscles and to develop the eye-hand coordination needed to make picking up an object or playing a complicated game like tennis a smooth and efficient process.

It takes a lot of practice for a baby to learn to grasp an object.

Johnson and Johnson

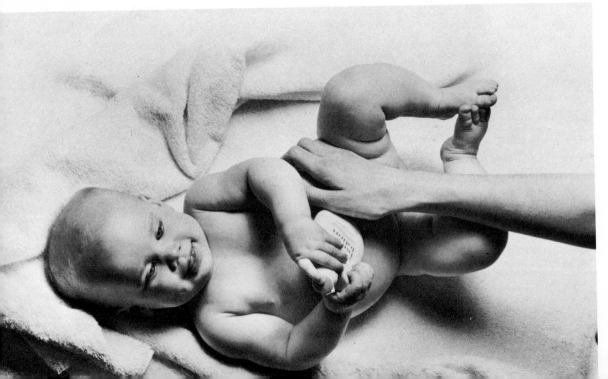

It is easy for us to reach out and pick up a small object. Notice how clumsy the baby is about it at first. Just reaching out and getting near the object is hard for him. His hand lands near it but not on it. Sometimes in his efforts he pushes the object away from him rather than bringing it closer. When he does reach it, he scoops it up with the palm of his hand at first rather than with his thumb and fingers as we do.

Before he is a year old he begins to use his thumb, not just as something to suck, but as a useful thing for grasping. With the thumb and forefinger he develops a "pincer grip" which gets results and which will serve him the rest of his life. It has taken weeks of practice. Now he reaches for everything, the tiniest speck of dust or a bit of paper. He gives himself plenty of practice. We need to watch carefully—the object picked up usually goes into his mouth.

He must feel great satisfaction in being able to accomplish this feat of controlling his thumb and fingers to get what he sets out to get. How discouraging to him if someone always snatches the thing away from him, with no appreciation of his achievement. He will continue to work at practicing his skill but the effort may seem less satisfying if he feels that people don't appreciate what he is trying to do. You may need to give him another object if you take something away from him.

Sucking and thumbsucking.   Since babies need to do a lot of sucking, some babies may like a pacifier to suck on when they feel uncomfortable or restless. Sucking on a pacifier may mean they do less crying which makes them easier to live with. Some babies do a lot of thumbsucking. We are not sure why they differ in the amount of thumbsucking they do.

Children may suck a thumb when they are sleepy or tired or not feeling well. This comforts them. They need comfort for they are in a new, strange world. They may feel more safe and secure with a thumb in their mouth. Watch how a child confronted with a new person or an unexpected noise or a strange situation may put his finger into his mouth. As he grows older, he will feel safer and more confident. He may no longer need this kind of support.

Carlos N. Crosbie

We should not feel too concerned when the young child sucks her thumb. Sometimes she needs the comfort of her thumb.

In some cases a baby or an older child who sucks his thumb is having trouble feeling that the world is a good place, so he retreats to the comfort of a thumb. He knows that he can depend on his thumb. It is always available. It is easy to see that we only make matters worse for this kind of child if we pull his thumb out of his mouth or cover it so he can't get to it. Sucking a thumb seems to be a natural safety valve which children use. It may do harm to deprive them of it.

It is better just to feel comfortable about letting infants suck if they want. We can try, too, to make sure that their world is really comfortable, without too much strain in it and with plenty of love and attention. When they are older, we can help them find other things to play with and other ways of finding satisfaction, so that they need their thumb less and less. If a child gives up thumbsucking before he is five or six years old, his teeth are not likely to be made crooked by his sucking. Thumbsucking may be a sign of emotional trouble in an older child, but is not apt to be serious for a toddler.

Often it is the children whose parents have fought with them over the habit who keep on sucking the longest and the hardest. As we know, the toddler is trying hard to assert himself and be independent. If someone tries to *make* him take his thumb out of his mouth, he may use this as the issue to take a stand on. He raises the flag of independence. He insists on having his thumb.

One quiet little girl of three who sucked her thumb when she was tired or unhappy was taken to the dentist. The dentist happened to be one who tried to discourage any thumbsucking. He told her she must stop the "bad habit." Her mother kept reminding her when she saw the thumb go into the child's mouth. The child's answer was to keep the thumb in her mouth more and more of the time. As a quiet, timid child, she didn't feel brave enough to assert herself in many other ways, but she could defiantly suck her thumb. She did less thumbsucking when the family dropped the issue, leaving the matter up to her.

Our feelings about thumbsucking usually come from the feelings our parents had toward it. Our feelings may be especially strong if we happened to have been scolded by our parents for sucking our thumb. If we had to try hard to overcome the habit, we aren't likely to enjoy seeing someone else thumbsucking contentedly!

Readiness and maturation. Learning things like grasping an object is more than just a matter of practice. It is a developmental matter, too. A baby or a young child gains control over his body because there are changes taking place in his muscles, his bones and skeletal system, and the pathways in his nervous system which make it possible for him to acquire the skill. The possibility of using the thumb in opposition to the fingers in a "pincer grip" appears as a child nears the end of the first year because of his physical development then. His body is "ready" for him to learn to grasp objects. He seizes every chance he can get to practice and perfect the skill.

L. de Victoria

Children will practice skills for which they are developmentally ready and will work at what is most appropriate for them to learn at the time.

J. Peoples

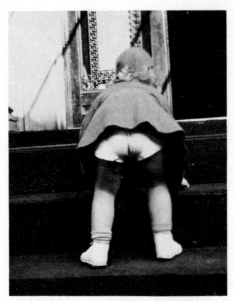

C. S. Dixon

Skill in stair-climbing comes with maturation. But she likes to practice!

We call this readiness *maturation*. Maturation means that growth has taken place which now makes it possible to do a thing, such as opposing the thumb and forefinger, that had been impossible before a certain level of development was reached. Doing the thing then becomes easily possible. It gives the child satisfaction to perfect his control over muscles.

Stair-climbing is a good example of a skill which depends on maturation. Most children are nearly four years old before they walk up and down stairs smoothly the way we do, one foot to a step. Before the maturation of this capacity (which depends on physical growth in the body), children use two feet to each stair step. The adult way of walking up and down stairs appears in a child not because of our efforts to teach him, but because he has matured to the point where he is able to do it this way easily.

A child will usually practice those skills for which he is developmentally ready. It helps a child to have opportunities to practice when he is ready. It is discouraging to him to be urged to practice skills for which he is not ready, like trying to catch a ball when he is only two or three years old. He likes to throw the ball but catching it is difficult. Left alone, with plenty of chance to do what he wishes, the child will usually work at what is most appropriate for him to learn at the time, from sucking to picking up things, to sitting by himself, to standing and then walking and throwing balls.

Maturation, or the "readiness" to do a thing, and then a chance to practice doing it are what a child needs in developing motor skills. He finds satisfaction in exercising his skills as well as in our pleasure at seeing him be successful. He likes to know that we approve and are pleased with him. He begins to feel good about himself.

A baby soon gets to know special people.

Social relationships. At first a baby knows people by the way they pick him up or by their voices. A baby's eyes do not focus well enough at first to see people as we do. But babies soon begin to know special people such as their mothers and fathers. They stop crying more readily in that person's arms or even when they hear his or her step.

Toward the end of the first year the baby may be apprehensive of strangers.

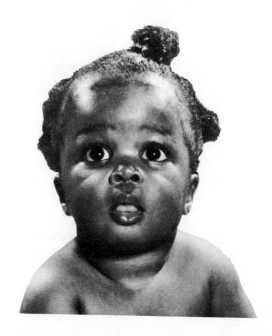

Winthrop Laboratories

Some babies are very ready to smile.

By the end of the first two months a baby is beginning to smile. By the time he is three or four months old he usually smiles at a person who makes a friendly approach. Babies become more discriminating at five or six months. They show more pleasure in being greeted by people they know than by a strange face. Around eight or ten months they may even cry if a stranger approaches. This means they are realizing the significance of the differences between familiar people and ones strange to them. Later they will be friendlier and more interested in strange people.

Almost from the beginning babies begin to show their own individual patterns of making contacts with people. Some babies are very ready to smile and invite approaches. Others want to take their time with people. Some babies may be busy exploring so many other aspects of the world that they don't want to be bothered by attention except when it's needed. But most babies like attention and like to watch other people, especially children.

Play.   Toward the end of the first year most babies have begun to enjoy simple games like "pat-a-cake" or having someone cover up a face and then reappear. Too much of this kind of play makes them tired and may lead to crying. Babies should be played with for only short periods of time. The best play comes during the daily caring

Most babies, even solemn ones, like attention.

The best time for playing is while the baby is being bathed or dressed.

Rubin

Johnson and Johnson

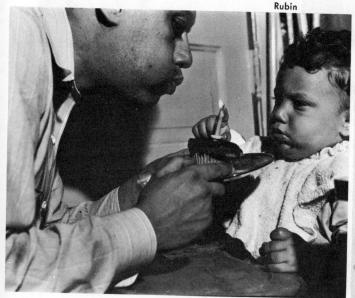

for them while they are being bathed and dressed. Here is the time for that extra bit of attention. It is good to allow time for splashing in the bath, for talking and singing while you bathe and dress the baby and while you are getting his cereal ready. It will be fun for both of you.

A baby's change and growth during his first year is amazing.

W. Schmidt

THINGS TO PLAY WITH

Watch a baby and see what he plays with. He should have:

something that can be *safely put into his mouth and can be washed* and easily kept clean, such as a terry cloth animal;

something that is *hard* and feels good on his gum when he bites on it, such as a hard rubber teething ring;

something that is *soft* and feels good when he squeezes it and bangs it with his hands, such as a soft rubber doll;

something that is a *bright color,* such as colored plastic cubes;

something that *moves,* such as a mobile;

something that makes a *sound,* such as a rattle;

something he can *grasp* in his hands, such as a small lid;

something *light in weight* without sharp edges or points.

At the end of twelve months. By the end of the first year, the baby has changed from an unknown and unknowing newcomer to an individual admired and admiring. He has progressed from a milk diet to one including some solid foods. He has discovered some things about himself—his hands, his toes, how to manipulate himself to crawl and, perhaps, to take a few steps. He has discovered some things about his world—the security and affection of parents, the fun and play of brothers and sisters, that a smile gets a smile, and that crying also gets a response. The change and growth in a baby during his first year is amazing.

TO DO AND DISCUSS   **ACTIVITIES**

1. **Visit a home where there is a baby. Before you visit, decide what you will want to observe and what you will want to ask the mother about the baby. Afterwards write a report of what you learned. Be sure to mention the age of the baby.**
   a. **What did you learn from your observations of the baby?**
   b. **What additional information did you obtain from the mother?**

    c. How much control does this baby have over his body? his hands? his arms? his legs?

    d. How does he respond to people? What are the differences in his responses to familiar people and strangers?

2. Arrange to watch a mother as she gives a bath to a baby less than a year old. Describe what the baby does. What are the steps the mother takes in bathing and dressing the infant? List the things she uses at bath time.

3. Visit a baby who is being bottle fed; watch the mother prepare the bottle. Find out just how it is done. You may need to know about getting a bottle ready if you are taking care of a baby. Watch how the mother holds the baby when she gives him his bottle.

4. Make a list of some play materials which are safe, such as rubber rings. What makes these things safe? Observe a baby at play. Did the baby you observed have any playthings which seemed unsafe?

TO THINK AND WRITE ABOUT

1. What are five changes married couples can expect in their lives when their first baby is born?

2. What are some of the things a pregnant woman does to insure the best health for her child and for herself?

3. Which daily activities may a pregnant woman safely continue to do? What activities would better be suspended until after the baby is born?

4. What are some of the reasons that breast feeding of babies is recommended when it is possible?

5. How does the mother of a newborn baby make him feel that the world is a nice place?

6. Why is it important for a baby to live at home with a family rather than in an institution?

7. List at least ten ways in which a newborn baby is helpless and must depend on others.

8. What are some reasons babies cry? Why do some cry more than others?

9. What is a three-month-old baby like? a six-month-old baby? a twelve-month-old baby? What are some ways babies of each age show that they are individuals?

10. What differences have you observed in the way babies respond to your approaches to them? Does the same baby always respond in the same way to you? If not, what seems to make the response different at different times? For example, who is holding the baby at the time you approach him?

11. How do you feel about seeing a baby or a small child sucking his thumb? What do you remember about your own experiences in connection with thumbsucking? What differences in attitudes are there among members of the class?

PAMPHLETS AND PAPERBACKS   REFERENCES

Auerback, Aline B.
How to Give Your Child a Good Start
New York: Child Study Association of America, 1961

Carson, Ruth
Having a Baby
Public Affairs Pamphlet No. 178
New York: Public Affairs Committee, Inc.

Carson, Ruth
Your New Baby
Public Affairs Pamphlet No. 353
New York: Public Affairs Committee, Inc.

Castallo, Mario
Getting Ready for Parenthood: A Manual for Expectant Mothers and Fathers
New York: The Crowell-Collier Publishing Company, 1962

Graves, Judy
Right from the Start—The Importance of Early Immunizations
Public Affairs Pamphlet No. 350
New York: Public Affairs Committee, Inc.

How Your Baby Grows
New York: Dell Purse Books, Dell Publishing Company, Inc., 1965

Infant Care
Children's Bureau Publication No. 8
U. S. Department of Health, Education, and Welfare, 1962

Prenatal Care
Children's Bureau Publication No. 4
U. S. Department of Health, Education, and Welfare, 1962

Spock, Benjamin
Baby and Child Care, Revised Edition
New York: Pocket Books, Inc.

Spock, Benjamin
Dr. Spock Talks with Mothers: Growth and Guidance
New York: Crest Books, 1961

Spock, Benjamin, and John Reinhart, with photographs by Wayne
  Miller
A Baby's First Year
New York: Pocket Books, Inc., 1956

When Your Baby Is on the Way
Children's Bureau Publication No. 391
U. S. Department of Health, Education, and Welfare

Wolf, Anna W. M.
*The Parents' Manual: A Guide to the Emotional Development of Young
  Children, Revised Edition*
New York: Frederick Ungar Publishing Company, Inc., 1962

BOOKS

DeSchweinitz, Karl
*Growing Up: The Story of How We Become Alive, Are Born, and
  Grow Up*
New York: The Macmillan Company, 1965

The Encyclopedia of Child Care and Guidance, Revised Edition
Gruenberg, Sidonie, ed.
New York: Doubleday & Company, Inc., 1963

Ets, Marie
The Story of a Baby
New York: Viking Press, Inc., 1939

Gruenberg, Sidonie
The Wonderful Story of How You Were Born
New York: Hanover House, 1959

Winnicott, D. W.
Mother and Child: A Primer of First Relationships
New York: Basic Books, 1957

Wolf, Anna W. M., and Suzanne Szasz
Helping Your Child's Emotional Growth
New York: Doubleday & Company, Inc., 1954

Children Who Are One and Two Years Old

3

The child who is one or two years old is beginning to learn about his world. He is discovering he is a person, and it is important for him to feel that he is a person of worth. He has a strong urge to be independent, but he feels safe and is safe only when someone is near to care for him. He needs discipline that is gentle but firm. He is learning to fit into a world of other individuals by talking, walking about, and acquiring some social customs.

Curiosity and play are very important to the toddler's development. His exploring may lead him anywhere—he likes to wander and to touch everything within reach. A wide variety of play experiences helps to develop his muscular coordination, as well as providing the basis for future learning.

73

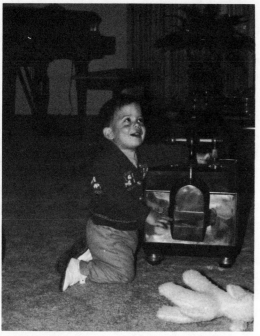

Jonathan Mach

Caring for a toddler is a full-time job. He is always trying new things, exploring his world.

WHAT ARE TODDLERS LIKE?

"I'm really somebody." The toddler presents us with a challenge. Caring for him is a full-time job. He is active. He is learning to walk and do some things by himself. He often says "No," which usually means that he is trying to say, "I'm discovering I'm really somebody. I want to do things my way."

In spite of feeling he is somebody, he depends on us to protect him and keep him safe. We have to see that he doesn't fall into holes, get into the street, or pinch his fingers in the door or eat inedible things. We have to be very alert to keep up with him.

We need to help him but we want to do it in such a way that we leave him with that wonderful feeling, "I'm really somebody!" This is a good feeling for anyone to have. We all do better when we feel we are "somebody." We want him to keep the feeling that he can assert himself and be somebody.

When we protect him, we want to be sure that we do it in such a way that he does not feel afraid to try new things, or afraid to be wrong (this is a terrible way to feel), or does not feel that he is just little and worthless. We want him to keep the feeling that it is wonderful to explore on his own. We want him to find out how to do it safely, when to use help, and what the limits are. The young child isn't very "realistic" when he begins trotting around. It takes experience to learn about the world and what's in it.

The desire to be independent vs the need to be babied. A young child has a strong desire to be independent. It has been said that at this age he is trying to discover whether he is a man or a mouse. He may run the other way when we want him to come with us. He may refuse to put on a shoe when we are trying to dress him. He may turn his head away when we try to feed him.

Ringle

We want to be sure that she is not afraid to try new things.

It helps to remember that we can expect him to act like this many times. It is part of being a one- or two-year-old or even three or four. It has little to do with us or our methods of managing him. It is not the beginning of "bad" behavior. He has just learned that he *can* run away or refuse things. He is practicing his independence. Perhaps the shoe doesn't really need to go on just at this minute. We can wait. Five minutes later he is delighted to put the shoe on—provided we have not been too insistent the first time.

We can wait with the spoonful of food when he turns away. The last mouthful may not be completely down. There is just not room. Maybe he is a child who likes to take his time and we are hurrying matters. Maybe he has really had enough. Forcing him only makes him more resistant and he will eat less rather than more. After all he is the authority on how much he needs to eat. We do well to accept his decision and not push him. Giving a two-year-old many chances to be independent and to make the decisions which he is able to make encourages healthy personality growth.

Watch a toddler run away from his parents. He runs a little way and then turns and looks back. If his mother or father waits and smiles reassuringly, the child may run happily back into his parents' arms. He is learning that it is all right to go away on his own. He is learning that his parents feel all right about it. A wonderful bit of learning!

He is independent at times but he is often a baby, too. In the process of growing up he needs to be free to retreat to babyhood

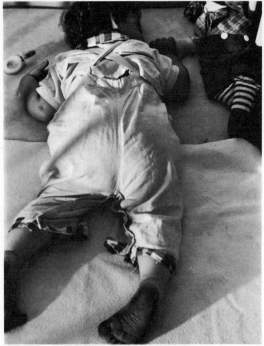

Rubin

The toddler needs to be free to retreat to babyhood with its pacifier and favorite sleeping toy.

when he finds the world a bit too frightening without feeling ashamed of acting this way. He may hang on to his mother's skirt and refuse to leave her in a strange place or he may cry bitterly when something startles him. Yet he is the same child who was climbing up high or pulling a wagonload of leaves or wearing a big cowboy hat a few minutes earlier. But now he wants to be accepted as little just because he *feels* little.

We should approve of him when he acts in grown-up ways, but we do not disapprove of him when he acts like a little child. In this way he can be comfortable about his ups and downs of feeling and become better able to manage *all* his feelings.

It is important for us to know how he feels because we are better able to help him when we understand. If he hides his feelings from us, he is showing us that he does not trust us or himself as he should. If he is angry at us, for example, it is better for us to know it and better for him to tell us directly. Anger is hard to bear alone. We will talk more about this later on.

The child likes to take his time. The child needs *time*. When he goes walking, he really strolls—if he isn't running! He stops to touch the fire hydrant and feel its knobs or pick up a stone and then drop it for the next one. He stands and watches. Sometimes it is hard to figure out which way he wants to go. He really enjoys a walk when he can go at his own rate. We can't always go at this rate, of course, but he is entitled to do it whenever it is possible.

Having to hurry makes a child irritable for he sees no purpose in it. Only later can he understand about being "on time." It makes no sense to him at this age. He is busy learning about other things.

He wants time to play with the crackly leaf or the crumbling clod of dirt and poke his finger into the crack as he walks along. We will enjoy giving him this time if we appreciate how important it is to his development. He is laying foundations for understanding and living.

The magic of distraction.   When parents manage the toddler's wandering, exploratory gestures in an understanding way, they satisfy his urge to test out his independence. During a walk, he may then become interested in a bright flower or a stick along the way. He devotes himself to a thorough exploration of this fascinating object. It becomes a scientific adventure. The objective of the walk has taken a different form. This change suggests an important principle in guidance—the magic of distraction.

Young children are easily distracted. They may be sobbing one minute because they can't have a shiny pair of scissors, but their tears stop and a smile breaks through at the sight of a shiny lid from a cottage cheese carton which can be set spinning. If one can't have one thing, there is often another. The world is still a good place.

It seldom gets us anywhere to beat our heads against a stone wall, as the saying goes. If we keep insisting, "No, you can't have the scissors," the child will be unhappy. He may become less likely to want things—a pretty unfortunate way for anyone to feel. With a little imagination and resourcefulness, we can usually think of something to substitute or some way to distract him and make life livable again for him and for us. We are helping him, too, with an important step in personality growth. Everyone has to learn to live within some limits and feel *comfortable* about doing it.

Play makes him healthy.   The child of this age needs plenty of time and opportunity to play. Play keeps him healthy. It may sound strange, but play is essential for a child's health.

At this age, he will usually need to play near us or keep in touch with us, reassured by a smile or a word and knowing that we feel interest and pleasure in what is happening and that we can be depended on to see that all goes well. He needs this if he is to play freely. Notice how much more freely some children play than others.

Children of one and two need plenty of time to play with "their" adults nearby.

Play is a way of feeling big even when one is still little. It is a way of making things happen as one wants, quite different from the world the child lives in. It is a way of overcoming fears. For example, the child himself can make things disappear and reappear in play by covering them up and then uncovering them. He grows less afraid that people will leave him. Play is a way of anticipating things and getting prepared, trying to understand what it is like to be a mother or a father or a doctor or a policeman. In play he can act as if he were these people and feel bigger.

Play is a way of learning what all kinds of things are like, and how one solves the problems they present. It is absorbing business and the child needs plenty of time if he is to lay a good foundation. He creates through play, stretches his imagination and brings his fantasies in touch with the real world through play.

S. Altman

S. Altman

Play is a way of learning what all kinds of things are like, of stretching the imagination, of feeling big. Play is an absorbing business.

B. Sierles

He does not need many playthings. He plays best with just a few things at this age. He repeats things over and over. He is mastering his world. Although his interest span is usually short at two, he will be satisfied to play in water for long periods of time. He likes mud and sand and sticks and stones and pans and perhaps something to serve as a doll. Simple activities entertain him, repeated over and over. He watches moving objects and people. He listens to sounds and makes some himself. He tries to pick up tiny objects. He examines every article he finds. He is two and is discovering the world in his own ways.

Two-year-olds enjoy the company of other children. They like to play near others, but they tend to treat other children like objects, pushing them down or out of the way. They take things from each other and seem surprised if the response is tears. They are learning that children are not like adults. When two-year-olds play together, they need adult supervision.

ATTITUDES AND DEVELOPMENTAL TASKS

"What's it all about? Who am I?" the child wonders. What is the answer? Will he find he is a person who manages pretty well, who can discover, who lives in an interesting world, who can depend on people and yet is not interfered with all the time? Or is the answer—a person who is always in trouble, who lives in the kind of world that is always hurting one, who lives with people who are always interfering and do not comfort one or keep one safe?

Attitudes are learned early.   Attitudes toward himself and the world are among the most important things that the toddler learns. Out of all his many experiences in these first years of rapid growth, he builds up his ideas about the kind of person he is, about what others are like, and about what he can expect in the world.

If he is fortunate he learns to feel that he is an important person, a lovable person, a successful person; one who can explore and discover, enjoy and create; one who can have things and do things. In

Anne R. Smith

**A child is fortunate if he learns to feel that he
is a person of worth and ability.**

other words he develops self-confidence and self-respect. These attitudes grow out of experiences of being treated with respect from the
beginning. Of course he will have many kinds of experiences. It is
important that the largest number of his experiences be the kind that
help him feel confidence in himself and trust in the people around
him.

A mother was talking about her daughter who was attending
college. The daughter was having real trouble because she thought
that she could not do anything successfully. She would sit and look
at her books and try to study, but she always thought, "I'm just
stupid. I can't learn. I always fail. Other people are so much better."

As she talked, this mother began to remember certain things.
She remembered that when the girl was quite small, she had been
given a tricycle. It was really too big for her. The family lived in the
country where there was no sidewalk. Her parents tried to teach her

to ride the tricycle but it would tip over. She couldn't make it go. She would cry and try pushing it around, but she was told that wasn't the right way. Her older brother laughed at her. He could ride it easily. This girl finally learned to ride the tricycle, but, unfortunately, she developed some ideas about herself. She learned to feel that, regardless of how hard she tried, she would fail, even when she wanted very much to feel big and to please her parents.

Probably many other things like this had happened to this girl as she was growing up. The ideas she built up about herself did not happen to be true in many respects. She really was not stupid. She did not need to fail, but because of her early experiences, she felt convinced that her efforts could lead only to failure. Later she did change her attitudes about herself. She was able to build a different "image" of herself, but only after someone else had helped her see more clearly what things had really been like for her. And she had been pretty unhappy and discouraged for a good many years.

Attitudes about the kind of person one is are learned early in life. Many experiences of failing to please one's parents or of failing to get approval result in handicapping attitudes about oneself, as with the girl who found it so difficult to ride her tricycle. She could not trust herself to be successful in anything.

You may have seen a child who seems to feel that the only way to get attention and feel important is to act silly and make people laugh. Perhaps he is really a quiet, timid child who never received much notice. One day he happened to put his father's hat on backwards. To his great delight everyone laughed. No one had paid attention when he succeeded in opening a door by himself or in building a big tower. No one seems to value the things that are important to him. From the response of other people he learned that one gets attention by showing off, so he continues to try it. But he does not get the satisfaction he should.

We all need attention, especially when we are young. You may know a child who has found that the best way to get attention is to be noisy and disturbing, forcing people to notice him. Another child may be very quiet, seeking attention by climbing into the adult's lap and sitting, watching what others are doing. If this child is a slow-moving, placid child, she may be content in doing this. If she is an active, impulsive child, she may do this only because she is unhappy and resentful. These children have found different ways of coping with the problem of finding the attention and approval they need, but not all the ways they have found are healthy ways of finding one's place in the world.

Attitudes and patterns of eating. "By two years of age many children can do a pretty complete feeding job, if not a neat one." (*Your Child from One to Six*, p. 11) They are far less messy than they were earlier. They still use their fingers a good deal. They still play with food in a purposeful way to find out more about it, such as its texture or temperature.

The child who is fed toward the end of the meal may eat more, but we should not force her to eat more than she wants.

By the age of two, many children can feed themselves—if somewhat messily!

Gerber Products Company

Gerber Products Company

If he is fed toward the end of the meal, a two-year-old may eat more. But we need to be sure that we do not try to get him to take more than he wants. The rule is *no urging or coaxing*. The extra mouthful gained this way may be more than lost if it lessens his appetite or gives him a distaste for the food or builds a resistance to eating. Remember he has a strong urge to be independent and to resist pressure! Relax and let him be the judge of the amounts of food he needs.

Our part as adults is to serve simple, attractive, well-balanced meals to the child under comfortable conditions. This means a chair which fits him, with a support on which his feet can rest if they do not reach the floor. It means a spoon, a fork, and a glass he can hold easily. It also means avoiding issues about eating. Appetites fluctuate in young children. They may eat a lot one day and want very little on another day. We need to let the child be the judge of how much he wants at any meal. Likes and dislikes change, too, and there are big individual differences here. Some children are eager to taste new foods while others are very conservative. They stick to the familiar and only slowly learn to enjoy new tastes. Some children go on food "jags," eating a lot of one food day after day until they are satisfied. The wise mother accepts most of these individual idiosyncrasies. She knows there are many ways of getting the nutrients one needs. If a child dislikes one food, she serves another he likes which has about the same food value. While she does not cater to his preferences alone, she tries to serve some of the foods he likes. She uses many finger foods which are easy for him to eat—carrot sticks, raw cauliflowerlets or broccoli, strips of celery or turnips, apple slices, meat in bite-sized pieces.

Appetite is related to growth spurts and becomes more stable with age. Acceptance of a variety of foods becomes easier with experience. A healthy child enjoys eating. While individual differences are present in what he prefers, he learns to like an increasing number of the foods which are served him unless there are issues about foods, or he has examples of finicky adults to imitate.

Some children satisfy their hunger by drinking a lot of milk so that they eat less of other foods which they need. In this case it may

Be sure children practice sanitary habits such as washing their hands before meals. (Chapter 5)

Flyer

Climbing is fun but requires careful supervision. (Chapter 5)

L. Dittmar

A mother should never leave without telling the child that she is going. (Chapter 5)

Flyer

The child learns through many experiences with people, activities with children and with play materials, and numerous educational media in the everyday world around him. Watch a child gain new skills through his observations and the use of his five senses. (Chapter 6)

Toys

Mattel, Inc., Toymakers

Art media

Binney and Smith, Inc.

be necessary to limit the amount of milk they drink before they have eaten other foods. On the other hand, if the child drinks only a small amount of milk his mother will serve milk in other forms such as custard, ice cream, or by adding powdered milk to other foods to make sure he is getting his quart every day. She avoids sweets or rich foods which take away the appetite. Desserts are usually fruits or custards. She is not too concerned with manners in eating at this age. She gives him time to master the whole process of eating at a table, using implements some of the time, and learning to like a variety of wholesome foods.

Learning to talk.   The two-year-old is learning to talk. He has been making speech sounds since he was a few months old. Babbling and vocalization precede using these sounds as speech to communicate wishes.

Progress in learning to talk depends on hearing speech. We mentioned earlier the importance of talking as we care for a baby so that he is familiar with the sound of voices and patterns of communication. Most two-year-olds love the sound of words and repeat them over and over. They practice talking. They are pleased with any success in using speech to get what they want. We need to pay attention when they try to communicate something to us in words. Our response and our approval are important in encouraging them to learn to use language.

The two-year-old loves simple stories of a few sentences—repeated—about what he did. Try making up one about what the child did. Repeat it for him as you are dressing him. Tell him in simple words what is going to happen:

> "Bobby is getting dressed now—first his shirt—now his pants—now his socks, one on this foot, one on the other foot—next his shoes, one for this foot, and one for that foot— then his sweater, over his head."

In this way he learns about language and how to use it this way. He learns how things are put into words.

W. Schmidt

A toddler should have a good example of correct speech—no "baby talk," even from brothers and sisters.

Here again there are individual differences. Some children enjoy sounds of words more than do others. They are fascinated by almost anything they hear. They listen for quite a long time. Other children will not listen as long. But they all need to *hear* speech if they are to develop well in using language. It will help if we speak slowly so that they can understand more easily.

It is important to learn good patterns of speech. People are handicapped if they use incorrect grammar and speak in harsh, unpleasant voices. These habits are hard to change, so we need to be careful to set an example in using correct grammar, enunciating distinctly and watching the quality of our voices. The child is a great imitator. He will copy our speech habits.

We give the two-year-old plenty of opportunities to use speech, but we do not call attention to his mistakes. We know he will learn correct speech in time if he hears it. Correcting him, trying to make him repeat words, may only interfere with his learning. If speech does not develop, the reason may be in conditions such as defective hearing or slow mental growth or even an emotional blocking in growth. These conditions require special treatment.

Toilet training.   *Learning to control elimination is a step toward independence.* For a child at this age, learning to follow the customs of adults in the use of the toilet is a real accomplishment.

Some mothers take pride in seeing how early they can "train" a child to stay "dry" or "clean." We know now that while this may be convenient for the mother, it may not be good for the child. A wise mother will usually wait until after the child is walking before she starts his toilet training. She may try to "catch" a bowel movement much earlier than this if his movements come at a regular time, but this is a matter of convenience to her.

A child receives real satisfaction from learning to control elimination when he is developmentally ready.

Baby Toilette, Hamilton Cosco, Inc.

The child needs help in learning to use the toilet properly, but he needs the right kind of help. Just responding to the contact of a cool potty on a warm bottom is a passive process in learning. It is an active kind of learning when the child uses the potty by his own choice, doing something which he knows pleases others. There is real satisfaction for the child in developing this kind of control. It is worth waiting for. With automatic washing machines and dryers it is easier for mothers to wait.

Toilet training can be a step for the child in becoming more responsible and more grown-up and independent. Since being independent is an important step in development, we want to protect him in this feeling.

Some children who are afraid of a flush toilet may respond better on a chair of their own.

Michigan Plastic Products, Inc.

A child gives signs of his readiness to learn control. One sign is that the intervals between wetting are longer. Another sign is the interest the child shows in the toilet habits of the people he lives with. He may suddenly get interested in the bathroom, coming in to play or watch family members there.

Now is the time to have a potty chair or toilet seat available. Children who are afraid of a flushing toilet may find it easier to sit on a chair of their own. Other children like trying the regular toilet seat, especially if there is a solid place, such as a box or step, to rest their feet so they do not feel any danger of falling in. A child will often sit with no results at first, but in sitting on the toilet for even a minute or two he becomes familiar with the process. When he gets the idea, he will be successful in imitating adults here as he does in so many other ways. If he resists, he should not be forced. Forcing him to sit on the seat may build up his resistance to the whole idea. It delays sound learning.

Some children seem to take on toilet habits easily and fairly early. Others are not ready for this learning until much later. The majority of children are ready to learn somewhere between 18-27 months, but the timetable is a flexible one. Some children take only a few days and some children take several months before they can be relied upon to be dry most of the time. Probably a good deal depends on the child's own development in motor control along with his confidence that he can do what others expect of him. Perhaps just as much depends on us and our confidence that he will learn when he is ready.

There are a few general procedures parents should follow in toilet training, but if they have been matter-of-fact about the child's elimination, have changed his diapers with no fuss about the messes he made, he should have no special problem in learning to stay dry and clean when he is ready.

When the child is successful in urinating in the proper place, he needs plenty of approval. It *is* an achievement! We should show our pride and pleasure. But we can expect plenty of failures, too. When he wets or soils, we should never scold or shame him. If we do, he may completely lose confidence in his ability or come to dislike the whole process. It is enough to say hopefully, as we change his pants, "Next time you can use the toilet."

At first it is the adult who needs to be responsible for seeing that the child gets to the toilet. We can say, "Time to go to the toilet. Let's run inside." Saying something such as "Which way shall we go?" or "You *are* a big boy now," to make the idea attractive to him will help. It is up to us to be responsible and to use all the skill we have in helping the child be successful. We should approve every success.

We need to be careful about praise, however. Praise that is out of proportion to the effort may make a child anxious. Failure may seem too serious for him to accept comfortably. He is almost sure to fail many times.

It is better to take off diapers and use training pants when the child seems ready to learn. His clothes should be easy to slip off—for his sake and ours. He may come running to us in a hurry and we need to be able to hurry. We must help him keep dry if he is to learn. By taking off diapers and putting on pants we are showing confidence in his ability to learn. Diapers are a symbol of babyhood. When his clothes are easy to manage he is likely soon to use the toilet without adult help and to enjoy being independent and feeling grown-up.

If a child comes and tells us he has already wet, we can take that as a sign that he is at least getting the point. We should take him to the toilet and see if he can "finish" in the right place and be pleased about it if he does. In time he will learn to come and tell us *before* he has wet.

Accidents are likely to happen when the child is under the strain of a new experience like starting Sunday school or nursery school, or if he is excited by having visitors or sick or even afraid. But these lapses will get fewer with time. Successful toilet training is an important milestone in development. But we should not be in a hurry to reach it. The child should set the timetable and we should be content to help him.

Successful learning here helps him with the feeling that he is really "somebody" in this world.

A child cannot learn everything at once.   A very young child is finding out what he is like, what other people are like, and what the world is like. But he cannot learn everything at once.

He feels more confidence if we try to help him learn those things which are understandable to him, and which he is able to learn most easily at his stage of development. He needs to find the world manageable. We need to trust his capacity to learn the necessary lessons with time.

For example, we do not expect a two-year-old to remember to say "please" and "thank you." He is only vaguely aware of relationships among people. He is mostly concerned about himself. We can help the child by using the words ourselves, by saying them for him at appropriate times, and much later by letting him know when these words are expected of him. We can give him approval when he does use them properly. In this way we help him with successful learning. He feels competent. Insisting on the child's using these words when they are meaningless to him may confuse him. A child may say, "I said 'please' so you *must* give it to me." These words seem to have magic powers to him.

Learning table manners is another example of behavior which is learned step by step. At first the child is concentrating on getting food into his mouth. This is an achievement. He uses his fingers instead of a spoon or fork when it is too hard to use the implement. He can feel quite discouraged if we expect good manners from him at this stage. Expecting too much may make him less likely to be successful later.

There are many lessons to be learned about property rights and sharing, too. The two-year-old is finding out that some things are his and some things are not his. They belong to others. He is learning to possess. "Mine! Mine!" he cries. It is difficult and often confusing to master the concepts of property rights.

The two-year-old must learn something about possessing before he is ready to learn about sharing. A neighbor comes in with a child, and his mother takes *his* toy and gives it to the visitor. He snatches it back, not because he is selfish, but because it seems part of him. It is *his,* which means he can have it. A wise mother proceeds with

Rubin

The toddler develops a strong sense of "Mine!" and often
finds it difficult to share.

care here. She does not insist on his sharing at this age. She may
help him give one of his less treasured toys to the visitor. This is a
good compromise and represents progress. When he enjoys playing
with other children, he really may want to share toys with them.

The child is not ready to do much sharing, not only because he's
learning that things belong to him, but also because he has not
reached the stage of being concerned about the needs of others. He
is still pretty much wrapped up in himself and in the business of
asserting himself. Gradually he will discover other people and be
interested in a relationship with them. He will *want* to give to them,
and this feeling is the basis for sharing. Until the child has this feeling, he may learn the wrong things if we push him into giving up
toys when he is unwilling.

There are other situations in which we build the child's confidence and self-respect or weaken them. He faces another big lesson

in dealing with frustration and angry feelings. The toddler is little and often feels helpless and hopeless in trying to make things happen as he wants them to happen. Frustration leads to anger or even depression. He must live with these difficult feelings and not feel too overwhelmed by them. All of us know this is not an easy task even for an older person. The little child is helped in this task if we are calm and reassuring, and give him the confidence that even these feelings can be managed. He must have confidence that he will be accepted as he is with all the less lovable parts of him, accepted as a person who at times feels angry or resentful or afraid. He must have some assurance that we can and will help him manage these kinds of feelings.

TAKING CARE OF A TODDLER

When we are taking care of the one- or two-year-old, we usually feel ready for a rest ourselves when he falls asleep. Fortunately he

A toddler likes to investigate everything.

Miami-Carey Division, The Philip Carey Manufacturing Company

takes naps. But when he is awake, he is likely to be into things constantly so that if he is quiet we know that we had better find out what's up. He may be into the soap powder or pulling towels off the shelf or putting the latest magazine into the toilet. It is useless to scold him or punish him for he usually is not sure what the scolding is about. We have to be the person responsible for keeping him within safe and acceptable limits. In doing this we are helping him learn what the limits are.

We must watch him if there is no fence to keep him out of the street. We must put away the things he should not touch or be there to say "No" and give him something he *can* touch. His strongest urges are to touch and explore. By touching he finds out what things are like and what one can do with them. We have to learn to work *with* these urges, not to disapprove of them.

The toddler learns from every experience. He may run down a slope and fall. We comfort him if he wants to be comforted. Sometimes comfort isn't necessary for he gets right up and goes on. When we do comfort him, we don't act as though a fall was a "major calamity," something to be frightened about. We just give him some extra loving, take care of the scratches, and send him on his way. Next time, we may take his hand and walk down the slope with him saying, "Walk slowly."

Taking his hand and *walking* down the slope with him, then letting him go as fast as he likes up the slope will help him learn how to manage himself on hills. Much later, he will learn more things about inclines and forces. Now he is learning how to manage himself on a slope with *confidence*. Beginnings are always important and especially those in the development of a personality.

Personality traits develop in these simple, early experiences. Self-confidence for the toddler grows out of being able to manage himself on a slope which seems steep to him. It grows out of success in exploring something new or climbing over an obstacle or even in saying "No." He does not develop confidence if he experiences more failure than success. In the way we care for him, we are helping him build healthy personality traits, as well as keeping him physically safe.

Anne R. Smith

The way a toddler is cared for can help him build healthy personality traits while he is finding out what the world is like.

The toddler is fortunate if he has a lot of things to touch and to feel and find out about, simple things that he can grasp both with his hands and his mind. He likes playing with the pans from the kitchen cupboard, for example, fitting lids on over and over again. He practices his skills. He explores sizes, shapes, form relationships. He squeezes things. He crumples and tears things like paper. He is learning about materials—the soft, the hard—about differences in texture. Some things tear and some things don't. He often puts things into his mouth. We have to watch him to see that harmful things are not popped in. He's testing things out in all kinds of ways, not only by touch but also by taste and sound. What is this world really like?

Never threaten to leave a child.   Because a young child is really dependent on adults, he needs to feel sure that he can find them or reach them whenever he needs to. There is no worse panic for a child than to feel that he is lost, that his mother or the person caring for him has abandoned him. It terrifies him because he knows he is helpless without her. It is cruel to say, "I'll go away and leave you," as a threat to get him to do what we want him to do. We hear thoughtless people say this, but it does real damage to the child even though it may get results for the adult.

A parent can say, "It's time to go now," (or whatever she intends to have him do) and take steps to see that he does what she asks, but a thoughtful parent never threatens to leave a child. The threat may make the child stop trying to be independent. He may become very anxious and this is unfortunate for him.

Let the child know when you must leave. A child is usually content as long as he is sure his mother is near. A wise mother never goes away without telling him she is leaving. He may cry. He may not like having her leave, but he will recover, and he will come to trust her. If she slips away without letting him know, he is likely to grow anxious even when she is around for fear she might leave, not knowing when she might. He doesn't trust. He may grow more dependent.

The child who has been left many times by his mother is often a child who finds it difficult to have her leave. He has had too many of these experiences, too early, before he has built up enough trust in himself. Or, a child who has been left many times may become almost too eager to make friends and to reassure himself about being safe. He is *too* dependent on pleasing others and ignores his own wishes. He goes from one person to another without the depth and closeness of feeling which are good for all of us to have with the most important people in our lives.

What about discipline?   Our approach to discipline should be consistent. The steps we take to remedy any situation should occur every time that situation or a similar one arises. There are beginning steps which we should use to help a child learn to control his actions in ways that are acceptable to us. What approach should be used and what steps should be taken to establish sound discipline? Once sound discipline is established, how can we maintain it?

When a toddler hits another child, for example, what should we do? The first thing is to stop the hitting, of course. We don't permit a child to keep on hitting. We don't punish him, however, for he won't understand why at this stage. He may think we don't like *him* which will only make him feel more like hitting other children!

We may help by trying to show him how to touch the other child gently. Hitting is often a way of making social contact and he may be fascinated by the noise he can evoke by hitting another child—like a live music box which responds to a punch. He can learn to make a contact less roughly and therefore more acceptably.

We may help him say the other child's name so he can learn to use words instead of blows as a way of being social.

We stop a child firmly and then we show him what to do—patting or speaking or offering something or just turning back to his own business. When he uses the acceptable method of managing himself, we approve, "Fine." We have helped him with the right kind of learning and shown our approval of his success in learning. The process will need to be repeated many times before it is fully learned.

If we ourselves are really good at forestalling things, we may be able to stop the child *before* he hits, saying "No" as we do it. This is the effective time to say "No," before, and not after the deed. We want him to learn to stop *before* he hits, not afterwards.

Now look at another kind of situation. Suppose the child starts to run into the street. We bring him back with a firm, "No," and show him something he can do which may be interesting to him. But suppose he heads for the street again. We must *do* something about the matter.

A good thing to do is to take him into the house and close the door, telling him he must play inside because he has not stayed in his play yard or on the sidewalk. He is likely to be very mad at us. He may lie on the floor and kick and cry. We don't get mad at him in return. We remain pleasantly neutral, but we may state the problem clearly for him, again, "When you are outside, you *must* stay on the sidewalk or in the yard." It is his problem, and he has to face it and suffer the consequences. It does not hurt a child to cry. We can bear his anger. We do not need to be upset about it.

When he calms down, we should be friendly and make him comfortable. We want him to *accept* the limit, not resent it. If he is quite young, there is no need to keep him inside for a long time since a short time seems long to a child, but we *make sure that he stays in for a time.*

When he goes outside again we keep a close watch. He may go toward the street again. If he does, it does not mean that the discipline is no good. It only means that he is testing out his conclusions as any scientist would do! It's important that the *same* result happen, a firm "No" and immediate removal to the house in spite of protest. You are big enough to carry a two-year-old even if he is kicking and screaming.

If you are firm and sure in what you do, the lesson is clear and he should learn it quickly. You can leave the learning to him. Threats or attempts to frighten him may only make him confused. He may learn all kinds of things that are not true—that streets are always dangerous or that cars are sure to hurt him—which may give him nightmares but may not keep him out of the street.

Sometimes spanking works, but we know that often a child learns the wrong things from it, things we didn't intend, like "people hurt you" or "I'm bad," and he is less clear about the real lesson which is simply, "You must stay on the sidewalk."

We want to be effective in discipline. To be effective we must say and do what will be clear and make sense to the child. The trouble with using spanking in such a case is that being spanked really has nothing to do with the problem. If we spank him, he may feel that he is quite right in being mad at *us*. He thus avoids facing the real problem and his responsibility for managing his impulses. Spanking only muddles his learning. He learns from facing the consequences of an act rather than from punishment.

GROWING INTELLECTUALLY

There is a great deal of evidence today that even a two-year-old needs a variety of experiences in order to grow intellectually. Learning to use words helps him grow in this way, but he also needs experiences to talk about. He needs to see a variety of objects, animals, and people, and to watch a variety of events if his mental capacities are to develop. These experiences nourish his mind. They give him the raw material for thinking, wondering, talking, and thus growing intellectually. Taking him on walks or for rides where there are new things to see, giving him time to watch, talking in simple language about the object or about what is happening are important for him.

A two-year-old is also ready to be introduced to the world of books. Select picture books with bright colors and only a sentence or two of text on a page. The pictures and text should be about things with which he is familiar, such as animals, everyday objects, everyday experiences, and children. A book will help him learn by reinforcing his discoveries about the world. An enjoyment of books opens the door to many kinds of learning.

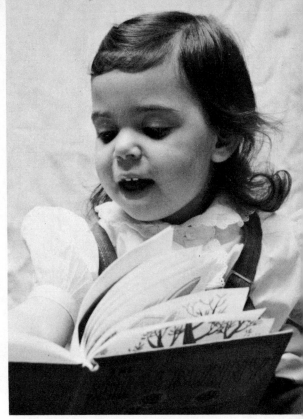

S. Altman

Books for young children should be about the real world and about familiar, everyday experiences.

If he is interested in sounds and rhythm, he may especially enjoy the language of poetry. Not only nursery rhymes but also simple, lovely poems which he may not understand but which he can enjoy because of the sound and the rhythmic language, will open doors for future satisfying experiences.

Music offers another experience in hearing sounds. A child of this age enjoys listening to singing and instrumental music. He enjoys making sounds, high ones, low ones, soft or loud ones. He enjoys songs we make up about what he is doing just as he does such stories. Children need to hear a variety of good, simple music. When music accompanies rhythmic activities, they respond with special pleasure. Try singing to a child as you swing him. Notice how often a child's movements as he plays are in tune with the music which is being

Dunn/dpi

A sense of humor is a help to everyone. We can encourage
a toddler to laugh at the things that seem funny to her.

played at the time. All these experiences increase his awareness of
sounds and his feeling for the rhythm of language itself. They develop his capacities.

A sense of humor is a help to everyone. There are already individual differences in two-year-olds. More things are funny to one
two-year-old than to another. We can encourage them all, however,
to laugh at some things, to play games that have an element of
humor. Almost every two-year-old enjoys hiding and having someone
find him—quite quickly—or finding the adult quickly. They all have
enough experience to know that putting a hat over one's face instead of on one's head is funny.

We need to be sure that a child is not puzzled and bewildered
or even frightened by something we see as funny. If it isn't funny to

him, it isn't funny. We should help him understand what really happened. The big job for him is to get things straight, understand them clearly, and not feel confused. It is not fun when people laugh at things that one doesn't understand. It only makes one feel little and helpless rather than independent and adequate. Part of growing is to understand better and to see things in a better perspective. It is good when we can laugh about some things.

The most significant thing that happens to the child one and two years old *is* to find that he is a person, that he is respected and that he can feel good about being independent, and about exploring and discovering more and more about the world and the people in it, including, most important of all, himself.

WHAT WE KNOW ABOUT TODDLERS

We can summarize what we know about toddlers in this way:

1. *Physical development:* At two years of age some children are steady on their feet. They walk well, and enjoy walking. Others are unsteady and likely to fall. Their walking skills are less well developed.

The second and third years are still a period of rapid physical growth. The child's body is changing and he needs—and wants —plenty of chance for exercise. He needs space to run and play both indoors and out.

He develops coordination of his large muscles through *climbing, pushing* and *pulling* things, *riding* kiddy cars or a small tricycle, and *carrying* objects which are large (for him) and lightweight.

At two years, some children are steady on their feet, while others still tumble.

R. MacKenzie

His finer muscles develop through activities such as these:

doing part of his *dressing,* putting on his socks, his shoes,
   pushing his arm into his sweater as we hold it for him.

hanging his jacket or coat on a low hook.

feeding himself, with his fingers or with a spoon.

playing with blocks of different sizes and shapes.

manipulating toys, as wooden rings on a stand and simple
   puzzles.

2. *Social development:* The toddler is finding out that he is an
individual, and it is essential for him to feel that he is valued, loved,
and respected by the important people in his world.

Although he urgently desires to be independent in some ways,
he still needs adults for emotional support, encouragement, and care.

He is learning to feed himself, to like more foods, to control his
elimination, and to talk. In accomplishing these things, he is growing
into the society in which he will live.

A toddler is learning about the world and his place in it as he
begins to respond to people and their expectations for him.

3. *Play:* At this age, when play is so important to the child, a
variety of experiences provides the foundation for future learnings.
Play becomes even more important to him as a three- or four-year-
old, but at two he has begun all his significant approaches to learning. He is curious and tries to find out. We make sure he is safe and

The toddler is finding out that he is
an individual as he responds to people and their expectations of him.

Gerber Products Company

let him go ahead and discover. We help him with words, the tools for thought and communication. We see that he has opportunities for many different play and exploration experiences.

Here are some things to remember when selecting play materials for a child of this age.

Choose:

Things that *feel* different.

Things that can be used *many ways*.

Things that a child can manipulate successfully *by himself*.

Things that are *raw materials* such as water, sand, and mud.

Avoid:

Things with sharp edges or points.

Things that splinter.

Things that get broken easily.

Things that have only *one* use, such as mechanical toys.

TO DO AND DISCUSS

ACTIVITIES

1. **Observe a toddler in his home for 30 minutes.**
   a. **See if you can keep a record of the objects he touches or looks at, the things that he notices and seems interested in.**
   b. **What kinds of responses does he make toward people?**
      his mother   other grown-ups
      you   other children
   c. **Describe what he does in one ten-minute period at play. What do you think he learned in this time?**
2. **Plan one day's meals for a preschool child after you have read the section on food in *Your Child from One to Six*, Children's Bureau Publication No. 30, 1962, pages 66 to 71.**
3. **If you know a family with a preschool child, ask the mother to tell you what the child had to eat yesterday. Write it down and check the foods with the list on page 67 in *Your Child from One to Six*.**

4. Prepare to discuss in class: What are children of one and two years like? How do they differ? Compare descriptions with other members of the class.

TO THINK AND WRITE ABOUT

1. How does the mother of a one-year-old help him develop his intelligence?

2. Why is the mother of a two-year-old busier than she might be with a child of any other age?

3. List some of the experiences which help a two-year-old develop self-confidence.

4. How may the mother of a two-year-old provide opportunities for learning?

5. Why is play the important work of little children?

6. Why is it important for children of all ages to have limits set for them? What kinds of limits should there be? What is the importance of enforcing these rules consistently? Do you think there should ever be exceptions to the limits or their enforcement?

7. What is the difference between discipline and punishment?

8. Why is it important that mealtimes be pleasant times?

REFERENCES   PAMPHLETS AND PAPERBACKS

Auerback, Aline B.
How to Give Your Child a Good Start
New York: Child Study Association of America, 1961

How Your Baby Grows (Chapters 2 and 3)
New York: Dell Purse Books, Dell Publishing Company, Inc., 1965

Hymes, James L.
Enjoy Your Child—Ages 1, 2, and 3
Public Affairs Pamphlet No. 141
New York: Public Affairs Committee, Inc.

Lowenberg, Miriam
Feeding Your Baby and Child
New York: Pocket Books, Inc.

Spock, Benjamin
Baby and Child Care, Revised Edition
New York: Pocket Books

Wolf, Anna W. M.
Your Child's Emotional Health
Public Affairs Pamphlet No. 264
New York: Public Affairs Committee, Inc.

Your Child from One to Six
Children's Bureau Publication No. 30
U. S. Department of Health, Education, and Welfare, 1962

BOOKS

The Encyclopedia of Child Care and Guidance, Revised Edition
Gruenberg, Sidonie, ed.
New York: Doubleday & Company, Inc., 1963

Gardner, D. Bruce
Development in Early Childhood
New York: Harper & Row, Publishers, 1964

Greene, Margaret
Learning to Talk: A Parent's Guide for the First Five Years
New York: Harper & Row, Publishers, 1960

Hymes, James L.
The Child Under Six
Englewood Cliffs, New Jersey: Prentice-Hall, Inc., 1963

Janis, Marjorie Graham
*A Two-year-old Goes to Nursery School: A Case Study of Separation
    Reactions*
Washington, D. C.: National Association for the Education of Young
    Children, 1964

Spock, Benjamin
Problems of Parents
Boston: Houghton Mifflin Company, 1962

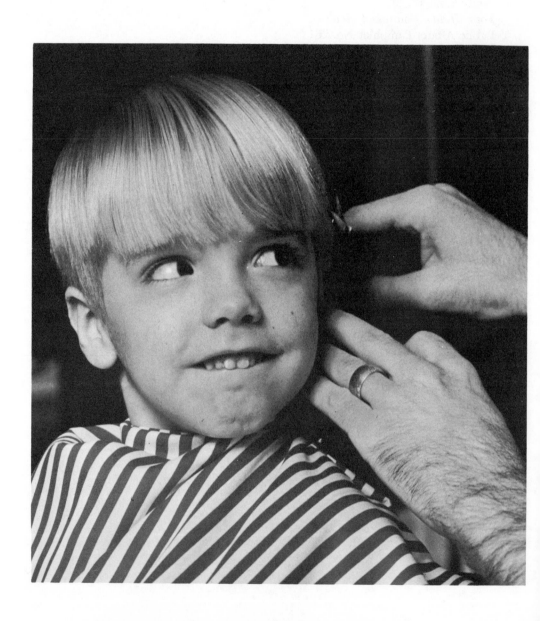

Children Who Are Three and Four Years Old

4

Children three and four years of age like to explore, to investigate, and to imagine. They like to pretend that they are mothers or daddies or doctors or cowboys or anyone else. They are now playing together in more purposeful ways. Their speech is more equal to the expression of their needs. Their feelings of anger or fear or joy are strong and are often strongly expressed although they struggle to fit themselves into civilized patterns. When they misbehave, they feel uncomfortable and guilty for they have the beginnings of a conscience. They are very much in need of firm but loving discipline. They are eager for attention and approval from adults and for contact with other children. We can see more clearly the unique personality patterns of each individual. Each one has begun the task of discovering what kind of place he or she may expect to have in the big world. Growth is taking place in all areas—physical, social, emotional, intellectual, and ethical.   107

DIFFERENCES AMONG CHILDREN

Children of three or four look very different from one another. They behave differently and these differences are easy for us to observe.

Some of these differences are the result of all the things which have been part of living for each child through his prenatal months and the months since he was born. Each one has been surrounded by different sights and sounds. More important still, he has been surrounded by people who have behaved toward him in different ways and set different patterns for him as he perceives and responds to the world. He may speak English or he may speak Italian, for example, depending upon the people with whom he has lived. He may be friendly or unfriendly, afraid of dogs or fond of them, depending on his experiences. He is developing patterns of behavior for coping with difficulties. He is developing characteristic ways of reacting to situations.

Children of three and four are developing characteristic ways of behaving.

George A. Hormel & Company

GROWTH CHANGES IN THREE- AND FOUR-YEAR-OLDS

Let us look at some of the growth changes which have taken place in the child of three or four. He looks different from the toddler. He has changed in appearance from a chubby baby to a pre-school child. His individual pattern of growth, whether he is a slow grower or a fast grower, for example, is pretty well established. In most cases, it will stay fairly constant throughout his childhood.

The child of three and four no longer looks like a toddler. Compare this young lady with the toddlers in the previous chapter.

Today's Health, published by the American Medical Association

His legs are getting longer and straighter. He tends to be knock kneed rather than bowlegged as he was at first. He still has a potbelly. By the time he is four or five his feet are not growing as fast as they were earlier. A lot of muscle growth is taking place throughout his body. This means he needs a great deal of active play to exercise his growing muscles. He tires quickly and recovers quickly. His bones are still soft and flexible. He gets tired sitting in one position. He often does a lot of wiggling.

He needs loose-fitting clothes which let him move freely. He needs shoes which fit well. He needs a firm mattress for sleeping and, when he sits down, a chair in which he can put his feet comfortably on the floor if he is to develop good posture.

He has gained skill and balance in walking and running even though he is not very graceful yet. By the time he is four he is usually walking up and down stairs in the grown-up way. He climbs a great deal and tries jumping from boxes and planks. Most

He needs a great deal of active play in loose-fitting clothes which let him move freely.

American Telephone and Telegraph Company

The three- and four-year-old needs clothes which he can manage by himself.

Pak-Nit ® Shrinkage Control

children do not skip easily until they are five or six. Roller skating is also a five-year-old activity for most children.

The child of three or four can dress himself with only a little help if he has the proper clothes. He cannot tie a bow knot yet. He will not be ready to learn to do it easily until he is six or seven. He can cut with scissors after a fashion, and he loves to draw with a pencil or a crayon. He uses his right or left hand consistently.

The preference for one hand over the other is usually established around twelve-eighteen months although sometimes it is not established until the child is much older. We think now that it is wise to encourage the use of the right hand in ways such as passing an object so the child finds it easy to reach for it with his right hand. But we think it is *not* wise to force a child to use his right hand if he persists in using his left. In some children changing hand preference leads to difficulties in learning and in speech.

The child of this age talks a lot and is adding words to his vocabulary rapidly. The muscles involved in speech do not always work together smoothly. His words tumble over each other and he may stutter. He just needs more practice and this is what he is getting. Our part is to listen and not to comment on his lack of skill.

The child of this age has learned to manage a spoon and fork pretty well but he does not find it easy yet to use a knife for cutting. He can pour from a pitcher if the pitcher is not too heavy.

The young child is far-sighted at this age, but he may hold an object close to his eyes in order to make it look bigger. Spending much time looking at small things or doing close work at this age is undesirable. It may result in nearsightedness. Binocular vision (use of both eyes to focus on an object and perceive depth correctly) is not fully developed until the child is six or eight years old. A child younger than this will often misjudge distance in jumping. Reading puts more of a strain on him than on an older child. Print in books for even seven or eight year old children should be large.

The child of three or four usually has all of his baby (deciduous) teeth, and the permanent teeth are developing in his jaw. He should start visits to the dentist. Some tooth decay (dental caries) occurs with most children. Cavities in the baby teeth should be filled in order to keep the mouth in good condition and protect the permanent teeth.

Research has shown that tooth decay is less frequent where (1) the child's diet is well balanced with plenty of protective foods, (2) the sugar intake is reduced, and (3) there is a small amount of fluoride in the water.

CHANGES IN PATTERNS OF EATING, SLEEPING, AND ELIMINATING

The three- or four-year-old follows the family meal schedule. He often needs a snack between meals to restore his energy, but he should not "piece" constantly or have a snack just before meals. His appetite may be less than when he was a toddler. It is often unpredictable. He may eat a lot of one food and very little of another. He thrives best if nourishing food is put before him with little comment about the food, and he is free to eat what he wants of it. He develops poor eating habits if his food whims are constantly catered to or he is urged to eat more than he wishes. Plenty of active play will take care of his appetite. (See *Your Child from One to Six,* Children's Bureau Publication, No. 30, 1962, on foods and snacks, pp. 67-68.)

A three-year-old will need sympathy after a bad dream—common at this age.

UNICEF Photo by Jack Ling—India

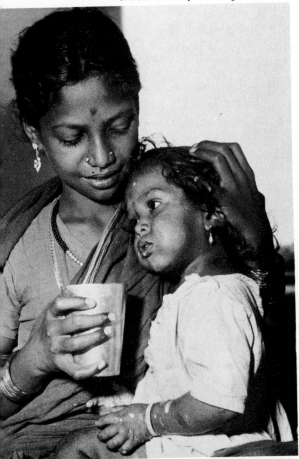

He continues to sleep about twelve hours a night and to need a rest during the day. Most children take a nap at least part of the time, sometimes sleeping an hour or two. Some do not take a nap, but only rest. Bedtime is usually accepted with less protest at this age. Each child will have his own routine and may still depend on a favorite toy or blanket at bedtime.

"Bad dreams" are common at this age and go along with the fears and the active imagination of the child at this stage. They may be connected with the struggle the child is having to control his "bad" impulses and become a civilized person. He needs comfort and sympathy but not indulgence. He should stay in his own bed.

Most children of this age have a reasonably good mastery of toilet habits. They are dry in the daytime most of the time although they still may have toilet "accidents" when upset or excited. They are pretty dependable at night, too. The timetable for completing this learning varies with individual children. Unless circumstances are quite unfavorable, children learn these habits of control. We continue to be matter-of-fact in our attitude toward "mistakes" and try to build up their confidence in succeeding.

TASKS IN PERSONALITY GROWTH

By three or four years of age the foundations for the child's personality are laid even though many changes may take place in the years ahead. Let us look at some of the personality characteristics which appear in children by this age.

Developing a feeling of trust. We have talked about the importance of helping the infant develop a sense of trust in his world. Developing trust is the first basic task in the development of a healthy personality. The infant learns to trust as he finds that he will be fed when he is hungry, kept safe, and given attention when he wants it. Through these experiences he begins to trust the world and its people and himself. With a foundation of basic trust he is helped in meeting the disappointments and frustrations which are sure to come as he goes on in life. Trust is the basis on which his religious faith will grow later.

S. Altman

If the personality is healthy, the feeling of trust that began in the first year of life continues to grow.

A child can face any experience, even a visit to the dentist, when she has developed trust and confidence with the help of understanding adults.

Susannah Spencer

Bakers of Wonder Bread

Changes due to physical growth help the child develop independence.

If the infant's early experiences have satisfied him, his feelings of trust in others will be greater than his feelings of mistrust. If this kind of balance is not achieved, he may find the world a frightening place. We all know people who are suspicious of everyone, who always expect the worst and get very depressed over what would seem a trifle to someone else. They are the people who have not succeeded in developing a sufficient amount of trust over mistrust. We all may have moments of feeling like this, and we know how hard it is to live with these feelings.

With a healthy personality the feelings of trust which were built up in the first year or two keep on growing. The child develops more trust in himself through being able to cope with the experiences which come with living. Under favorable circumstances the three- or four-year-old child continues to strengthen and extend his feelings of trust in the world while he is also perceiving the world more realistically than he did as an infant.

Developing a feeling of independence. A child of three or four also continues to work on the task which was most important when he was in the toddler stage. He was discovering then what it was like to be independent and no longer entirely dependent and helpless. Achieving a favorable ratio of independence and dependence is the second basic task in healthy personality growth. It is not simple to develop feelings of independence when one continues to be dependent on others, and the child must learn to balance his wish to be independent and his desire to be mothered. How well he succeeds in achieving this balance will, in a large measure, determine the kind of adult he will become.

The changes which are part of his physical growth help the child cope with this task. He is now able to use his body in ways which make it easier for him to be independent such as in walking, reaching, and climbing. He really can do things for himself. We help him by seeing that he has clothes that he can manage himself, for example, so that he can begin to dress himself and use the toilet without help. We help him by seeing that he has play materials that he can make into whatever he wants without having to ask for help. We help him by keeping his things where he can get them and can also put them away easily.

Watch for signs of this urge to be independent in the children you observe or care for. Listen for words like, "Let me do it," or, "I can do it myself." Words like these show that there is a healthy balance of independent feelings in the child. If you often hear words such as, "I can't," or, "You do it for me," you may wonder whether this child has had enough chance to be independent in his own way and at his own rate. You will know that he needs help in feeling that he *can* do things and that you value his being independent.

None of us can be entirely independent. In fact we wouldn't really want to be entirely independent. But it is often hard to have to depend on others when one wants to be independent, just as it is hard to have to be on our own when we would like to have someone to depend on. Things seldom work out for us in this respect just as we would like. The little child is really up against it here. A healthy amount of independence is hard for him to achieve because he is little and there is much that he cannot manage on his own. It takes a large measure of trust on his part if he is to achieve healthy growth toward independence.

One child may seem to find it easy to move along the road toward being independent. Another child will have more difficulty and may keep retreating to the much easier stage of being like a baby and needing more help. He may need encouragement if he is to become independent in a healthy way. There are individual differences in development here.

We sometimes fail to give a child the help that we might because of the way we feel ourselves. It may seem pleasant to have a child prefer sitting on our lap to playing with others. Of course it is nice to know that he prefers us. But we may be making it easy for him to remain a dependent person. He may even feel that it is good to please people by dependence.

Of course there are times when it may be all right to hold a child on our lap. He may need, at the moment, the reassurance of feeling safe and loved. Being held in someone's lap replenishes his store of secure feelings. But it is a sign that all is not well with him if he keeps retreating to a too-inviting lap. It is a good thing to show a young child that we like him and enjoy having him sit on our lap. But it is also a good thing and very necessary for him to get down from our lap and go about the business of play, the business of reaching out toward new and sometimes difficult experiences, the business of finding his place among children. A child needs to know that we really *want* to see him grow in independence.

Developing initiative.   While the child of three or four years continues to work on the "unfinished business" of the earlier stages in developing a healthy amount of trust and independence over mistrust and dependency, he is also spending a lot of energy on the next developmental task in personality development. He is working on the task of finding out more about himself and the place he may expect in the world. He is ready for this task to the extent that (1) he has learned to feel safe with people and (2) he has found that he can assert himself in independent ways and still be accepted. He is now ready to discover what his place in the world may be.

This third task in personality growth has been called the development of a sense of initiative. The child is working on it when he wonders, "What will I become?" It takes a good deal of initiative to explore the possibilities of what one can become. What will it be like to be a mother or a daddy? Or a fireman or a soldier or a nurse or a doctor? What will it be like to be big and powerful? In his play the child acts "as if," pretending he is all these things. He exercises his initiative in play.

If one is to explore and learn in creative, imaginative ways, he needs to have a sense of initiative—a desire to go ahead and discover.

We all need this feeling of daring to try out new ways and take on new responsibilities. We are hampered in this if we are afraid of being blamed or of being held responsible and found guilty. Guilt and the part it plays in healthy growth will be discussed later. A sense of guilt usually interferes with the development of initiative. It is important for the child of four or five to develop his sense of initiative in greater amounts than his sense of being to blame for things. We need to make sure we give support to the behavior which represents initiative whenever we can. Encouraging his initiative helps him in healthy personality growth. Initiative means daring to do, to imagine, and to learn.

After developing feelings of trust and independence, the child is ready to develop a sense of initiative.

Many things help him with this third personality task. He now should have fairly good control of his body. He can walk, run, climb, and jump. He can ask questions even if he does not understand all the answers. He can imagine and pretend. He has had a variety of experiences to draw on to help him with his thinking about things. He now enjoys some experiences away from home for short periods of time, especially with other children. He is ready to test things out on his own. He explores and experiments. As he uses his initiative, he moves toward making a place for himself in the world.

BECOMING A PERSON

The child is becoming the person he is going to be. What kind of person will he be? What kind of world will he live in? What kind of "world" will he create for himself?

It is important to be clear about what is in the outside world. This world is observable to others as well as oneself. It is also important to be aware of the inner world, which is not observable by others, but which can be shared with those who understand. Both worlds are part of a whole, and life is enriched when they both can be experienced fully.

His feelings are strong.   This age is a time when *feelings are very strong*. A child this age gets very upset. He gets angry. He gets anxious. He gets very discouraged. He gets very excited and delighted. He is often difficult. He is also often a delight.

He responds with all of his being. The world is fresh and new, and he has a feeling of wonder at the things around him. At times he may feel overwhelmed at the multitude of things and "dos" and "don'ts."

What does he expect of himself? What does the world expect of him?

We can appreciate something of how he feels because these questions are never completely answered. We can understand how overwhelming they must seem to the child who is just becoming aware of them and has had so little experience with the world and the people in it.

A child develops self-reliance by doing—brushing her teeth, dressing herself, or performing some small task "for Mommy."

Joan Mach

He has an active imagination.   The child's imagination is so active at this age that he may develop many fears. He is likely to see bears in every corner of his room at night! He is often confused about whether what he is saying really happened or not, for his stories seem so vivid to him. Truth and fantasy get mixed.

Children of this age have many fears because they often misunderstand what they do see and hear going on around them. A child may be afraid of real things, and he may be afraid of imagined things which seem real to him. When he tries to tell us about his fears, his stories may sound pretty wild to us. He often tries to hide his fears and thus gets more confused.

Slowly we try to help him distinguish between the real and the pretend kinds of things. We are careful not to make fun of his stories for they are serious to him and for him. We don't confuse him by passing judgment on what he says as though he were an adult. That is, we do not label his story a "lie" before he knows what the truth is. We try to help him get clear what is pretend and what is real. It is fun to pretend, and imagination is a precious quality to be guarded carefully.

He needs playmates.   A child three or four years of age seeks other children and needs them. Playing with others, he finds a new kind of relationship. He is an *equal,* not just a little person with a lot of big people and perhaps a new baby in addition at home. When he is with other children, he finds out much more about what he is like, the kind of person he is, and what it takes to build a place for himself in the world.

To imaginative children their dolls are real people.

Most three- and four-year-olds actively seek out other children. They may watch or they may take part in play with groups. They like and need to be around others, to have experiences in giving and taking, in finding friends, in standing up for their rights or their ideas in situations where they are among equals or near equals. They like and need experiences in sharing and cooperating with friends or even in arguing and fighting with them.

Some children have an imaginary playmate during this period. We do not encourage this fantasy, but there is no need to deny

Most children of three or four like to be with other children.

Nursery school or play groups are important for children of this age.

it. We can remain neutral. Real playmates have more to offer. The best course of action is to satisfy the child by treating the imaginary playmate with respect and to wait until "it" fades out of the picture.

At this age nursery schools or play groups become important for children. Experience with other children is essential for the healthy growth of most children.

While relations with other children are very important to the development of a healthy personality, relations with grown-ups are also important so that the child can discover what he may be like in relationships with people different from his parents, such as nursery school teachers or Sunday school teachers.

He begins to understand the role of a man and of a woman. In wondering what his place in the world will be, each child explores ideas about the roles of men and women. What is it like to be a man? What is it like to be a woman? In dramatic play as they play house, children enjoy dressing up like adults, putting on a long skirt, or a hat or a belt. Girls usually dress up as ladies and boys as cowboys, but sometimes they try out reversing roles. They all can play home-making roles with which they are familiar. It is harder to play out roles filled by working parents, for many children have had little contact with the work roles of their fathers or perhaps of their mothers.

Children need contacts with a man. Boys need to have experiences with men so that they have an idea of what men are like and can identify themselves imaginatively with masculine roles. Girls, too, need contacts with a man to become clearer about their feminine role. It is especially important for children growing up in homes without fathers to have these contacts. Some nursery schools are using boys as assistants or volunteer aides when possible. The group seems to become more stable with fewer conflicts when there is a man teacher at least *part* of the time. The children respond differently.

Accepting one's own sex is essential for future adjustment in adolescence and maturity. A three- and four-year-old, or even a two-year-old, is working on identification with his or her sex. We need

Quaker Oats Company—Corn Goods

Wearing manly clothes helps a boy identify his sex role.

to give children all the help we can at this age. Fathers have a very important role to play here. They need to spend some time with their children, both girls and boys. They need to take opportunities to do things with them—errands, jobs around the home, walks, trips. In recalling events from their childhood, many people report that special experiences with their fathers stand out in their memories. Both mothers and fathers are important, of course, for they are both needed if the child is to understand the roles of the sexes, the part they each play in making a home as mothers and fathers, and as contributors to the life of the community. In different families the roles men and women play may differ. We know these roles are changing and should change, but the child needs to understand and to feel good about these roles. If his father is harsh and unreasonable in his discipline, for example, it is hard for a four-year-old boy to identify with the male role. If a mother is demanding and exacting and perhaps prefers her son to her daughter, it is hard for the girl to identify with the feminine role. She may try to be a tomboy to please her mother or even her father.

Each of us as a parent or as an adult whom the child knows well is giving him experiences in learning what it is like to be a man or a woman in an adult world.

He learns more about his body. Just as during his first year he learned about his fingers and toes by touching and examining them, he now learns about other parts of his body. All children discover the different parts of their body and do some touching of their genitals. It is nothing to be distressed about. If this is done often, it may mean they need more things to play with or more activities to interest them. One should use correct terms with a child from the beginning, such as penis, bowel movement, urine. The child needs them in his vocabulary now and will not have to relearn them later.

Children of this age will be interested in what other children look like, too. In nursery school boys and girls use the toilets together. This gives them a chance to watch others going to the toilet, to make comments and ask questions as they wish. They are learning about some of the physical differences between the sexes.

He is interested in where babies come from. Questions about where babies come from may keep coming up. It is a hard matter to get straight. Simple, truthful explanations will need to be repeated.

The baby grows in a special place inside the mother. This is where you grew. The father starts the baby growing. When the baby is big enough he comes out through a special place. This is being born.

We shall have more to say about these questions in a later chapter.

ACQUIRING INNER CONTROLS

The four-year-old is developing a conscience.

Janet Mirer

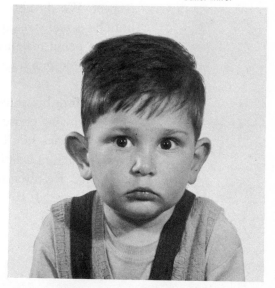

The development of inner controls is a necessary part of being civilized. This involves recognizing that there is a right and a wrong way to act. It means facing the reality that each of us has impulses that are bad as well as impulses that are good. It means facing the fact that we sometimes behave in undesirable ways.

He develops a conscience. It is at this age that the child's *conscience* begins to develop. He now feels guilty for things that he does that he feels he should not do. He begins to feel responsibility. Insofar as he is an independent person and can act on his own he must begin to take responsibility for what he does. Being responsible means feeling guilt for wrongdoing. The child at this age has special problems because he still is not clear about which things are wrong. It is not easy to be clear even when we are much older, as most of us know. He is not even clear about the part he plays in making things happen. He may think he is responsible for an event with which, in reality, he had no connection.

We take an important step when we begin to accept our responsibility for managing our actions. We would all prefer to deny the anger, the cruelty, the resentments that we harbor inside us, but denial does not help us deal with these feelings. It is probably confusing to a child to be told that we love him but we don't like what he does. It suggests the primitive notion of a demon which makes us behave in ways for which we cannot be held responsible. We are responsible for our acts. What we do is an expression of ourselves. It is better to help a child feel that, although we may disapprove of his behavior and thus of him at the moment, our love is strong enough to stand this strain. We love him for better or for worse. We love him because he is himself, and we are here to help him strengthen the good part in him. It may be frightening to a child to feel he is loved only as a good boy. Because he knows he is also a bad boy, he may fear that he will lose love if the bad shows.

Conscience is a tremendous force and should be treated with respect. We do not ask a child to be responsible for his behavior until he is really ready. He may become inhibited and fearful or just give up being responsible because he is afraid of being wrong. He may feel too much guilt or guilt for the wrong things.

Guiding his conscience. It is possible to take advantage of a child's growing conscience in a way that is really harmful to him. If we try to *make* him feel guilty when he does something wrong, impressing on him how bad he is to act like this, we may make him feel *too* guilty. He often feels more guilt than he can bear. He may become depressed. He may feel confused as to just what he did that made us angry. As a result, the guilty feelings spill over into other acts which he thinks are connected, and he becomes afraid to do these things, too. He feels less confidence in himself. He may also feel resentful toward us for making him suffer. These are not good feelings to have.

We may think it is fine when a child is very good and never gets into trouble, but it sometimes means that he has lost his capacity to dare to do things. This is very undesirable. He may be unable to act freely in desirable ways. Because he is afraid that he may be considered naughty, he may become afraid to explore and use his initiative. This is not what we intended when we scolded him, but it may be the result. At this age his conscience tends to "run wild" and pile up a heavy burden of guilt. Instead of being too good, on the other hand, he may become defiant and "mean" because he feels hopeless about keeping out of trouble.

Most of us have had the experience of *feeling* guilty because of what someone did or said to us even though we knew we had no reason to feel this way. Conscience is a necessary and fine thing but it can get on the wrong track or spill over where it doesn't belong. Many of us suffer at times because of a conscience that got out of bounds and made us needlessly afraid of being wrong.

We should be very careful to avoid blaming a young child or shaming him or trying to *make* him feel guilty. We just tell him what he can do or what he can't do and what the consequences are if he does. We see that these consequences happen. We are firm without getting angry. We may show him that we are displeased and that he is responsible, but we let *him* struggle with his own conscience and sense of guilt. We don't add to his burden of guilt by trying to increase it, or by *making* him feel ashamed, "You naughty boy, shame on you."

Guilty feelings can do a lot of damage to a personality in its early stages of growth when it is very important to develop a sense of respect for oneself.

He may feel confused about his responsibility.   We help a child by avoiding giving him too much responsibility. A four-year-old who

Mattel, Inc., Toymakers

We help a child by giving her appropriate responsibilities. She can be responsible for using her toy with care.

is told he must be responsible for keeping an active two-year-old off the street is pretty sure to get interested in play and forget. If the two-year-old goes into the street and gets hurt, the older child has an impossible load of guilt to manage, a load that he never should have had.

Adults should not place these kinds of responsibilities on a child. A child should be responsible for things that he has a good chance to be successful in doing and where his failures are not serious. He *wants* to be responsible and big. He is trying to build this kind of "image" for himself and he needs success, not failure.

The child sometimes feels as though he were responsible for things that happen even when there is no real connection, as mentioned earlier. As a toddler, he pulls on a cloth hanging over the edge of the table. A whole shower of dishes and things spills onto the floor. His mother says, "Look what you did!" She is very angry. He is startled and thoroughly bewildered. It must feel like magic to him. One little tug and all this happened! He tugs other things with no such results. Or he may push a button on one wall and a light flashes on in an entirely different spot. No wonder the child often thinks he has caused something when he is not really responsible for it.

Circumstances may occur which confuse him. A child may have played with a baby sister a bit roughly and the next day the baby becomes seriously ill with the flu. The child feels responsible and guilty. He does not understand that he had no connection with the germ which caused the illness. No one realizes that he feels as he does and he suffers real misery.

Children have feelings of guilt often enough so that it is always wise to reassure a child when an accident happens. "Nothing we did made it happen." One mother reported that when her car skidded off the road, the four-year-old sobbed, "I didn't do anything." His mother could reassure him in this case, but children often don't put it into words like this.

Guiding the sense of responsibility. It is important, too, that when a child *is* responsible we make it clear just what he did that led to the happening (so he does not imagine other things). We share the burden with him if it is in truth part of our responsibility. We may say, "I'm responsible too. I should have been watching."

We don't use, "It's only an accident" as an excuse for not being careful. While accidents happen to all of us, accidents happen to us sometimes because we are not doing much to prevent them. A child pushed another child off a box and climbed on, answering the other child's protest by saying, "It was an accident." She did not feel a sense of responsibility for her action.

Guilt feelings may make a child passive and obedient but they also make him unhappy and sometimes cruel and unable to grow in healthy ways. He will be less likely to develop the amount of initiative he needs to be a creatively functioning person. As we help children learn, we can give help in ways that increase their confidence and feelings of self-respect. We can help them develop a conscience which promotes responsible behavior without inhibiting initiative. This kind of conscience belongs to the mature, creative person.

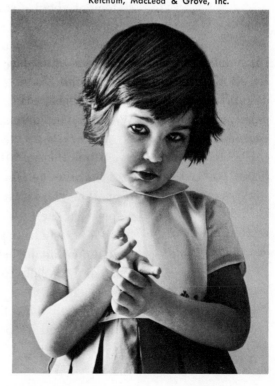

Guilt feelings may make a child passive, unhappy, and unable to grow in healthy ways.

Ketchum, MacLeod & Grove, Inc.

DISCIPLINE AT THIS AGE

If we discipline in a firm, kindly way, depending on the child's conscience but not provoking unnecessary guilt, we teach the child what is reasonable while allowing him to feel that he is a person of worth as he learns. He will not be afraid to try things. He will not be too hard on himself.

At this age he is ready to learn quickly and with eagerness, to become "big" in the sense of sharing in responsibility and discipline and achievement.

By the time a child is four, he does not respond to "distraction" as he did when he was a toddler. He is able to bear unpleasant situations and to accept responsibility for his behavior. He understands more about reasons for things. When he fusses or sulks he is often *not* helped by our attempts to turn his attention to something else or distract him. It may be better to let him face the situation, work through his feelings and then recover. It shows more respect for him and his capacities than if we coax or offer substitutes or indulge him in order to make up for some unpleasant reality.

When it is time to stop his play outdoors and come in to get ready to go to bed, for example, the fact need not be sugarcoated by trying to take his mind off it. It can be made more acceptable by a statement about a story to be read as soon as he is ready for bed, but he must face the necessity of stopping his play and getting ready for bed. If we feel uncertain ourselves or dislike dealing with his fussing or sulking, we may be tempted to try to distract or bribe him. But we should be friendly and firm. He is no longer a baby. He can face difficulty if it does not come in "doses" that are overwhelming. We can bear his fussing without getting upset by it.

From what has been said, we can see that punishment does not have much place in the guidance of children of this age. We should be firm and friendly and help children learn to act in acceptable ways. The child who feels that he is loved and who is treated with respect has the best chance of learning. Equally important, he and his parents will have a better chance of discovering real pleasure and companionship in being together. They can enjoy sharing experiences and can help each other grow. Punishment interferes with this kind of growth.

Through these first years the child has learned and grown a great deal, and his personality patterns have been laid. He remains

**He remains absorbed in discovering what the world is like.
When he enters school his world will become larger.**

absorbed with the task of discovering who he is and what the world is like, but as he enters school he will begin to find more and more satisfaction in his accomplishments and achievements. What he does and makes will become as important as the processes of doing and making. He will find enjoyment in accomplishing things with other people. If his earlier experiences have prepared him well, he will be able to cooperate with others while keeping a sense of his own identity as a person. He will be ready to take his place among others.

| ACTIVITIES | TO DO AND DISCUSS |

1. Observe a three- or four-year-old for half an hour.
   a. Describe his appearance.
   b. Describe what you observed about his physical development. (How active was he? What did he do which showed you something about his motor coordination, large muscle coordination, and small muscle coordination?)
   c. Describe what you observed about his social development.
      (1) Did you observe him learning something? Describe it.
      (2) Did you see an example of reasoning? Describe it.
      (3) Give some examples of his speech.
      (4) What did he do that told you something about his imagination?
      (5) What did his interests seem to be?
      (6) What else did you notice about this child?
   d. What comments would you make about each of the following?
      (1) His sense of trust.
      (2) His amounts of independence and dependence.
      (3) His sense of initiative or confidence in exploring.
   e. What kind of person does he seem to be at this stage? What do you think he would be like with other children? Why?

2. Observe a three- or four-year-old child and try to write down exactly what happened for five minutes. This will give you some practice in becoming an accurate and objective observer.

   An objective observer is one who records what takes place without passing personal judgment on it or coloring the report with his or her individual way of looking at a particular bit of behavior.

   "She was selfish when she played in the sand with Jane." This is a subjective statement. "She took a spoon from Jane and used it in filling her pan with sand." This is an objective record.

TO THINK AND WRITE ABOUT

1. A child falls, and you feel sure that he has not been hurt, but he begins to cry loudly.
   a. What would you do
      (1) if he is at home and you are his regular baby-sitter?

(2) if he is at Sunday school or nursery school and it is his first day there without his mother?

(3) if he is with a group of children whom he knows, but he has just had a fight with one of his best friends?

   b. Be prepared to discuss in class your answers in each of these situations and the reasons for each answer.

2. How does the mother of a three- or four-year-old help him to develop good habits in regard to cleanliness, eating, and sleeping?

3. How does the mother of a three- or four-year-old help him become independent in such matters as dressing, eating, and taking care of his things?

4. Why are games like playing house and playing store important to a child's development?

5. Why is it important for parents to use good speech and the correct words when speaking to children?

6. What is the mother's role in helping her child develop a feeling of trust?

7. Why is it important for a child to develop a sense of initiative?

8. Think back to your own childhood at the time when you were developing a conscience. Describe an incident in which you wanted very much to do something, but your conscience prevented you.

PAMPHLETS AND PAPERBACKS

REFERENCES

Adair, Thelma, and Rachel Adams
When We Teach 4's and 5's
Philadelphia: (Geneva Press) Westminster, 1963

Arnstein, Helene, in cooperation with the Child Study Association of America
What to Tell Your Child
Indianapolis: Bobbs-Merrill Company, 1962

Burgess, Helen S.
How to Choose a Nursery School
Public Affairs Pamphlet No. 310, 1961
New York: Public Affairs Committee, Inc.

Freedman, David, and Dorothy Colodny
Water, Sand, and Mud as Play Materials
Washington, D. C.: National Association for the Education of Young
    Children, 1959

Hymes, James L.
Three to Six—Your Child Starts to School
Public Affairs Pamphlet No. 163
New York: Public Affairs Committee, Inc.

Reeves, Katherine
When We Teach 3's
Philadelphia: (Geneva Press) Westminster, 1962

Ridenour, Nina
Building Self-Confidence in Children
Chicago: Science Research Associates, Inc., 1954

Ridenour, Nina
Some Special Problems of Children Age 2 to 5 Years
Chicago: Science Research Associates, Inc., 1947

Stolz, Lois Meek
Our Changing Understanding of Young Children's Fears
Washington, D. C.: National Association for the Education of Young
    Children, 1964

What to Tell Your Child About Sex
Child Study Association of America
New York: Permabooks, 1959

Winicott, W.
The Child, the Family and the Outside World
Middlesex, England: Penguin Books, Ltd., 1964

Your Child from Three to Four
Children's Bureau Publication No. 446
U. S. Department of Health, Education, and Welfare, 1967

BOOKS

Gruenberg, Benjamin C., and Sidonie Gruenberg
The Wonderful Story of You: Your Body, Your Mind, Your Feelings
New York: Garden City Books, 1960

Hymes, James L.
The Child Under Six
Englewood Cliffs, New Jersey: Prentice-Hall, Inc., 1963

Langstaff, Nancy, with photographs by Suzanne Szasz
A Tiny Baby for You
New York: Harcourt, Brace & World, Inc., 1955 (for a child)

Read, Katherine H.
The Nursery School: A Human Relationships Laboratory, Fourth Edition
Philadelphia: W. B. Saunders Company, 1966

We Learn Through Experiences with Children

Young children are everywhere. They may be part of your family or live in the apartment above you, or they may live in the house next door—or in all these places! Have you ever thought about the ways these children may all be alike and the ways in which they are different? Children of different ages are not alike in every way—neither are children of the same age. What makes all these children "tick"? How can you learn to understand them?

To understand children we need to have actual experience with them. Just to read about children is not enough. Select a child whom you can observe. You can watch the ways in which this child learns, the ways in which he meets difficulties, what pleases him, and what disturbs him. You can try the "teaching skills" to be suggested. You can report what you learn from your experiences with this child.

SELECTING CHILDREN TO STUDY

Any child is likely to enjoy attention from someone who is interested. You may know a child in the neighborhood or in a Sunday school, or have a brother, sister, nephew, or niece who is under six.

Relations with a younger sibling (a brother or sister) will be different from the relations you may have with children in the neighborhood or in school. The relationship is a closer one. You may find your younger brother or sister more irritating at times. You also like him in a deeper kind of way. Because you are close to him, it is harder to observe him objectively, that is, without letting your own feelings color what you see. But it also may be more important to try to see what *really* happens. It may make living with him more comfortable for you and much more rewarding to him. An older sibling is a very important person to a young child.

Observing a child "at work" or at play can be a rewarding experience for an adult or a teen-ager.

Today's Health, published by the American Medical Association

You may decide to select a child to observe outside your family even if you do have a young sister or brother. The child may be one in the neighborhood, or may be one that you know through a baby-sitting experience. You may wish to observe the same child or you may wish to observe children of different ages, a baby one week, a two-year-old another week, a three- or four-year-old the next week.

Besides observing one child you will also want to have some experience with young children in groups so that you may understand more about the growth and development of children. When children are playing together, you can see how different each one is from all the others. You see the ways in which a child reacts with people on his own level, not just with older people. You see important aspects of his personality.

You may arrange to observe in a Sunday school where there are groups of preschool children. You may visit a library which has a

One opportunity for observing young children is during story time.

story hour for young children. You may find a day-care center where children come whose mothers work outside their homes, or you may find a nursery school or play school where you can observe. You may arrange to observe in the kindergarten in your own school.

You and your teacher may arrange to invite a group of children for a play experience in your own classroom. This is another way to learn more about children. You will want to have an experience in some way with a group of children as well as with an individual child.

When you are with children, you will need to develop skills in guiding them. As we have said earlier, it makes a great deal of difference to a child what kinds of experiences he has with people. A child should feel more self-confidence as a result of the way others treat him. He should feel that he is a likable person. This is a good way for anyone to feel. He should feel that people are friendly and that the world around him is an interesting place. If he feels these ways, he has laid a good foundation for his growing personality. He has had skillful guidance.

With less skillful guidance a child sometimes feels that he is a person whom nobody likes very much. He may feel uncomfortable about himself. He may feel afraid of people or experiences. He may learn to draw back inside himself and be unhappy because he may not even like *himself* very well. Or he may learn to fight with everybody and complain about everything. In such cases the guidance he has received has not given him the help he needed.

Of course it takes more than one poor experience to have much effect on a child. Children are pretty well made to withstand the hazards they may meet, both physically and psychologically. We are

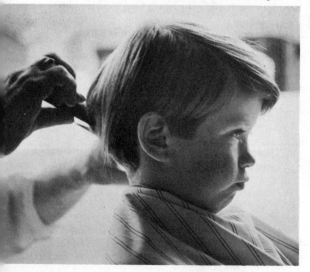

Sometimes a child feels he is a person whom nobody likes very much. However, it takes more than one poor experience to have much effect on him.

The New Book of Knowledge

sure to make many mistakes with them. But it is the mistakes in guidance which are repeated and repeated that damage children and change the kind of person each may become. It is like the many small drops of water dripping long enough to wear away the rock.

Understanding more about growth and guidance of children not only helps us guide them more wisely but also helps us respect them and enjoy them more. We are likely to be more successful with them when we understand and this makes us feel good.

Here are some "Guides for Guidance." Read them carefully and try to apply them in your experiences with children. With your teacher, plan for some firsthand experiences with a child each week, so that you can practice using these guides. Keep these "Guides for Guidance" in mind, too, when you are with the special child you have chosen to observe and work with.

Report your experiences to the class, describing how you used one of the "guides."

Be sure the child is appropriately dressed for the weather.

American Telephone and Telegraph Company

GUIDES FOR GUIDANCE

SUPERVISING GROUP PLAY

1. Supervise for Good Health.

a. *Be sure that each child's clothing is adjusted to the weather.* Be sure that he takes off his coat or sweater if he begins to get hot or puts on one if he begins to get cold. See that he has on rubbers if the ground is wet.

R. MacKenzie

**Be sure that the active child has some rest time
and that she sits on the sled instead of the snow.**

b. *Be sure that children practice sanitary habits.* See that the children do not use the same glass or bubble pipe, for example, until it has been thoroughly washed. Be sure that children wash their hands before eating at snack time and after going to the toilet.

c. *Protect the child's health.* In cool or damp weather be sure that children do not sit on the ground. Be sure that the children have some rest time. If children have been running about, you might have them sit quietly and read or tell a story to them or have them play in the sandbox for a time. Be sure to observe any special restrictions that a child might have—a child recovering from an illness, for example, may not be permitted to run and climb.

Assume responsibility for these things yourself.

2. Supervise for Safety.

a. *Check equipment to be sure it is safe to use.* Be sure that ladders are firmly fixed, for example, or that boards are not likely to slip. If you see a loose nail, remove it or pound it in.

American Telephone and Telegraph Company

R. MacKenzie

Watch the child closely when he is using play equipment or material that could be dangerous.

L. Dittmar

b. *Watch children closely when they are using play equipment which may present dangers.* Give special attention to the safe use of a swing or a teeter. Show children how a piece of equipment can be used safely. "Walk around the swing," or, "Get off the teeter slowly," or, "Put the wood in the vise before you start to saw it."

c. *Stand in a position to prevent trouble.* Stand so that you are in a position to prevent possible accidents. Stand close to a group of children who are using the teeter or climbing. If you are helping one child, stand facing the other children so that you can also keep your eye on them.

TEACHING SKILLS

1. *Give your suggestions or directions in a positive way.* This means telling the child *what to do* rather than what not to do. It is easier for a child to follow directions if you turn his attention to what he should be doing. He is less apt to resist. Be sure to make your directions simple and specific. Use a *do* rather than a *don't*, as "Keep the sand in the sandbox," or, "Dig in the sand," when you wish to redirect a child who is throwing sand. Say, "As soon as you are quiet, I will read the story" when you are helping a noisy group settle down for the story period.

2. *Use a quiet, confident tone of voice.* When you speak quietly to children, they will pay more attention than when you raise your voice. When you speak in a confident tone, they feel more confidence that you mean what you say; they find it easier to comply. If you use a demanding, bossy tone, the children are more likely to resist. It makes them want *not* to do what you direct, just as you yourself might feel if you were in their place.

Give your suggestions in a quiet, positive tone, using simple words.

Armstrong/Rapho-Guillumette

3. *Give your directions in as few words as possible and use simple words.* It will be clear to the child who is learning to use the toilet, for example, if you say, "Time to go to the toilet," as you hold out your hand to him. He will not need any long explanation. Children often do not listen to involved reasons or explanations.

4. *Offer the child a choice only when you intend to leave the choice up to him.* When we are unsure of ourselves, we often make a request in the form of a question because of our own uncertainty. Listen to yourself when you are with a child whom you do not know very well in a situation which is new to you. "Are you ready to go?" may be a request for information or it may be an attempt to suggest going to the child. If it really is time to go, it is better to state the fact, "It's time for us to go now," and then help him bring his play to an end. You may ask, "Would you like to go outdoors?" if he is free to choose whether he wants to play inside or outside. Avoid putting a direction in the form of a question. If you want him to close the

A bedtime story for children should be carefully chosen. It should not frighten or overexcite them.

National Fuel Oil Institute

Julia Richman High School, New York

Help the child learn to share by respecting his right to possess things of his own.

door, say, "Please close the door." Be clear in your own mind whether you wish to give a direction, offer the child a choice, or ask for information.

5. *Give the child plenty of time to finish his play if it is possible.* A child may resist if he feels that you are hurrying him. He may want and need time to park his cars or finish a job before he changes to another activity. We need to respect the child's purposes just as we like to have our purposes respected.

We can respect his purposes without permitting "stalling." If we find him thinking of one thing after another to delay matters, we can say firmly, "It really is time to stop now. You must come as soon as you have put that one car in its garage." Then, when he has put the one car away, we can quietly take his hand and see that he complies. Perhaps we will make it easier for him if we start a conversation about something else as we do this.

6. *Make desirable behavior interesting.* Things like picking up play materials can be made more interesting by the use of a little imagination. A suggestion such as, "Let's pretend we're deliverymen taking these blocks back to the shelves," may help when children seem to feel that picking up is a chore.

7. *Encourage the child to be independent.* Give the child only as much help as he needs and only when he asks for help. He can manage to put on his own coat or his boots, for example. It may take him more time, but it gives him satisfaction to do it himself. Give him an opportunity to take responsibility. If he spills some water or paint, let him wipe it up himself.

He may be able to climb into the swing himself if we steady it for him. This is better than lifting him into the seat. If he wants to reach something, we can show him how to make a step with a large block and get it himself. When we can help him in this way, we are teaching him to solve his own problems and to be independent.

8. *Let children use all art media such as paints, clay, crayons or collage materials, as avenues for self-expression, without models to copy.* Making a model for a child to copy in a drawing or in clay or in other art media provides him with an activity, but it prevents him from developing his own ideas or his imagination. Copying may effectively block creativity in children. When children paint, draw or use clay, they should use these art materials as avenues for *self* expression.

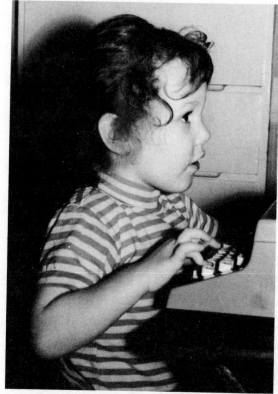

L. Dittmar

The attention and approval of adults give a child motivation to learn and to develop self-reliance.

Avoid drawing pictures for a child. He is less likely to draw his own picture then. When you play with clay, avoid *making* anything. Squeeze it or pound it or roll it. The process involved in using clay is important for the child rather than the product although we may value what he makes. We should make such comments as, "That is a lovely color," or, "Tell me about your picture," or, "The clay feels good, doesn't it!"

9. *Depend on motivating the child by encouragement and approval.* When we give attention and approval, we give the best form of motivation for a young child. When we show our pleasure in what a child does, we encourage him in his efforts. He feels respect for himself and values what he has succeeded in doing. Doing something that wins the approval of the adults whom the child respects

A child will make a tremendous effort to master a skill, when given encouragement.

gives him satisfaction and also gives direction to his further efforts. He is motivated.

When we try to motivate children by making comparisons between one child and another or getting them to compete with each other, we only increase the feelings of rivalry and jealousy which are always present. These feelings are especially difficult for young children to manage. They interfere with the development of good social relations and make it harder for them to get along with others. Most young children have not yet built up enough confidence in themselves to face the failures which are inevitable in all competitive situations.

The best reasons for making an effort to do something well are because we get satisfaction from the doing and because the thing is worth doing. We should do something for this reason rather than because we want to get ahead of someone else. Children are capable of making a tremendous effort when they are given encouragement and approval. They gain in confidence and self-respect. These are feelings which we all need if we are to be successful people.

A child is helped when we say, "You carried that glass of milk very carefully, without spilling a drop," or, "That's fine. You remembered to put all the blocks back in the box."

Children receive satisfaction from doing things with an approving adult.

Roberts/Rapho-Guillumette

 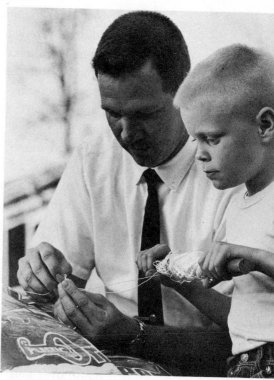

BUILDING GOOD SOCIAL RELATIONS
AMONG CHILDREN

Our goal is to help children like each other more because of the guidance we give them in getting along together.

Children are individuals, and, as we watch them together, it is easy to see how different they are. In any group of young children we see children who are friendly and like to play with others. They are the secure, satisfied ones. We see children who usually play alone. They may be the timid ones. We see children who seem to want to play with others but are often not included. They are the frustrated ones. We see busy, purposeful children, children with few interests, imaginative children, unimaginative children, children who persist, children who give up easily, and many others. Children are people with the differences we all show.

Children need and want to play with other children. They learn some of their most important social lessons through play with other children. They often need help in understanding the behavior of others and their own feelings. They need help in understanding what behavior is acceptable.

If there are plenty of resources for play, plenty of space, and a minimum of interference from adults, most children can settle their differences most of the time. They learn from doing it. Others will need more help. Children who feel sure of their place in the group will need the least help.

Conflicts usually arise over possessions, over using equipment, or over carrying out purposes. Scolding children for their mistakes does not help them learn. It may only make them prefer to play alone. Telling them what they can or should do in a situation makes it possible for them to learn and to enjoy being with others.

A child may be having difficulty in being accepted by others. We may say, depending on the circumstances,

"Knock at the door and ask if you may come in."

"I think Mary and Jane don't want you in their house just now. Sometimes people want to play by themselves. You might build a house over here and ask Helen if she'd like to play."

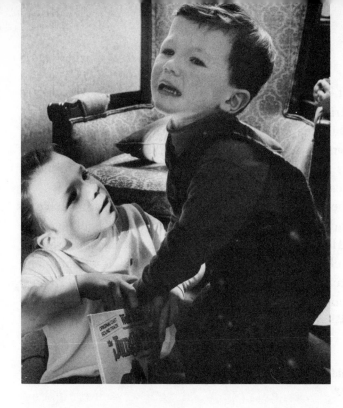

Conflicts may arise
over possessions.

Uzzle/Magnum

A child may need help in working out a solution. We may say,
"If you want the truck he is using, get another truck and see if
he will trade with you."

"Tell him why you want it."

"That tricycle belongs to Mary. You will have to use another
one."

"Bill and Dick are using the shovel. You may have it after they
finish digging their hole."

A child may need help in draining off anger so that he can have
a better chance of getting along in the group. We may say,

"It's hard not to have the truck when you really want it, I know.
It makes you feel pretty cross. Go ahead and bang the big can."

"No hitting people. It hurts. Bill doesn't like being hit. I know
you are cross with him. You can go over and punch our dummy
figure."

Sometimes it is important to encourage a child to stand up for
himself. Some children need help in learning that they do not have
to do everything that other children ask but can carry out purposes
of their own. "It is yours. You do not have to let him take it when

you are using it." We need to help them stand up for themselves effectively in a friendly way, with words instead of by hitting.

Help the child learn to share by respecting his right to possess things of his own. If possible, avoid insisting on his sharing things when he objects strongly. As he comes to enjoy and have fun with friends, he shares because he wants to.

A child is helped to accept "taking turns" if he doesn't have to wait too long and if he has a chance to get the object back again in another "turn." He learns then that sharing does not mean just giving up an object. A child is also helped to accept "turns" if we show him that we understand his feelings. "*I know that you really want to keep it,* but you've had your turn. It is his turn now. I'll see that you have another turn." Words like these will really help a child.

Through play children learn such social behavior as taking turns and fair play.

Owen/dpi

For good discipline, be sure the children understand the rules of behavior.

DISCIPLINING

Firmness with friendliness is the basis of good discipline.

State clearly what you expect of the child, what the rules or limits are, and the consequences, if there are any. An example of appropriate consequence is removing an object which was used to hit another child with. Maintain these rules or limits consistently. A child will learn quickly if we are firm and matter-of-fact in maintaining *understood* limits or rules.

If the child engages in play which is not safe for him or for others, *stop* the play, explaining the reasons to him; then show him what he can do.

A child may not like being kept from doing something. He may get angry. But if we are firm and do not get angry in return, the child will soon recover and will be helped in learning to control himself.

Hammid/Rapho-Guillumette

Whenever possible, let children handle their own conflicts.

Let children handle their own conflicts whenever they can. Sometimes it is enough merely to walk over closer to the children. Your presence is a steadying influence.

When you attempt to settle a conflict, speak quietly, getting the children's attention first and calling them by name. Help them look at the problem. If you understand the reasons for what happened, interpret the behavior of one child to the other. If you don't understand, tell them so. Trouble is often reduced by understanding or making an effort to talk matters over and understand circumstances better.

If conflicts are repeated, observe closely to see at what point the difficulty starts and help the children change what they are doing at that point. If a particular child seems to be causing most of the trouble, remove him from the situation. Talk the matter over with him. He may need to play alone for a while until he is better able to maintain his own controls. Be alert to what is happening and to particular combinations of children playing together. Some children often have trouble when they play together. They may play well with different children.

Forestalling (preventing) is the most effective way of managing problems. Learn to foresee and prevent rather than to "mop up" after troubles start. Make a suggestion to change the play *before* difficulties start whenever you can. As you come to know the children well, you will find you can often prevent trouble from arising. You will be a skillful teacher!

Remember that children learn from having conflicts and settling them constructively. Without conflicts there would be very little growing. We are concerned about giving good guidance to children in their struggle in growing.

TO DO AND DISCUSS   ACTIVITIES

EXAMPLES OF TYPICAL SITUATIONS IN GUIDING CHILDREN

On a separate sheet of paper, for each situation put the letter of the statement which describes most nearly what you think should be done. Then give the reasons you think it is the most desirable thing to do in the situation. In class discuss these reasons. See how much agreement there is as well as how many differences in points of view. Perhaps you will change your opinion in some cases as you talk it over.

A. *In a nursery school*
  1. It is the first day of school. Mary's mother has just brought her to the nursery school. At the teacher's approach, Mary, who is three, clings to her mother. She is an only child and has not had much experience with children or been away from her mother. The teacher:

_____a. suggests to Mary's mother that she say goodbye and leave, assuring her that Mary will soon be all right.

———b. takes Mary's hand and invites her to join the children in their play.

———c. smiles at Mary and asks Mary's mother to sit in a chair near where the children are playing.

2. Three children are walking up a steeply inclined board and climbing onto the jungle gym. Three other children are playing in the sandbox nearby. The teacher who is supervising the play yard stands:

———a. close to the children on the inclined board.

———b. close to the sandbox.

———c. halfway between the two groups.

3. Some three-year-old children are playing together in the sandbox at nursery school. Jane, a shy, quiet child, stands for some time watching them. The teacher:

———a. asks Jane if she wants to play in the sand.

———b. puts a spoon and truck near Jane.

———c. asks the children to invite Jane to play.

4. Three-year-old Jane, who has taken almost half of the available clay, starts to reach for some more. Several other children are using the clay. The teacher says:

———a. "Aren't you going to let the other children have some of the clay?"

———b. "You must not take any more clay, Jane. The other children want to use it, too."

———c. "Use the clay you have, Jane. The rest of the clay is for the other children to use."

5. Jane is playing in the housekeeping corner when she notices a teacher sitting nearby. She looks at the teacher a minute and then says, "I don't like you." The teacher replies:

———a. "Oh, I'm sure that you do. You like everyone in school."

———b. "I like you. Maybe you'll like me when you know me better."

———c. "You should not say that. It's not nice."

6. John is angry because there isn't time left for painting. He shouts at the teacher, "You old stink pot." The teacher says:

———a. "I know how you feel. It makes you pretty cross not to be able to paint when you want to."

_____b. "Let's talk about something pleasant, John."

_____c. "You mustn't talk to people that way, John. They won't like you."

7. Mary, who has a new baby brother at home, is at the table using crayons with several other children. She has ten crayons in her lap protecting them from the others. The teacher:

_____a. makes sure that there are enough crayons for the other children so they do not need the ones Mary has.

_____b. says, "It's selfish to take so many crayons, Mary. You'll have to leave the table if you can't share."

_____c. says, "You need to use only one crayon at a time, Mary. Put them on the table. We share them with all the children."

8. The teacher finds three-year-old Janet in the toilet room watching Joe as he urinates. Janet looks a little uncomfortable when she sees the teacher. The teacher:

_____a. says, "You mustn't stay in here watching the boys. Come, we'll go out and play now."

_____b. takes her out of the toilet room saying, "You are through. You are ready to go out and play."

_____c. says, "It's all right. You want to see how Joe goes to the toilet. Boys stand up. Girls sit down," and the teacher talks with Joe as they both stand watching.

9. John is an active, aggressive three-year-old. For no apparent reason he hits Jane as she walks past him on her way to the sandbox. Jane runs to the teacher crying, "John hit me. He's a naughty boy." The teacher says:

_____a. "John, you mustn't hit children. We don't do that at nursery school."

_____b. "That's too bad. I hope it didn't hurt much," and then adds, "Were you going to play in the sandbox?"

_____c. "You can hit him when he does that. You needn't come to me."

B. _At home or school_

1. John takes a big bite of mashed potato, spilling some of it in his lap. Mother says:

_____a. "Don't take such a big bite, John, and then you won't spill."

———b. "Take little bites, John. See what nice little bites Janet is taking."

———c. "Take little bites, John. Then it will all go in your mouth."

2. Bill, who is nearly four, comes in from his play outdoors, pulls off his hat and coat, drops them on the floor. His mother:

———a. picks up his hat and coat, goes after Bill and gives them to him saying, "Your hat and coat were on the floor. They belong on the hook in the closet. Take them back and hang them up before you play."

———b. goes after Bill, saying, "Your coat and hat are on the floor. They need to be hung on the hook in the closet; then you'll be ready to play." She returns with him while he picks up his wraps.

———c. picks up his hat and coat and hangs them in the closet for Bill, realizing that he is already busy with play and might object to coming back to hang up his wraps.

3. A mother sees four-year-old Bob hitting his playmate, Mary, because he wants the tricycle she is using and she won't give it to him. The mother stops Bob, saying:

———a. "You are a naughty boy to hit like that. You go into the house and play until you can behave."

———b. "You should hit him right back, Mary. That will teach him not to act that way."

———c. "Mary's using the tricycle, Bob. You can tell her you want it when she's through. I'll help you find something else to do while you're waiting."

4. One rainy day Betty and her friend Mary are making pictures, using paste and scraps of colored paper. They put lots of paste on both sides of the scraps of paper and they rub their fingers over the paste. Betty's mother sees them. She:

———a. says, "Do it this way. Just a little paste on one side. And try to keep your hands clean."

———b. smiles and says, "It's fun, isn't it!"

———c. says, "What a mess you've made! That's enough! You are just wasting the paste."

5. Louise is helping pick up the toys scattered over the floor when she runs off to the other end of the room and starts playing. Her mother says:

——a. "Louise, if you'll come back and help, I'll tell you a story about what I saw this morning out the window."

——b. "If you don't come back and help, you can't go out to play with your friends."

——c. "Louise, you need to finish picking up. When the toys are all picked up, I'll tell you a story about what I saw out of the window this morning."

TO THINK AND WRITE ABOUT

1. Try to describe some of the experiences you have had or things people have said to you which have increased your self-confidence.

2. Describe experiences you have had or things people have said to you which undermined your own self-confidence.

3. Why is it important to tell children what they should do rather than what they should not do?

4. Why is it better for a young child to do something because he has received encouragement and approval rather than through a spirit of competition?

5. How can a baby-sitter help a child who is too shy to play with other children?

6. Why are some conflicts between children a necessary and even desirable thing?

7. Describe some experiences you have had in which you used the "Guides for Guidance" suggested in this chapter.

8. Describe a situation you faced which involved discipline.

PAMPHLETS AND PAPERBACKS   REFERENCES

Cohen, Dorothy, and Virginia Stern
Observing and Recording the Behavior of Young Children
New York: Bureau of Publications, Teachers College, Columbia University, 1958

Gilkesen, Elizabeth
Let's Talk About Our Children—Teacher-Child-Parent Relationships
New York: Bank Street College of Education

Ilg, Frances, and Louise Bates Ames
The Gesell Institute's Child Behavior
New York: Dell Publishing Company

Jones, Eve
The Intelligent Parent's Guide to Raising Children
New York: The Crowell-Collier Publishing Company, 1961

Mayer, Morris Fritz
A Guide for Child Care Workers
New York: Child Welfare League of America, 1963

Mead, Margaret
A Creative Life for Your Child
Children's Bureau Publication
U. S. Department of Health, Education, and Welfare

Suggested Guide for Training Workers in Child Day Care Centers
U. S. Office of Education
U. S. Department of Health, Education, and Welfare, 1964

Teachers for Young Children—The Person and the Skills
New York: Early Childhood Education of New York, 1957

When Teen-Agers Take Care of Children: A Guide for Baby Sitters
Children's Bureau Publication No. 409
U. S. Department of Health, Education, and Welfare, 1964

Wolf, Anna W. M.
*The Parents' Manual: A Guide to the Emotional Development of Young
    Children, Second Revision*
New York: Frederick Ungar Publishing Company, Inc., 1962

BOOKS

Hymes, James L.
Before the Child Reads
New York: Harper & Row, Publishers, 1958

Read, Katherine H.
The Nursery School: A Human Relationships Laboratory, Fourth Edition (especially Chapter 4)
Philadelphia: W. B. Saunders Company, 1966

Rudolph, Marguerita
Living and Learning in the Nursery School (especially pages 145-170)
New York: Harper & Row, Publishers, 1954

Rudolph, Marguerita, and Dorothy Cohen
Kindergarten: A Year of Learning
New York: Appleton-Century-Crofts, 1964

6 Children Learn Through Activities

In this chapter we shall discuss activities which promote children's learning about the world. Whether you care for one child at home or whether you have a group of children in a play group or a nursery school, you will be interested in activities which form a "curriculum" and promote learning.

If a child is to have the best chance for a well-rounded development he will need experiences in play which help him learn in all areas: language, literature, music, art, science, and social science—including psychology. We shall discuss each of these areas, beginning with play itself.

161

PLAY

First let us look at play as a way of learning. Teachers as well as parents of young children are concerned with children's play. Some of our most important teaching is done when we are guiding the play of children. Play is the really important business of early childhood just as school becomes the important business of later childhood and adolescence, and a job is the business of the adult.

Peggy, a three-year-old, was at play. She kept jumping down from the third step of the stairs in the apartment house where she lived, repeating this feat with a pleased expression on her face. With each succeeding jump she hesitated less. Even though she always fell forward on her hands and this must have hurt, she eagerly jumped up again, rubbing her hands together, and dashed back up to the third step to try again. When her mother came out, she said excitedly, "Do you want to see me jump off the steps?" Her mother replied, "Yes, I really do." Peggy jumped again and said, "Did you know I could do that?" When her mother answered, "No," with a smile, Peggy said confidently, "Well, I can. Do you want me to do it again?" Her joy in mastering this skill was apparent and her mother said, "Yes, just once more and then I have to get back to my work."

All of us learn most easily when we enjoy what we are doing. Perhaps you recall something you enjoyed doing very much as a preschool child, not necessarily the most exciting thing you remember, but something that made you feel content and happy and pleased with what you had done. What do you think you may have learned through doing this thing or having this experience?

The world is changing rapidly today, so that some of the things you may recall are not easily available for many children today. If you recall taking care of a pet duck or playing in the tall grass of a

Play is the really important business of childhood and the gateway to adulthood.

Rubin

meadow, you have enjoyed experiences which are often not possible for a child growing up in a city. It takes a good deal of imagination to provide children with a rich variety of satisfying experiences for fun and learning in some of the places where children are growing up today. It takes planning on the part of the citizens in these communities.

Every healthy child plays. He plans, builds, organizes. He makes things and discovers what materials are like and what he can do. He begins to feel part of the world of workers. A five-year-old who had been to the zoo drew a picture after his visit there. He put in many animals but he also added a truck and workmen whom he imagined had been at work making the zoo. Thinking of how the zoo was built seemed as important to him as the animals he had seen there.

Rubin

Through play every healthy child discovers what materials are like and what he can do.

Values of play. In play children *practice* skills as Peggy did. They also *experiment* as the toddler does with fitting lids on his pans. They *discover* as the child does who picks up a leaf or a rock to examine it. They *solve problems* as the child does when he builds with blocks, balancing pieces and planning the structure. They also *imagine* and *create* as they play, whether they are making sand or mud pies, using art materials, or using words in making up stories.

Learning in play is the foundation for intellectual development. A child who has a rich variety of materials to use for play and a breadth of play experiences is getting preparation for formal learning. Without the firsthand experiences which come through play the child would be less well equipped to deal with the concepts and symbols of later stages of learning. Intellectual learning is part of play.

C. S. Dixon

A rich variety of play materials and a breadth of play experiences are preparation for formal learning.

Operation Headstart programs are designed to give children who have lacked a variety of play-learning experiences a chance to have these essential experiences, so that these children may have a better chance of success in school.

We can promote learning through play by the variety of materials and experiences we provide. A variety of things to touch and feel, to manipulate, to combine, to make into other things can be found among discarded articles, such as an old clock, old pots and pans, lids, scraps of material, egg cartons, boxes, plastic bottles, lengths of hose, boards.

Excursions to places such as a park, a zoo, a hatchery, a barn, a packing plant or warehouse, a fire station, a laundry, a railway or bus station, an airport offer a variety of firsthand experiences.

Make a list of things a child can use in play and which one does not have to purchase. Make a list of places in your community which might provide learning experiences of interest to a preschool child.

We can also promote learning as we encourage language—attaching names to objects, asking questions, calling attention to qualities, to similarities and differences, and helping the child organize and classify as he is interested. When we are with children, we can comment, "I wonder what will happen if we use the egg beater in the soapy water?" Or we can answer a "why" question by saying, "Tell me what you think." As the child picks up a smooth stone we can label its qualities, "It's a smooth stone. Are there some stones that feel different? Sort the stones you find into smooth ones and rough ones and let's see which pile is bigger. Are there more smooth stones or more rough stones?" And then, "I wonder why?" Comments such as these encourage the processes of learning. We can make up games for organizing and classifying objects or experiences. The child will develop his own games as he approaches other experiences in play. Our interest and our comments will help the child organize his experiences in ways that develop the ability to learn concepts.

R. MacKenzie

C. S. Dixon

C. S. Dixon

Excursions to see animals provide good firsthand experiences.

List some of the concepts which are within the child's level of comprehension, such as up and down, above and below, light and heavy, loud and soft. What are possible play experiences in which he can use these concepts and can verbalize ideas about them?

Play is a way to deal with anxieties. The child uses play for this purpose. He is anxious about many things—about being little, about being helpless, about being left alone, about being left out or not liked, about failing to please. Many of these anxieties persist to some extent throughout life as we all know. Play is a way of reducing one's anxious feelings. A child can play he is big and strong, a cowboy or a soldier with two guns or a policeman or even a wicked witch. He can make things happen in play as he wants. He can be the one who does the spanking or the scolding or the one who goes off and leaves the little ones crying. He can comfort them and care for them. He can do things to others or to dolls or even to materials instead of having things done to him. Dramatic play is a great healer of fears. Playing doctor makes having "shots" less upsetting. Escaping into

Dramatic play provides escape—she can be grown-up; he can be a hero.

Arkansas Rice Growers Association

roles such as these makes it easier to live in a real world where one is only a little boy or a little girl bossed around by almost everyone else.

Even when we are older, we continue to need to escape into fantasy sometimes. We imagine ourselves behaving with great bravery or being very beautiful, and we feel better able to live with the somewhat more limited selves we possess. Paul Bunyan legends grew out of just such feelings because people may need to imagine themselves more powerful than they are. They enjoy the thought, at least. We may imagine ourselves "telling off" a teacher or taking revenge on someone we don't like. We wouldn't really do these things, but imagining doing them relieves our feelings and leaves us with more energy to give to the actual, everyday situation we face. We are better able to sit in the class because we have drained off some of our irritation. It is a desirable thing as long as it helps us deal with reality more comfortably. It is not a desirable thing when we use it only to escape from facing real situations.

Play is also a way of expressing and communicating ideas and feelings. In many types of dramatic play children are expressing their feelings about the world around them and the people in it. Homemaking play is the most common expression of feelings in play, taking the role of father, mother, or baby, or perhaps doctor or nurse. In play the child expresses his feelings about all these roles. In his block building, in his play with clay, paints, sand, or any other material the child is expressing ideas, thoughts, and feelings. He often thinks we understand far more than we do. He will break off his play suddenly if he finds this play-expression too disturbing for him at the time.

Play may be a means of expressing feelings—she is jealous of the newborn, so she is pushing "the baby" away.

R. MacKenzie

Watch a group of children playing house and see what they seem to be thinking about as shown in their play.

Children often use play quite openly as an avenue for communicating and thus relieving their feelings. A child may be upset because his mother has scolded him. He is angry with her. He feels like doing something "bad" to her so he goes out and digs a hole and buries his favorite toy, or throws all his sand toys into a big heap and then becomes interested in the tunnels he can make through the heap. His feelings have changed. Or he may get his gun and swagger around playing he is shooting up the neighborhood. As he plays being a dangerous bandit, he can show his mother how angry he is without really hurting her. Play helps restore a child's emotional balance.

Children who are emotionally ill can often be helped through a process known as *play therapy*. Play therapy takes place under the guidance of a trained therapist. After the child has come to trust the therapist, he is able to deal with his fears and conflicts through playing them out in the presence of the therapist who can respond with understanding.

A very important value of *play* for children *is* that it is *a means of establishing social relations* with each other. Children come to know each other through playing together. At first children play side by side, often talking without listening, but enjoying the activity more because of the presence of another child. This is parallel play. Later, children will play in pairs. These pairs may shift frequently, so that in a few minutes a child is playing with a different companion. Next children form groups briefly around an activity or to accomplish a purpose. Group play gradually becomes more frequent by the time the child is four. By the time the child is five he plays in groups much of the time. His language and social skills at this age are more nearly equal to the demands which group life makes. He has learned these skills through playing with others. In playing together children both lead and follow, cooperate and disagree. They use all types of techniques in getting along together. In play they

Children who have come to know each other
through playing together may share other experiences with pleasure.

Children need plenty of time for play.

Donmoor

have a chance to find the satisfactions which lie in companionship and in having friends. They have a chance to discover more about what they themselves are like. They can stand up for themselves. They give and take. Out of their successes and their failures they build patterns of living and working together. These experiences are part of the world of play and are an essential part of the process of socialization. Children need plenty of time for play.

PLAY EQUIPMENT

Many good types of play equipment can be made with soft wood and simple tools. A good piece of equipment should have most of these characteristics.

It should *have more than one use,* preferably many possible uses.

It should *be safe,* as with no sharp points or edges. It should *be sturdy* and able to stand up under all kinds of treatment.

It should *encourage imaginative* types of *play.*

It should *offer possibilities for learning about the world*—such as learning about forces from using a pulley or about forms from fitting puzzles.

It should *invite use by more than one child at a time,* as a sandbox does.

Plan or make something which a preschool child can use in play.

LANGUAGE

Children are busy learning to talk. As we all know, talking is important! It is useful to be able to speak easily and comfortably, using correct grammar, and to understand a large number of words. Language enables us to develop ideas and concepts, to communicate them, and to learn from other people.

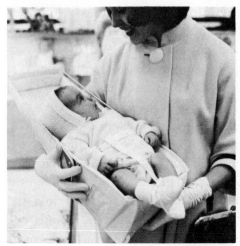
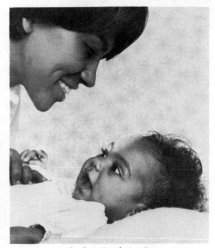

Infanseat   Gerber Products Company

**Babies need to hear speech if they are to
learn to make words out of sounds.**

Have you ever had the experience of thinking you understood
something but when you tried to put it into words to explain to
someone else you found you were not clear about the point at all?
It is not always easy to put ideas into words, but it is important to
master the skill.

Babies cry and make sounds, all the sounds from which words
are formed and many more. Babies need to hear speech if they are
to learn and make words out of these sounds. Talk to a baby as you
bathe him or dress him or feed him, not "baby talk," but the speech
which you would use to anyone else. Give him good speech patterns
to copy. Speak clearly and not too rapidly and you will make it easier
for him to learn. Sing to him and repeat words and phrases. Rhythm
and pitch differences are part of speech. He needs to hear sounds
that are rhythmic, that are high and low, loud and soft.

A child enjoys practicing speech. He repeats words and phrases
over and over. He chants them. He sings or talks to himself as he
plays. Speech for him is not just a matter of communicating with

Miranda Spencer

It takes time and practice to learn to talk.

At first one word—or sound—may express a whole idea.

R. Boxer

someone. He thinks out loud. He enjoys expressing himself through language without any thought of a listener. He also uses speech for communicating with others.

A word may stand for a whole idea at first. "Me" may mean "I want it. Give it to me." It will help him learn if we put in all the words for him, "You want it. I'll give it to you." This helps him to realize that there is more to it than one sound. Sometimes it is better *not* to understand the child too easily. Not understanding his sounds encourages him to make the effort to learn to use speech to get what he wants.

A child needs to have someone listen to him and show pleasure when he talks. A mother's delight at the "mamma" which the baby babbles by accident helps him remember and use that particular sound and associate it with his mother. In this way a word is born for him! It has been there all the time. The attention she gives when he says the word makes him value and repeat that word.

As he gets older, he needs to find that there are people who take time to listen to him as he stumbles and fumbles to convey something that is important to him. He needs to feel people are interested, too. We listen to children as part of helping them learn to talk.

Learning to talk. It takes time and plenty of practice to learn to talk. It takes time for speech muscles to function smoothly, just as it does for other muscles. In learning to play tennis, we may try to hit the ball but find we swing the racket and miss. The ball was somewhere else. So the child learning to talk has an idea of what he wants to say but it doesn't come out. He stutters over a word, or the words may tumble over each other. He misses the mark of easy flowing speech. But give him time. Don't tell him to talk more slowly. Listen as though you had all the time in the world, so he won't feel he has to be in such a hurry. Speak slowly yourself when you answer. When he pronounces a sound or a word incorrectly, don't call attention to his mistakes or correct him. Repeat the word correctly yourself, so he hears it pronounced properly. Do not make him repeat it.

Speaking serves complicated social and intellectual purposes and involves a whole system of muscles and nerve impulses. Learning to control them may take months and years of practice. There is effort involved. Most children go through periods of what we might call "stuttering" if we heard an adult talking this way. This is a normal part of speech development for a child and it is serious only if our comments make the child feel upset and afraid to try talking.

Many children have difficulty with some sounds. Try to say these sounds with special clarity when you speak to the child. There are exercises which make the tongue more flexible. These exercises are games which the child enjoys. They include a play on sounds which helps him become aware of differences in sounds. Playing games which exercise the muscles used in speaking may improve a child's articulation without making him self-conscious about his own speech. If he has not learned to say a sound correctly by the time he reaches first grade, he should get some help in school from a trained teacher.

Talk with a teacher of speech and get suggestions for speech-development games.

The important thing is to learn to use language freely, with **pleasure in all its functions.** Give a child plenty of experiences to

National Association of Real Estate Boards

Children need experiences to talk about.

L. de Victoria

talk about. Really listen to him and encourage expression in words. Avoid correcting him and making him afraid to try speaking.

Experimenting with words. As children learn to talk, they also go through periods of experimenting with words. They experiment with sounds, repeating new words that are appealing because of rhythmic qualities or repetition of syllables or associations. Children experiment also with the meaning of words and the responses they bring when they are used.

This kind of experimenting usually begins with toilet words such as "wee wee" or "poo-poo pants." By the age of three they may take delight in using such words at inappropriate times and places. When they are with other children, they often chant all sorts of nonsense words or phrases. These chants may include all the toilet words they know. Later children begin to add the swear words or the sex words which they have heard. They may call each other all kinds of names. They are finding they can be aggressive with words and can assert themselves verbally. They are just managing some control over hitting and physical aggression. Language is another way to be aggressive and is a step in growing.

This period in the child's growth presents a problem to adults. As a general rule, we deal with the problem best by ignoring most of this kind of language behavior. It is a phase which will pass. The child of this age uses swear words because he finds he gets a response. When he is angry, he may use an unacceptable word because he wants to disturb us. If we object, we can tell him so, "I don't like that word. If you want to say it, go where I can't hear you."

It may be important to help a child who is four or five years old understand how other people may respond if he uses certain words. "Most people don't like hearing that word. Say it if you want to, but not when you are with grown-ups. They won't like it and may be cross with you for saying it." If he tries it out, he will at least understand the reason for the response he may get, even though he still may not understand why people feel as they do. A child is really confused if he feels that the word itself is naughty and that he is doing something bad in saying it, like creating some kind of black magic.

Most of the time it is better to change the subject. It is enough to say that you don't like to hear the word, and then introduce another activity, begin a story or a game. Usually the less attention that is paid to bad language at this age, the less attraction it has for the child. His judgment about which words to use in different circumstances improves with age and experience.

Ringle

Children experiment with all kinds of sounds and words. Give most attention to those which will produce desirable language behavior. Usually the less attention paid to bad language, the less attraction it has.

Creating with words.   Children create with words just as they do with blocks or with paint. If we listen, we can hear the beginning of songs, poems, and stories. It is a matter of recognizing them. When you are with children, have a pad and pencil handy so you can jot down the song a child may be singing as he swings, or the story he is telling himself as he plays alone in the sand or the housekeeping corner.

He will enjoy hearing you read his own song or story back to him. Perhaps you can make a booklet of some of these songs or stories. Like keeping his paintings and putting them up on the wall, this shows him you value his creative efforts and encourages him to keep on creating.

Children usually enjoy very much a story you make up about their own experiences. It may be about something they have done or something which has happened to them. Try making up a story when you are with a child. Give the child a chance to join in through repeating a phrase or answering a question or adding details. You are helping him learn to create and express himself through language.

Some of you may want to try to write a story for a certain child or for a group of children, keeping in mind the ages and experiences of the children. Stories for young children should be about familiar things: other boys and girls, families, animals, firemen and policemen, or about childlike fantasies that are not frightening or confusing. Repetition, suspense, and brevity are important. Writing the

Children enjoy hearing stories and songs, especially those related to their own experiences.

Armstrong/Rapho-Guillumette

story on colored paper and illustrating it will add to its interest. Try reading the story to the child or the group. Maybe you will revise it somewhat after you have tried it out. Making up a good story for children takes skill. Some of you may enjoy developing this skill. If you are doing some baby-sitting, you can try out your stories and discover what children enjoy and what stimulates their imaginations.

Everyone needs avenues for creative expression, and children may find that one of the avenues can be creating with language. They can find real satisfaction in making up stories, seeing them put on paper, hearing them read and valued. If they go on creating, they have another avenue to help meet the stresses and strains of daily living.

Telling stories to children is fun, too, especially if one learns to do it well. A good storyteller learns a story, practicing it until he can tell it with expression. It is a wonderful skill. Children make a wonderful audience.

Look up a book by Ruth Sawyer, *The Way of a Storyteller,* or Ruth Tooze's *Storytelling.* Learn a story and tell it to the class first, using a tape recorder so that you may listen later and criticize your own performance. If you have a chance, try telling the story to a child or a small group of children. What stories do you find hold the attention of the children? What are the differences between storytelling to two or three children and to larger groups? You will find that every audience is different.

Books, especially picture books.   There are places in the world where people have very few books, where there are no public libraries like ours from which one can borrow a book. There are places in which few people have had a chance to learn to read. It would change our world to live without books—cook books, song books, picture books, comic books, school books, mystery stories, adventure stories, history books, biographies, novels.

There is not time to discover everything for ourselves even if we could. We read to find out more about things in the world, to

C. S. Dixon

We want children to discover the magic of books.

Sharing a favorite book with children may help them enjoy all books more.

Uzzle/Magnum

answer some of our questions, to learn about what other people have thought or discovered. Through books one can share in the thoughts and feelings of people who live in far-off places and of people who lived in other ages.

We want children to enjoy books, discover their magic, and be eager to learn to read and use books for all the purposes they can serve for us.

Being with people who, themselves, enjoy books sets a pattern for a child. If you like books, you can share your liking with the child. Read to him often. Read books that are attractive with good pictures and a text you can both enjoy.

SUGGESTIONS FOR SELECTING A BOOK

A book should have pictures. The pictures should be in color when possible, simple, easy to understand, but artistic and related to the story. They should be placed on the page with the part of the story they illustrate.

Books should be short, with only a few sentences or short paragraphs to a page. The language should be free of errors in grammar. Repetition of words, phrases, or ideas appeal to children.

The subject matter for two- and three-year-olds should be about things they know, such as children, animals, people. It is important that the facts be accurate. Older children like stories about familiar objects, but they are beginning to be able to distinguish fact and fantasy. They like fairy stories when they can tell what is real and what is pretend. The text in a good book for children does not distort the truth. It should help the child recall and understand better what he sees in the world rather than introduce him to new and strange things.

Books with humor and with suspense hold children's attention. Children enjoy funny things. These things should be funny to the child—not adult humor. Children love the dramatic, but they must be able to understand the humor and the drama. They can appreciate beauty in language just as they can appreciate illustrations that are beautiful.

There are wonderful books available for children today. Some are inexpensive as well as good, as for example, *some,* but not many, of the "supermarket-shelf" books. It is worthwhile to spend time selecting books for children.

SCIENCE—OR DISCOVERING THE WORLD AROUND US

We have said that the three- and four-year-old child is mainly concerned with the task of discovery, seeking to find "Who am I?" and "What is the world like?" and "What is my place in it?" All these questions make him a budding scientist.

Unfortunately he is discouraged far too often by replies such as "You're too little to understand," "Don't bother me," "Stop asking questions," "What a mess you've

Lees Carpets

Books for young children should have very little text on a page.

Children's books should help them understand what they see.

Rubin

Carlos N. Crosbie

Roberts/Rapho-Guillumette

The child is eager to explore the world around him. By the
time he is three, he is ready to question his discoveries.

made. Can't you learn to leave things alone?" "Don't touch things all
the time," or by being scolded for investigating.

He is seldom encouraged. He should be encouraged by having
his questions treated with respect, by simple answers which get to
the point and which don't offer more information than he is ready
for, by approval, and by more opportunities and more materials.

This is what we should do for him. He is eager, curious, and
ready to discover what the world around him is like. He is ready to
learn to check his observations. He is ready to be introduced to the
scientific method. We should answer his questions. If we do not
know the answers, we should try to find out with him. Investigation
is one way to treat a question with respect.

A definition of science is knowledge gained and verified by
exact observation and correct thinking. Children of four or five are
eager for experiences in which they can observe and check their
observations.

Actual experiences. How do we make the most of this eagerness to learn? We do it by providing plenty of firsthand experiences for young children. We do it by letting children *observe* for themselves.

In addition to telling stories about rabbits to a group of children, we can see that they have a chance to observe a rabbit, to pat it, to feed it, play with it. If the rabbit is a female, she can be bred and thus add to knowledge in an area in which children are keenly interested, that is, where babies come from and how mothers care for babies. You will probably have to learn some things about rabbits yourself if you are to answer children's questions and correct their misconceptions.

Children will talk about the rabbit, too. They may make up stories about bunnies, about this bunny and what he does or might do, real stories and fantasy ones. Reading about rabbits now is quite a different thing. Books verify experience. They extend it. Children are now clearer about the difference between the real and the imagined as they listen to stories.

The more experiences children have with a variety of animals, the more learning for them, even if the experience is limited to a visit to the barns or to an animal brought to the children for a visit. A goat, a lamb, even a baby pig or calf, a pet skunk, turtles large and small, fish, a bird, chickens, pollywogs, salamanders, guinea pigs, white rats, in addition to kittens and puppies offer opportunities for making observations and correcting thinking. These opportunities stimulate further investigation by the children.

If you are planning experiences for a child or for a group of children, first watch the children and see what they are noticing. Perhaps they discover roots as they are

Observing and caring for an animal is an exciting learning experience for a child.

General Motors Acceptance Corporation

Experiences with a variety of animals stimulate further investigation.

digging. The children stop to look, or to pull at the roots. Here is where you can step in and ask questions: "What are they?" "What are they for?" "Why are they there?" See if the children can discover the shrub or tree to which these roots belong.

Experiences with plant life such as sprouting some beans and discovering how the first roots start will now have meaning to these children. This experience is based on interest which grew from their discovery of a root system. Its meaning can be broadened by other experiences to see how roots develop. All children will not be equally interested, but if some children are extremely interested you have a good project. The children may discover seed pods. Then you can extend their interest in this area. Bring in seeds of different sizes. (There are many sizes!) Help children find answers to questions such as "How are seeds scattered?" "What different kinds of seed pods are there?"

From the children's point of view, seeds are slow in sprouting, even radish seeds. As scientists, the children may want to see what is happening to the seeds. You do not want them to take your word for things that they can investigate. Let them dig and discover.

We should be sure that children have some experiences with plant life.

C. S. Dixon

Suzanne Szasz

Digging leads to the discovery of worms—and to further investigation.

Limit the number of seeds to be dug up, if you can, and explain why, so the children can be aware of what the results will be if they dig up *every* seed. You might get some radish plants along with the seeds, so that the children can water and care for something visible from the start. They can perceive more of the cycle of growth.

A garden is fun because of the digging. Digging leads to the discovery of earthworms. Here is another area you can explore. What are worms doing in the garden? How do they live? You may need to become informed yourself.

Weather provides all kinds of opportunities for science experiences—for finding out, verifying, reasoning, and drawing conclusions. "You need your boots on. The grass is wet with dew this morning," said the teacher. The little boy who had come

Weather provides opportunities for science experiences. Why is there sun, rain, and snow?

C. S. Dixon

to school in a car and was sure that it hadn't rained looked at her with disbelief. He turned and ran out and felt the grass. Yes, it was wet all right. He went back inside and got on his boots. He was testing a statement in a scientific manner.

The sun dries dew. There is a difference between shady and sunny places on the grass. Objects cast shadows in sunlight. Ask questions such as, "Why is there shade?" "What makes shadows?" Notice the difference between shadows in the morning and around noon. Try marking out where the shadows fall at different times of day. Play with making shadows.

If it is cold enough, water in the puddles freezes to ice. Bring it inside and let it melt. Other things change in other ways. Gelatin gets firm. Clay hardens as it dries and changes color, too. Water changes to steam when it boils. Boil some water and collect some steam. Observe the operation at all stages.

Observe, test, find out. You will not understand all the "whys" but you first need to explore and find out about the properties of matter. Theoretical understanding needs a foundation of firsthand experiences. Questions precede answers. We can help children by asking questions of them as well as by helping them find answers to the questions they ask.

Observing while taking a walk. Another way in which you can help children learn about the world in which they live is through taking them on walks. A tractor may be at work in the street, or in digging the foundation for a new house. The nearest fire hydrant may be getting flushed out, or the street may be getting swept. Children learn from watching these things.

The grocery store, the feed store, the fire station are full of learning experiences. The children will be interested in some and not in others. Listen to their comments when they are there and try to clear up their confusions and enlarge their understanding of what they see. You will find yourself learning much as you look at things through children's eyes. The world will look new to you. You will see things you never noticed before and you will be teaching in a very good sense of the word.

Plan a walk with a particular child or with a group of children. Be sure to go first yourself so that you are thoroughly familiar with what the children may see or do on the walk. What is the purpose of the walk? What will you do to ensure a good experience for the child or the group of children?

Materials to investigate.   Sand, water, and mud are wonderful materials for investigation. Every child should have plenty of time to explore them. Of course, the most satisfying play material is water. Water fascinates all healthy young children. It offers the most absorbing play experiences. It pours. It spills. It runs down hill. Things float in it or they sink. What things? It splashes when hit, and the splashes are different depending on how one hits. What happens to things in it like sand or mud? Or like dirty clothes or dirty hands? What makes it change color? What objects can be used with water, like sponges, scrub brushes, paint brushes? Every child should have plenty of time for water play.

Water offers a variety of play experiences for a child.

Hoban/dpi

Discuss how opportunities for water play can be provided for children indoors as well as outdoors. What are some of the different materials that can be used along with water?

A can of water and a broad paint brush keep a child or a group of children busy being painters, painting fences, walks, walls. The possibilities for exploring, for observing, for testing observations with water are endless. It is safe and not frightening when there is not too much of it!

If you are planning for a group of children, ask yourself what experiences you can provide for them with water. How can you arrange these experiences so children can be free in their play? Putting a piece of oilcloth, for example, under a tub of water means that spilling is not serious. Putting plastic aprons over the children's clothes keeps them dry when it is not bathing-suit weather.

You will need to decide what limits you will set to children's experiments such as rules about no throwing of water indoors.

Bouncing a ball helps a child discover the world of physics.

C. S. Dixon

Be clear about these rules and enforce them with confidence. Not all investigations should be carried out! Stop children immediately, for example, when they start to throw water. Point out what they *can* do with it. If they persist in throwing, remove the water for a while. Behavior has consequences.

The world of physics. A child rolling a ball or building with blocks is discovering principles related to physics. The ball rolls down. When it's thrown, it goes up but soon comes down. Blocks piled too high or stacked unevenly will fall. A hammer and nails or a saw offer lessons related to forces and energy. Watch a child as he works with

Alison Leslie Gold

A child learns a great deal in a kitchen.

them. He has already learned a lot about physics from his own body, balancing and using it.

A magnet, a vise, a pulley, wheels of all kinds belong among his play materials. They are among the best toys for him. Many toys are a waste of money and precious time. They indicate little respect for the tasks of the child in his growing. These real things will be more fun and give more satisfaction.

A child learns a lot in a kitchen. First, it may be how a lid fits on a pan, how to stack bowls, pans, cans. The toddler with access to cupboards opening at floor level arranges and rearranges, tests out sounds, sizes, shapes, qualities of things. Later, he plays in water at the sink—warm water, cold water, sudsy water. He spends time pouring water, filling pans, maybe dissolving something in water as he helps his mother cook. He stirs and mixes, or he plays with dough, making cookies.

List possible science experiences for preschool children. Make sure that you have covered a *range* of experiences—in biology (plant and animal), chemistry, and physics. Carry out some science experiences yourself which might be suitable to try with children.

PLANNING A SCIENCE EXPERIENCE

Remember as you plan for science experiences with a child:

1. Begin with something familiar and interesting to him.

2. Let *him* do the discovering. Let him approach it in his own way, do what he likes with it. Try asking a question which will direct

his attention to something he may have overlooked. Give him a chance *to discover for himself rather than be told.* You know how you feel when you get a lot of directions!

3. Make comments and explanations simple. Use few words. Listen to *his* comments. Let children discuss among themselves. Quietly call their attention to something they may be missing, try to correct their misconceptions, but let them develop their ideas.

4. A child learns by using his senses—sight, touch, taste, smell, hearing. Provide experiences which let him use as many of his senses as possible.

5. You are helping him learn to use the scientific method. Every one of us needs to make use of this method. Every one of us needs some understanding of scientific principles and some scientific knowledge in all the possible fields. We will add to our own knowledge as we prepare to help children learn.

BLOCKS AND CONSTRUCTION

Blocks are a valuable play material for young children.

Anne R. Smith

Next to water, sand, and mud, the most valuable play material for young children is likely to be *blocks.* Not only boys but also girls like building with blocks and learn many things from using them. They learn about sizes, shapes, forms, numbers, and designs. They get creative satisfaction from making things from blocks. They often find fun in working out plans with one another. They give themselves lessons in cooperating with each other.

Blocks teach the child about forms and shapes and relationships and numbers. From blocks the child learns mathematical concepts. How many blocks will it take? Two short ones may equal one longer one. Understanding physics and mathematics is very important. The child needs many firsthand experiences in these fields—experiences which will serve as the basis for theoretical understanding later.

Children's building has more variety if they can combine things, such as small cars, airplanes, farm animals, or dolls with blocks. These materials suggest roads, airports, farms, homes, and towns.

Watch individual children of various ages playing with blocks. Watch groups of children who are playing with blocks. What age children did you watch? How was their age related to what they built and to how they built it?

The buildings of older children are often complex, extensive structures with interesting designs. Children are fortunate if they have *plenty* of building materials for construction play. They are fortunate if they have space for their building. And they are fortunate if they are left to their own devices concerning what to do or how to do it.

Imaginative children use many things for construction.

James A. Say

Imaginative children use many other things for construction. Cardboard cartons, wooden boxes, sturdy chairs on their sides, a card table with a blanket or sheet over it —all these things serve building purposes. We see individual differences here as in everything else. Some children spend a good deal of time in construction; other children spend only a little time.

Preschool children who have the chance usually enjoy a lightweight hammer (not a toy one), nails with large heads, and pieces of soft wood. It gives them a chance to gain motor skill and a sense of real accomplishment to make an airplane, for example, by nailing two boards together.

Sawing a piece of soft wood, held firmly in a vise on a low bench or table is an achievement. It is exciting to make two pieces where there was only one! When children use tools, they need responsible supervision.

Before you can supervise children's use of tools, you must know how to use them yourself. Make some simple wooden toy. This helps you appreciate the effort it takes. It helps you to remember the frustration of bent nails, pounded fingers, pieces that won't stay where you want them.

MUSIC AND DANCE

All children love to use their bodies in rhythmic ways. They march, swing, ride tricycles, run. In some places in the world, adults of all ages do a great deal of dancing. Children who watch adults dance begin to dance in more intricate ways early in their lives. For children music and body movements go together. They sing as they swing, or they make movements as they listen to music.

A child's sense of rhythm develops as a result of maturation. Children differ in their feeling for rhythm. Differences come more from inherent capacities in the child than from training. One child will keep good time to music at three years as he beats on a drum. Another child just beats! It is little use trying to teach the second child. Just give him time. His capacity for feeling rhythm may be maturing at a slower rate than that of the first child. Correcting him may only discourage him and prevent his enjoying rhythmic play.

Children use their bodies in rhythmic ways when they run and jump.

Bakers of Wonder Bread

Singing with accompaniment helps most children enjoy musical experiences.

W. Schmidt

Singing with children. A child's sense of pitch, on the other hand, is helped by practice. Singing with children, helping them hear the difference between high and low sounds, playing tone games will help them develop their "musical ear" and give flexibility and better pitch to their singing.

Most children like to pitch their singing lower than many people think for children's voices *sound* high to us because they are light. An Autoharp or an accordion is a fine instrument to play to accompany singing.

Sing with children around the piano. Sing with them when they are outdoors doing things like swinging or teetering. There are many good swinging songs, for example. You can also use songs the children themselves make up, singing with them. There are songs about rocking, walking, running through autumn leaves, which are short and easy to learn. Use them when the children are doing these activities.

Children often sing as they play when they are happy. Music is an avenue for expression of feelings. In the beginning, it is used without any formal teaching.

Teaching children songs is done by *letting them learn* through hearing the song, using it, and, perhaps, polishing off the learning by repeating phrases the child has trouble with. Much effort spent in memorizing songs or rhymes may interfere with the child's interest in creating his own songs. If you enjoy a song and sing it frequently, you will find the child singing it, too.

Songs with finger plays have action which a child enjoys. They are useful if you are baby-sitting and find there is little for the child to do.

Learn some finger plays to use as a resource when you may want them.

Creating songs or poems which express his own thoughts and feelings is worthwhile for every child. A parent can encourage the child in expression of this kind by showing interest. If a mother listens as the child sings, jots down the notes and words she hears, and sings them later, saying, "This is your song," she helps the child value his own creative impulses. He is more likely to continue producing music on his own just as he continues creating when we show our appreciation for his pictures, stories, and poems. Our interest will encourage him to use music as an avenue of expression and to be more aware of the music he hears.

If you have a play group, be sure to plan many experiences with music for the children. They can use sound-making instruments such as, bells, tambourines, cymbals, triangles, and drums of all kinds. For reasons of hygiene, it is better to avoid an instrument that goes into the mouth. You can make or devise many sound-making instruments yourself—drums from cans, wooden bowls, or nail kegs; cymbals from two lids of pans; bells on sticks or elastic wrist bands; rattles from small boxes with rice or dried peas inside; or tambourines from bottle caps on embroidery hoops.

Moving to music. Music and movement are closely related. Music experiences for children should include a great deal of body movement and action. Children are likely to express their feelings in rhythmic ways. They may do this as individuals or in a group.

Give young children plenty of chance to move to music but avoid teaching them *how* to move. Let them move in their own ways. Here again avoid "patterns." Play fast music or slow and see what they do. Maybe you have a song about an elephant. See how many different kinds of elephants you will have! If you dance yourself, do it because you like it but not because you want the children to do what you do. Let them discover dancing in their own ways. Leave children free to create their own patterns in music and dancing—patterns which express the ways they are thinking and feeling at the moment.

A group experience with children may involve imagination and dramatic play. Such dramatic play may be pretending to be various animals or people—soldiers, policemen, or Indians. The children may

A rhythm band affords children an opportunity to create "music" and discover dancing.

Yamaha International Corp.

"become" a different animal or person with each change in music. Marching to the sound of a trumpet or while using instruments themselves is also a wonderful experience for groups of children.

Listening to music. Listening is part of enjoying music. Children should have a chance to listen when they wish to do so. Some enjoy listening for only short periods. Remember that we want children to learn to *enjoy* music and to keep their spontaneous pleasure in sounds and rhythm. Children are not helped to do this if they are forced to sit quietly listening when they would much rather be doing something else.

When music is being played, you may notice that the child playing with dolls or running a truck will often move in response to the rhythm. He is listening as he plays. A child who may get tired of listening can play quietly without disturbing the other listeners. He learns about being considerate of others' wishes. His wishes have been respected, so it is easier for him to understand what consideration means.

A valuable listening experience for children is to listen while watching music being produced by different instruments. Most children have heard music on the radio or a record player, but they have not seen the instruments which make the different sounds. They do not know about the great variety of ways in which music is made.

There are the stringed instruments used to accompany folk singing. A ballad singer accompanying himself on an instrument will bring delight to children who enjoy music. There are violins. Invite a friend who plays a violin to visit, bring her violin, and play familiar songs. This gives the child a chance to become acquainted with a stringed instrument which is very

Listening while watching music being produced is a valuable experience

James A. Say

Audio Visual Products, General Electric Company

Children enjoy listening to records.

different from the piano. Wind instruments, such as the flute, the saxophone, or the trumpet offer another experience. Percussion instruments are different still.

A good listening experience may be one where the child can watch and listen to a school band as it practices or a drill in which drums accompany the marching. People who are studying music and practicing are usually glad to take time to play their instruments for a child when he comes to visit. They appreciate his interest.

Children are especially interested if they have the chance to touch and to try the instrument, to listen to a note they have played, and to explore how the sound is produced. A person who understands children as well as music can help the children gain much from these kinds of experiences.

Children enjoy listening to records. There are good records for children—with music and with stories. You will find individual preferences for selections. When you select records for children you can take into account these individual preferences. But remember that you are helping the child build an appreciation for music at its best. Select the records thoughtfully. Buy only those records that are well performed and well recorded.

All children profit from a rich variety of experiences in listening and learning more about music and the ways in which it is made. These experiences are good for an individual child or for children in groups. They help develop interest in music.

Group games with music. Games at this age should be very simple. It is hard for children to wait for turns, so groups should be small. "Ring around the Rosy," "London Bridge," or a simple choosing game are suitable for the fives and older fours. They will enjoy

196 games for only short periods of time.

Simple finger plays are fun for groups as well as individuals at this age. Finger plays have a place at the end of the day when children are tired and need a quiet activity. Finger plays are useful with an individual child when he may have to wait somewhere and has nothing to play with.

ART

Just as children love to move to music, children love to draw and paint. Have plenty of paper, crayons, chalk, and paint around. But *don't* make things for the children to copy. Throw out coloring books! We want children to develop their artistic capacities with all the satisfaction it brings. Art is too important to turn it into "busy work."

Here is a description of a child in nursery school who turned to the easel to paint after watching the group dancing to some very rhythmic music. It shows a child expressing his feelings about music and rhythm through his painting. It helps us see the relation between art and music. Eddie had not joined the group but had stood watching. Suddenly he turned and went directly to the easel. He was the only child there. He picked up two brushes, one in each hand, and began making sweeping lines and short staccato-like movements across the paper. He painted very rapidly. As he painted, Eddie's eyes sparkled, and there was a smile on his face. He attempted to remove the first painting when he finished but could not unclip it. A teacher stepped over and helped him with no comment. He continued with a second painting immediately. The second was similar

Children love to draw and paint.

Roberts/Rapho-Guillumette

to the first. Eddie made no attempt to control the drips. He was quickly finished with the second. It was removed, and Eddie began the third immediately. This time he took two brushes in each hand. He gaily blotched the colors on in a vigorous manner, dipping the brushes four at a time. He moved his whole body as he painted; it was delightful to watch. He painted intently, seemingly unaware of people around him. After the fifth picture he replaced the brushes and experimented for a second or two with mixing colors, perhaps as a result of placing the brushes in the wrong containers. His sixth and seventh paintings were done with two brushes. Now he made sweeping movements with great speed, covering the entire paper with paint. Before beginning his seventh picture he made a delightful musical sound. It was his only verbal sound during the experience. This seventh painting was like a grand finale. His movements became very intense. He gave a tremendous sigh as he finally placed the brushes back in the jars. As the teacher removed the painting from the easel, she asked, "Would you like to paint any more?" "No, I am finished," Eddie said and strolled away quietly.

The child's art work should express what she feels.

James A. Say

The child's art work should be an honest expression of what he is feeling and thinking. He may never be a great artist, but he should be able to express his thoughts and feelings through art as Eddie did in the paintings. For some children art seems especially important as an avenue of expression.

Art may be important to children as an avenue for expression because they lack the skill to express themselves as adequately in words or in music. It is not difficult to pick up a crayon or paintbrush and make a drawing, either a simple one or a complex creation. Finger paints offer a medium which requires little skill and brings satisfying results.

The child delights in expression and in representing the way things look to him. He paints what is important to him. If he represents a person, the face gets the biggest place in the picture. A door may be almost as large as the house. A bee may be larger than a flower. Perhaps he has just discovered bees or been stung by a bee. He uses the colors which please him. These colors may bear little relation to the actual colors of the objects he paints.

He enjoys using his imagination with freedom. We block his imagination if we tell him what to draw or how it should be done. We take away the joy of creating and of self-expression when we give him something to copy. Copying changes the whole experience for him. Children who have had coloring books tend to lose the capacity to perceive in individual ways and with spontaneity. When children are free to use art materials as they wish, they have very individual ways of making use of the materials. One child covers the paper, making large sweeping strokes with his brush. He uses several colors in parallel lines or in adjacent masses. One child's strokes may be light and delicate. Another child may press heavily on the paper and cover only a small area. We see these same individual characteristics repeated as these children play. One may use the whole playground while another restricts his play to one small corner. Each child is unique, a person different from all others.

Techniques or skills in drawing at this age are not important. We do not show the child how he should represent an object. The process is far more important than the product. What counts is the expression of feelings and of seeing things and the satisfaction and release which this expression brings. Eddie might not have painted his symphony if he had had a diet of coloring books or a well-meaning teacher who kept showing him how to hold a brush and how to draw "correctly."

There are things we can do to encourage a child's interest and pleasure in art experiences. We can see that art materials are readily available for him to use. We can see that there is a place where he can work without interruption. We can express our appreciation for what he does, "That is a lovely picture. I like it." We can also show our appreciation by putting the picture away carefully or by having a place where the picture can be displayed. Children need to feel that what they communicate through art is valued by others.

Some art materials have especially satisfying qualities for children because of the sensory experiences they offer. Finger paint is an example of such material. There is no brush between the child and the medium. He is touching it directly as well as seeing it. With one sweep of his hand he can destroy the picture, and then he can create another. Clay is another example. A child can put his hands in it, squeeze it, and pound it. He makes something. He can smash it. He is the creator and the destroyer. Clay is a good medium for releasing tensions. It should be soft so that it can be easily worked by small fingers. When children use paste they may want to use a lot. There may be more paste than paper in their product because they like the feel of the paste itself. Collages with materials in a variety of textures give children opportunities to enjoy the feel as well as the sight of what they create. Paper hangers' paste (the *non*poisonous kind) can be combined with sawdust, corn meal, even sand, to give additional sensory experiences.

You will find some children who are unable to enjoy a sensory experience such as these we have suggested. These children are afraid of getting dirty because getting dirty is associated with being naughty. They are unable to enjoy "messy" types of experiences. It makes them uncomfortable to touch a gooey mass of color as in finger painting. Usually they do overcome this attitude as they watch other children who feel free to explore sensory experiences. Many

Some children enjoy the sensory experience of finger paint.

children who are not able to enjoy messy play are confused as to when messiness is appropriate and when it is not. They have over-restricted themselves in learning what is acceptable and thus limited their experiences.

WHAT HELP DO WE GIVE WITH ART EXPERIENCES?

To help children experience art media with greater freedom and enjoyment there are certain *things we do.*

1. We provide materials for children—large sheets of paper (newsprint or unused backs of sheets of paper), crayons, washable paint in strong colors, including black, paint brushes, a smooth wet surface for finger painting, soft clay, paste, sheets of colored paper, bits of colored paper, scrap material for collages, blocks in different sizes and shapes, sand, and mud.

2. We provide a place and suitable conditions—plastic apron or old shirt to wear, protection for floor and table. He shouldn't have to give too much attention to the job of keeping clean.

3. We give him uninterrupted time.

4. We give him help as he asks for it as in mixing paint, or when he's puzzled over something and needs some explanation.

5. We see that he has plenty of the kind of experiences which he will want to think about and express in an art form.

6. We provide art as part of his familiar, everyday world. A good reproduction of a fine painting on the wall will appeal to a child. A lovely piece of pottery, flowers arranged artistically, or a piece of driftwood, fall foliage, color in the dishes he uses at the table, and an attractive place mat for his use help him appreciate beauty.

Patterns, cutouts, duplicated outlines, and coloring books have no place in creative art expression. If we draw for a child to "help" him, we actually stifle the development of creativity and make him dissatisfied with what he does produce. In helping a child with art experiences, there are certain *things we never do*.

1. We never give him a model or pattern to copy.

2. We never draw pictures for him.

3. We never criticize or show him how we think it should be done, as "This is the way to draw a man," or "That's not right."

4. We do not say "What is it?" (How stupid we are not to know!)

5. We never say, "You've painted enough." Instead, we may say, "It's time to stop painting. We need to get ready to go."

Use art materials yourself. If you are going to help children with art experiences, you will need first to explore art media yourself. One of the most satisfying is finger paint.

In finger painting you can create and destroy with one sweep. You can forget about the product and about being critical of what you make. You can enjoy the *process*. You can come closer to understanding what a child feels. You may find it difficult to overcome your feelings against the "messiness" of finger painting.

Try to use finger paints yourself. You can spread a sheet of plastic over the kitchen tabletop and paint on the plastic. Mix poster paint with wheat paste or starch so that it can be spooned on to a wet surface (wet butcher paper, a plastic sheet, or the tabletop itself). While you finger paint have plenty of paint, also have some music playing. Music with a strongly accented beat and then soothing, restful music. You will discover what it is like to paint with rhythm and to enjoy with more of your senses.

After you have tried finger painting, try playing with clay yourself, without making any special object. What does it feel like to you? Clay is a good medium for making and then destroying what one has made, getting out in an acceptable way the feeling all of us have at times of wanting to smash things.

Think back to your own childhood. Do you recall painting, playing house, or the comfort of a cuddly toy?

Congoleum-Nairn Cushioned Flooring

Lots of paste (mix up paper hangers' paste, being sure to avoid the poisonous kind) and things to make collages with are fun. Try these things yourself before you give them to children. At first children are likely to be most interested in just using the materials, especially the paste. Later they pay more attention to design. Let them discover for themselves what they can do with the materials you provide. Is it different from what you did?

Modeling dough is made of flour, water, and salt. Food coloring or poster paint powder can be added to it. Paper hangers' paste mixed with other materials which give it different textures offers other experiences. Try using as many of these materials as you can. See if you can recall using similar materials when you were a child.

ACTIVITIES   **TO DO AND DISCUSS**

1. Try making up a story when you are with a child, giving the child a chance to join in by adding details, repeating phrases, or giving replies to questions. The subject of the story may be an experience the child has had. It may be an imaginative experience. Which does the child seem to enjoy more? Is there a difference depending on the age of the child?

2. Select three books which you consider to be good books for a child whom you know. Make the selection in the light of what you know about his individual experiences and interests. Test out your selection by reading them to him and see whether your choices seem to be good ones.

3. Observe the story hour in your local library if there is an opportunity to do this. How does the children's librarian present the books to the group? What is the response of the children? How are problems of behavior managed?

4. Learn some simple songs which will be suitable for singing with children when they are swinging, marching, and carrying on other activities as they play. If you play an instrument, you might try accompanying the singing.

5. Use soft clay without trying to make any recognizable object. What are some of the feelings or sensations a child might get from handling clay?

TO THINK AND WRITE ABOUT

1. Why is the learning which comes from play a necessary foundation for later mental growth? Discuss at least five examples.

2. How does dramatic play, where a child acts out the parts of adults, help a child to grow into an adult? Give examples.

3. Prepare a list of toys which can be made at home out of low-cost materials which are on hand.

4. Discuss some of the ways in which adults help little children develop good speech habits.

5. What are the reasons little children like to use bad words? How should adults cope with this problem?

6. Why should children be introduced to simple story books at an early age?

7. Why are coloring books considered a poor art experience for children?

8. In what ways can parents create an environment in their home in which children will best develop their interests in art and music as avenues of self-expression?

PAMPHLETS AND PAPERBACKS

REFERENCES

Baker, Katherine Read
Let's Play Outdoors
Washington, D. C.: National Association for the Education of Young
    Children, 1966

Beyer, Evelyn
Nursery School Settings—Invitation to What?
Washington, D. C.: National Association for the Education of Young
    Children

*Books of the Year—For Children and About Children, Parents, and
    Family Life*
New York: Child Study Association of America (issued annually)

Chittenden, Gertrude, M. Murphy, and P. Williams
Essentials of Nursery Education
Washington, D. C.: National Association for the Education of Young
    Children

Frank, Josette
Children and TV
Public Affairs Pamphlet No. 323
New York: Public Affairs Committee, Inc.

Freedman, David, and Dorothy Colodny
Water, Sand, and Mud as Play Materials
Washington, D. C.: National Association for the Education of Young
 Children, 1959

Greenlee, Juleau
Teaching Science to Children
Dubuque, Iowa: William C. Brown Company, Publishers, 1951

Home Play and Play Equipment
Children's Bureau Publication No. 238
U. S. Department of Health, Education, and Welfare

Ilg, Frances, and others
The Gesell Institute Party Book
New York: Dell Publishing Company

Jones, Betty
What Is Music for Young Children?
Washington, D. C.: National Association for the Education of Young
 Children, 1958

Landeck, Beatrice
Time for Music—A Guide for Parents
Public Affairs Pamphlet No. 260
New York: Public Affairs Committee, Inc.

Larrack, Nancy
Your Child and His Reading
Public Affairs Pamphlet No. 278
New York: Public Affairs Committee, Inc.

Lindstrom, Miriam
Children's Art
Berkeley, California: University of California Press, 1963

Mead, Margaret
A Creative Life for Your Child
Children's Bureau Publication
U. S. Department of Health, Education, and Welfare, 1962

Omwake, Eveline
Basic Learning Begins With Play ("Teaching and Learning," pages 10-16)
New York: The Ethical Culture Schools of New York City, 1964

Omwake, Eveline, ed.
Teaching the Disadvantaged Young Child
Washington, D. C.: National Association for the Education of Young Children, 1965

Rasmussen, Margaret, and Lucy Martin, ed.
Play—Children's Business: Guide to Selection of Toys and Games—Infants to Twelve-Year-Olds
Washington, D.C.: Association for Childhood Education International, 1963

Tarnay, Elizabeth Doak
What Does the Nursery School Teacher Teach?
Washington, D. C.: National Association for the Education of Young Children, 1965

Wann, Kenneth, Miriam Dorn, and Elizabeth Anne Liddle
Fostering Intellectual Development in Young Children
New York: Bureau of Publications, Teachers College, Columbia University, 1962

What Are Nursery Schools For?
Washington, D. C.: Association for Childhood Education International, 1963

Young Children and Science
Washington, D. C.: Association for Childhood Education International, 1964

BOOKS

Association for Childhood Education International
Feelings and Learning
Washington, D. C.: Association for Childhood Education International, 1965

Arbuthnot, M. H.
Children and Books, Third Edition
Chicago: Scott, Foresman & Company, 1964

Beyer, Evelyn
Teaching Young Children
New York: Pegasus (Publishers), a division of Western Publishing Co., Inc., 1968

Christianson, Helen M., Mary Rogers, and Blanche Ludlum
The Nursery School: Adventure in Living and Learning
Boston: Houghton Mifflin Company, 1961

Carson, Rachel
The Sense of Wonder
New York: Harper & Row, Publishers, 1965

Feldman, Shirley, and Kathleen Merrill
Learning About Words
New York: Teachers College, Columbia University, 1964

Green, Marjorie, and Elizabeth Woods
A Nursery School Handbook for Teachers and Parents, Revised Edition
Sierra Madre, California: Sierra Madre Community Nursery School, 1963

Hartley, Ruth, and Robert Goldenson
The Complete Book of Children's Play, Revised Edition
New York: Thomas Y. Crowell Company, 1963

Hoover, Francis Louis
Art Activities for the Very Young: from 3 to 6 Years
Worcester, Massachusetts: Davis Publications, Inc., 1961

Hymes, James L.
Before the Child Reads
New York: Harper & Row, Publishers, 1958

Hymes, James L.
Teaching the Child Under Six
Columbus, Ohio: Charles Merrill Publishing Company, 1968

Johnson, June
Home Play for the Pre-School Child
New York: Harper & Row, Publishers, 1957

Kauffman, Carolyn, and Patricia Farrell
If You Live With Little Children
New York: G. P. Putnam's Sons, 1957

Lepper, Sarah, and others
Good Schools for Young Children
New York: The Macmillan Company, 1968

Matterson, Elizabeth, editor
Play and Playthings for the Preschool Child
Baltimore, Maryland: Penguin Books, Inc.

Moore, Sallie Beth, and Phyllis Richards
Teaching in the Nursery Schools
New York: Harper & Row, Publishers, 1959

Omwake, Eveline
"The Child's Estate" in Sally Provence and Albert Solnit, ed., *Modern Perspectives in Child Development* (pages 577-594)
New York: New York University Press, 1963

Read, Katherine H.
The Nursery School: A Human Relationships Laboratory, Fourth Edition (Chapters 11-13)
Philadelphia: W. B. Saunders Company, 1966

Rudolph, Marguerita
Living and Learning in the Nursery School
New York: Harper & Row, Publishers, 1954

Rudolph, Marguerita, and Dorothy Cohen
Kindergarten: A Year of Learning
New York: Appleton-Century-Crofts, 1964

Sawyer, Ruth
The Way of the Storyteller, Revised Edition
New York: The Viking Press, Inc., 1962

Sheehy, Emma
Children Discover Music and Dance
New York: Holt, Rinehart & Winston, Inc., 1959

Tooze, Ruth
Storytelling
Englewood Cliffs, New Jersey: Prentice-Hall, Inc., 1959

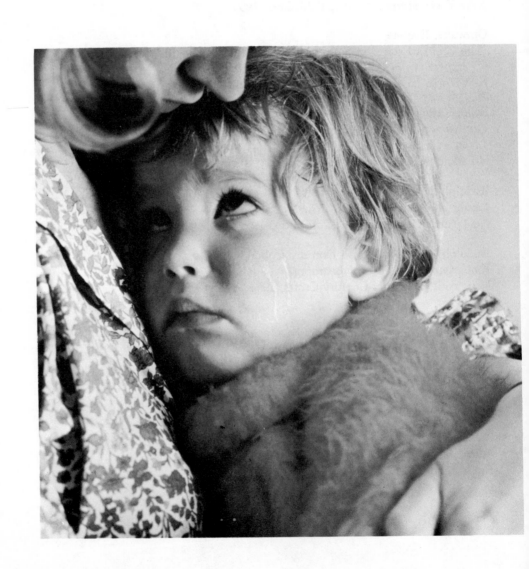

7

Discipline and Spoiling

When we talk about problem behavior, we may think of a "spoiled child." What words would you use to describe a "spoiled child"?

Your description will probably include all the kinds of behavior that you dislike. We often lump all the things we dislike about people under the label "spoiled"; then we end by saying that the person needed more discipline.

Have you ever wondered whether you might be just a little spoiled yourself? Probably most of us are, in one way or another. But what does "spoiling" really mean? How does a child become spoiled? Does discipline really make a difference? What is discipline? Are there different kinds of discipline and different ways to discipline? Can a spoiled child become unspoiled?

You may have other questions about spoiling and discipline. As you read this chapter, look for the answers to the above questions and to your own questions.

211

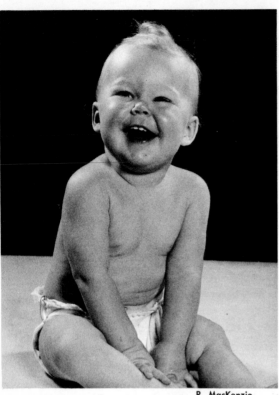

R. MacKenzie

A healthy, happy child is a joy. How can we keep her from being spoiled?

BEING SPOILED

A good many people are afraid of spoiling children. Because they are afraid, they may not give the child what he needs. They do not enjoy the child as much as they might and their relationships are not as satisfying. Other people say, "He's only a baby," and then go ahead and do what pleases them, but not always the child, at the moment. The next moment, they are cross with the child because he's not being the good baby they want. These are some of the ways of spoiling children.

We know that "spoiled" children have not been disciplined in a good way. They may have been indulged. They may have been denied a chance to be responsible and to learn from experience. They may have been given things that their mothers and fathers felt like giving them, but they usually have not had the things that they themselves want most. They want love and understanding, not just toys and gifts. Getting these things may seem like getting a candy bar when you are thirsty and wish for a nice cool drink of milk.

Because they get the wrong things, these children keep asking for more and more. They are never quite satisfied and often become discontented and disagreeable. Their parents don't bother to stop their doing unpleasant or naughty things. Other people get cross with them. Nobody seems to like them very much. Spoiled people are unhappy.

No wonder people are afraid of spoiling their children. It is worth understanding something about how *not* to spoil children. There is no foolproof recipe. Each child is different, and each parent is different. But we can learn something about how these things are likely to work out.

MUTUAL REGULATION

In the beginning of a child's life we can forget about spoiling. No baby a month old ever cried because he was spoiled! He cries because something is wrong. It is his only way of expressing his feelings and communicating.

In the beginning a good mother and father try to *satisfy* the baby's needs. They give freely to him—love, care, and attention—as

A great deal of mutual regulation takes place as mother and baby become acquainted. There is no danger of spoiling at this age.

Gerber Products Company

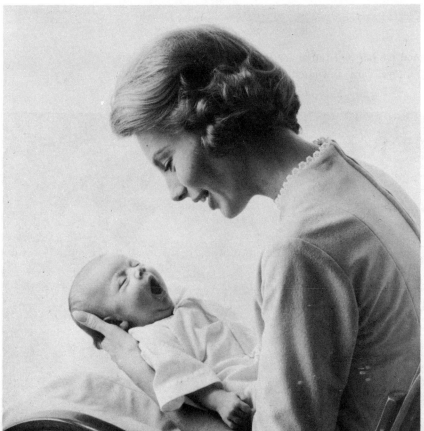

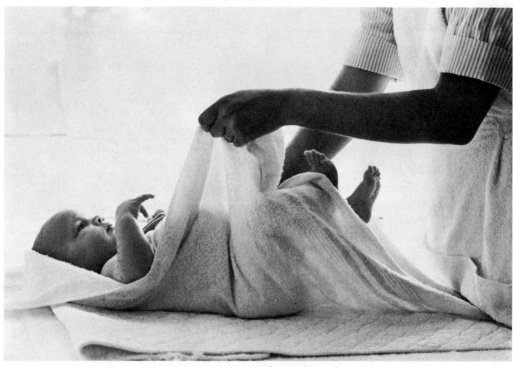

Winthrop Laboratories

At first, the good mother and father try to satisfy the baby's
needs by giving love, care, and attention freely.

Nel-King Products, Inc.

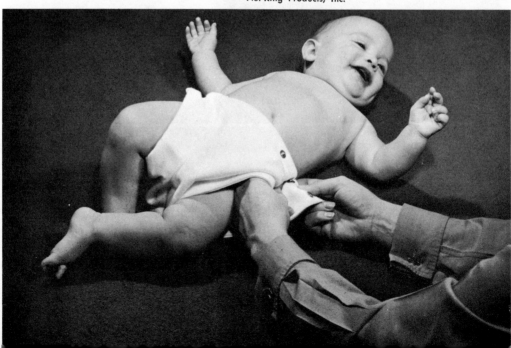

he seems to demand it. When they can satisfy him, they feel good and so does he. He begins to build some trust that he will get what he needs and wants. He wants only what he needs at first. His parents are unhappy when, for some reason, they are unable to satisfy him. The baby begins to learn what giving means, so that someday he, in his turn, can give freely to meet another person's needs. The roots of generosity go back to these first experiences.

But the infant has come into a world where the needs of one person often conflict with the needs of another. He can't have everything he wants. His mother gradually introduces him to this world with its limitations and frustrations as she senses that he is ready and able to take it without getting too discouraged and upset. He has come to trust her. She helps him understand that he is still all right even though things do not go just as he might like.

The needs of one person often conflict with the needs of others. Parents can help the child learn to live comfortably as part of a family.

International Telephone and Telegraph Company

He has to wait for his feeding while she finishes cooking the family meal. She may go out shopping and leave a friendly neighbor in charge. He is mad at first, but he may find something to watch which distracts him and he is quite comfortable in the neighbor's arms. He is able to tolerate these times if he has had a good balance of satisfying experiences to draw on. Gradually he becomes comfortable about waiting for longer periods. He finds it easier to accept substitutes when he cannot have what he wants. He begins to regulate his desires to the needs of the family without necessarily giving up his wishes.

It is a matter of *mutual regulation*. At first his mother does all the regulating and giving. Then, gradually, she asks him to do some. But she protects him from having to make too many adjustments or adjustments that are too great. She is careful to protect him from feeling overwhelmed by his helplessness. His father, too, adjusts his demands and expectations to the baby's growing capacity to cope

When he is waiting for supper, five minutes seem like forever!

American Telephone and Telegraph Company

with these demands. His parents try to make sure that he does not feel that he *never* can get what he wants. A baby's sense of time is not like ours. Five minutes without his mother when he wants her seems like ages. He may be in a panic. Later it will come to seem like the short time that it is.

As one writer has said, a baby needs to have the world presented to him in small enough doses so that he can get a feeling of being able to master the experiences. He should not feel anxious, afraid, deprived, helpless, lonely. If the "doses" of experience of not getting what he needs are regulated well for him, he gets the feeling that he can cope with such things. He enjoys the things that he has,

Babies should feel confident and secure, knowing their needs will be met.

The Equitable Life Assurance Society of the United States

or he finds other ways of getting what he wants—ways that fit in with the needs of his family and later the needs of other people. He is not spoiled.

BEING SATISFIED OR UNSATISFIED

Mutual regulation—give-and-take—is possible when parents give generously, with love, to the baby. In this kind of climate he learns on his part to begin to give to them. He learns to wait at times for satisfactions. If his mother is sensitive to his needs, she regulates wisely, asking from him only what is within his ability to give. His demands become less. Most of all his mother and father give him what he really needs more than anything else, *loving* care. This satisfies him. He can give up getting other things which he may desire but that are not really essential.

A baby needs loving care more than anything else. He is not spoiled by having this need met.

Winthrop Laboratories

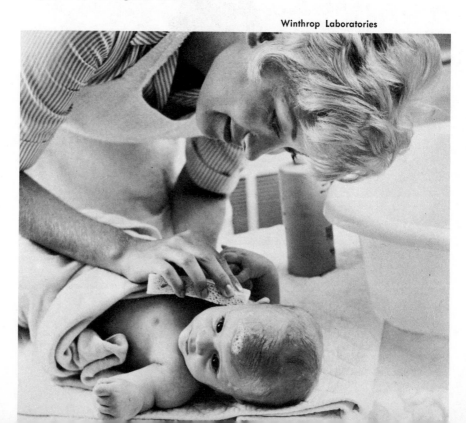

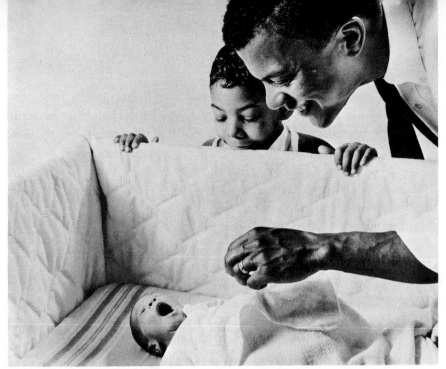

The Prudential Insurance Company of America

It is important for the father to give the child a feeling of strength, security, and reassurance.

A baby is not spoiled by love. Instead, the baby whose parents have not been able to give him enough satisfying love is the one who continues to be demanding. He feels overwhelmed with a sense of his helplessness. He struggles to combat this feeling by demanding more and more of *something*, and usually gets less and less of what he needs most, which is loving care. He gets all kinds of substitutes in the way of material things or of indulgences, which do not really satisfy. He goes on seeking and becomes "spoiled."

Of course all kinds of things can prevent a parent from satisfying a child in the beginning and from working through a good basis for mutual regulation. The mother may have had a severe illness which makes her unable to care for the child. The parents may be faced with some family crisis which takes all their energies. They have more than they can deal with, and there is no one available to give the baby the love and care he needs to help him cope with his adjustments at a critical point.

An illness for the child at a crucial time in his growing may also complicate the adjusting on his part. Difficulty between husband and wife is another thing which complicates the process of adjusting for the child, who must depend on his father and mother.

Even without problems like these, there are plenty of things the child has to struggle with at first—the change from prenatal living to living on his own, temperature changes, new food, gas pains, sights and sounds rushing at him. If loving care is lacking, he really is overwhelmed.

If he does not have reassuring care, he becomes more and more demanding, *or* he just gives up and doesn't care about anything. Both kinds of feelings "spoil" personality growth.

We know that children become spoiled, meaning that they want all kinds of impossible things and are selfish and show little consideration for others, but this spoiling is not the result of being *given* too much. It is the result of a ratio of giving and receiving which has

Children who have a good ratio of giving and receiving are not apt to be spoiled by being given too much.

American Gas Company

been wrong for these children. Mutual regulation has been lacking. They have had to take experiences in doses too great for them to digest well. They have not been protected by adults willing and able to deny children what they should not have or should not experience. These children have tried to defend themselves by behaving in ways we call "spoiled." They may also defend themselves in other ways like being passive and feeling it is safer to want nothing. We do not usually think of this as "spoiled" behavior because it does not bother us as much. But it may be just as spoiled from the standpoint of the individual.

What can we do about changing this kind of behavior?

BUILDING ANY NEW RELATIONSHIP

Mutual regulation is needed in building any new relationship. When you baby-sit with a little child for the first time, you do more of the "giving" in the process of getting acquainted. This may mean that you give your attention to all the things that the child wants to show you. You play the games he wants. If he is a shy child, you may offer him some of your most interesting songs or stories or folding paper tricks or just wait quietly until he indicates that he is ready for action. You regulate what you do with him. You establish a good relationship in which he can trust you and feel safe with you.

Then you are in a position to begin to expect some things of him. You try to be sensitive to this balance, sensitive to what will be enough—but not too much—to expect. After you have been with him a good many times, you can expect that he will be

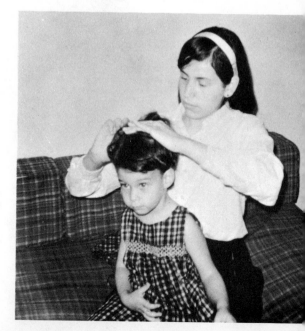

After you have established a good relationship with a child, you can expect some things of her—again, mutual regulation.

Flyer

able to look at what you need as well as what he himself needs. He will do things for you just as you have been doing things for him.

You will be firm. You may refuse to do some things. You may reprove him for something he does, telling him how you feel about it and what you expect of him. He may get mad with you, but he won't feel fear and panic as he might have before he learned to trust you. You are friends.

HELPING SPOILED CHILDREN

How do we help "spoiled" children? It's not easy and it may be impossible for any one of us to do. The trouble may go too deep. It began very early. But we can try.

We can begin by being a *giving* person with him. We do not always give a child what he may be demanding at the moment. But if it is all right to give the child what he asks for, we give it to him freely, not grudgingly. We want to give him the feeling that we are *glad* to give it. A child needs to feel that giving comes freely, not as a result of demanding. He needs to find that people give because they want to give. This kind of giving is important to all children, not just the ones we may consider spoiled. It is important to have this feeling when you give the child what he wants, for there are also times when you must deny

A child needs to feel that giving comes freely, not as a result of demanding.

the child what he asks for or refuse to allow him to do what he wishes. He will understand better the meaning of these denials and refusals if he knows that you are glad to give or allow when you can properly do it.

It is hard for a child when the giving is done reluctantly, the "Oh well, I guess you can have it. I think it would be better if you didn't," kind of attitude. He is not clear about what is really meant. It does not help to give in after you have refused and the child has cried or coaxed. He gets the feeling that, "Nobody really wants to give to me. I have to push and demand before I get anything," or "The way to get what I want is to cry and coax enough." This feeling makes it harder for him to take over control of himself in the future.

FIRMNESS

Try to give freely and willingly when you give to a child or when you do something for him. Then he won't have to push so hard. If you can't give him what he wants, say "No" firmly and immediately and be sure that you mean it.

Suppose you are taking care of a child and he demands his mother's large sharp-pointed scissors. You are right to say "No," and you say it quietly and firmly. He may fuss. He may get mad and storm around or call you names. He may even have a temper tantrum. Of course, he is upset. From his standpoint, he has a right to be upset, but you have enough experience to know that he has no right to the scissors. You try not

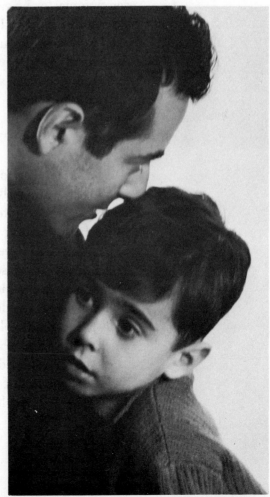

Firmness is a part of good discipline. Being firm does not mean being unpleasant.

Schreiber/Rapho-Guillumette

to get upset because he is upset. You are patient with his anger. You try to help him master it by saying, "When you get through fussing, I'll show you a way to fold a paper hat," or, "When you get through fussing, we'll go out and build those roads we were talking about." You don't bribe him by putting it this way, "If you'll stop, I'll fold a hat or build roads with you." There is a difference between the words "when" and "if."

He may be so angry that he starts throwing things. Again, you stop him firmly (holding him if necessary to show him you mean it), saying, "You must stop doing that. I know you are mad. I get mad, too." Here you may find that he will suddenly listen with great interest while you can tell him about some of your childish temper outbursts. It always helps to share these things.

He may need more vigorous action. Maybe there is a pillow he can pummel, or he can hammer if he has the equipment. Perhaps he can go outdoors and really throw something against a target. You make suggestions, but you do not get drawn into an argument. You do not have to justify your "No" at this point. Just remain firm. It is all part of good guidance or discipline.

DISCIPLINE WITH LOVE

All children need discipline. By discipline we mean direction and control of impulses. We undertake the task of disciplining ourselves as we grow into adulthood. It is not always easy to work when we feel like playing. It is not easy to manage our desires, or our anger, but it is necessary. In the beginning our parents had the responsibility; they set a pattern for being responsible for keeping our impulsive behavior within reasonable limits and giving it desirable directions. Gradually they expected us to assume more responsibility as we grew older and could understand what was needed.

Sound discipline grows out of experiences of mutual regulation as we have discussed. It is based on helping the child understand the consequences of his behavior as much as possible. He learns more readily when he can experience a consequence that bears a

Sound discipline grows out of shared experiences and mutual regulation.

relation to his act. He is playing with a stick and uses it to hit another child. It is taken from him. He cannot have it any longer. He does not stay on the sidewalk, but runs into the street. He is brought into the house. He cannot play outside until he can manage to stay out of the street. He takes something from another child. He must return it.

Sometimes we must set consequences because there are none which the child can face in the situation. When we do, we need to be consistent in maintaining the limits and the penalties.

Consequences of acts, penalties whose meanings are understood, definitions of what is acceptable behavior are all part of the guidance children need from us. A child learns when his relationships with the adult are good relationships. We might say that almost any method which is used with love, because we care about the child, will work. If he knows we care, he can accept our mistakes. Good discipline is based on mutual respect and confidence.

The use of the term punishment in the process of establishing direction and control of our impulses is sometimes misleading. It is often used to refer to methods which involve force or pain for the child. It assumes that a child suffers and repents. A mother bites a child who has bitten to teach him not to bite. A child may be beaten severely because he has disobeyed. We know that punishment of this type may change behavior, but it is likely to provoke impulses which are in turn difficult to manage. Fear and resentment and the feeling of withdrawing are not desirable feelings and do not help in self-control. Punishment of this kind is hard for the child to reconcile with love.

When a child behaves in unacceptable ways, he needs to learn how people feel about this behavior, but punishment like being beaten or bitten seldom teaches the lessons we intend. There are children who have received a great deal of punishment but very little discipline. They cannot control their impulses in socially responsible ways or direct their energies constructively.

Underlying all the seeking and demanding of a spoiled child, as of every child, lies the deep craving for love. Children want to feel that someone cares about them, that they are people of worth and value. Since spoiled children, for some reason, have not received enough loving to satisfy them, they often turn to objects to find satisfaction. They are greedy. They take from others. They want what others have. They have not had much expected of them. This shows a lack of respect for them as people. But what they really want and are afraid they cannot get is love. These children are often the very ones who are hardest to love. We have to draw on real understanding of their basic loneliness if we are to feel genuine respect and real liking for them.

The good mother does not keep on giving everything to the child. She helps prepare him for life by withholding some things from him, and by expecting some things from him as he grows. She regulates what she expects to his growing capacity to live up to expectations—hers and his own. He begins to do some self-regulation. He gets a sense of satisfaction in being able to meet demands. Children like to live up to expectations. They can stand failures if there are enough successes. They need parents who care enough about them to help them learn through sound discipline.

Spanking, scolding, blaming, and shaming a child may make the adult feel he is doing something, but these methods are not likely to give the child the direction he needs. Children may learn in spite of the method, or they may not. A cartoon once showed a big man with a little boy over his knee. As the man administers a spanking, he says, "I'll teach you not to hit other people." Confusing, isn't it?

Of course if you don't know what else to do, it may be better to spank than to do nothing. It may relieve your feelings so that you can tackle the problem of discipline in more effective, reasonable ways. It helps you more than it does the child.

WHAT IS GOOD DISCIPLINE?

1. If we are to discipline well, *we* must *care about the child.* We must like and respect him and want to help him. This kind of attitude is very different from one in which we really think he's a nuisance and feel he "ought to be taught a lesson" or "be made to suffer for his sins." Nothing we do will change his behavior, except for the worse, if we feel like this.

In good discipline, the child must know that we care about him.

Rubin

Of course, we all get angry and impatient with children at times. We get tired. We have our problems. We do not like all they do. We act hastily and are sorry afterwards. But they can survive times like these as long as there is a feeling of respect underneath. Children are remarkably hardy. We say we are sorry and go on from there. We are human and the child can appreciate this. We are sharing our humanness with him.

When we feel that the child does not amount to much and needs to be put in his place, he will resent whatever we do. He resists changing or feels hopeless about being able to change. The result is that any disciplining we do will not help much.

2. If we are to discipline well, *we* must *feel confidence in and respect for ourselves.* A rather surprising thing is that the more we feel respect for ourselves, the more we can respect other people.

Self-respect is a good trait to have if you are going to be effective in your discipline. It enables you to feel more confidence when you say "No" to the child. You are sure of your right to set limits as a responsible person. You trust your judgment. You are not so afraid of being wrong. You can afford to make mistakes. You know everyone makes mistakes. Making mistakes is one way to learn.

When you respect yourself, you give the child confidence by the way you act. It is easier for him to accept your "No." In addition he is learning something important about ways people can feel about themselves. You have set a good pattern for him.

We are better able to act in a firm, friendly way if we respect both him and ourselves.

3. In good discipline *we take the responsibility* for seeing that the child does what he is supposed to do. We don't leave it all up to him. It's a matter of mutual regulation again. With a toddler you take most of the responsibility. With a four-year-old who has had good experiences you can leave quite a bit of the responsibility for managing himself up to him. You have to estimate when the temptations may be too great and regulate yourself accordingly. For example, if he is playing ball near the street, he may be tempted to run into the street to get his ball. He had better play ball in the back

yard, although at other times you can trust him not to go into the street.

4. In good discipline, *we let the child learn from experience* and suffer a consequence from which he has a chance of learning cause and effect, or act and result, without any real harm. He learns what we mean when we say, "No, it's hot," if he touches the stove. We can say then, "I'm sorry, but now you know about hot things." If we can, we prevent his touching the hot stove by removing him, for the pain may leave him afraid of stoves. We do not want him to learn by being injured or by becoming afraid.

He learns most when the consequence follows immediately, occurs every time, and is directly connected with his act. He blows up a balloon and keeps on blowing. The balloon pops and is gone.

Anne R. Smith

In good discipline, we let the child learn from experience. We make sure that no harm will come to him.

5. In good discipline, *we are consistent* in what we do and say.

Sometimes people feel that a method of discipline is no good because the child repeats the same behavior later. It may only mean that he is testing things out. He asks himself, "Does it always happen? Or does it depend on how she feels?" Children really test out and probe for any loopholes. We have to see that things happen the same way if we really expect them to learn.

6. *We are firm* and follow through with what we say. Sometimes people feel uncertain about discipline because the child gets upset. We have a right to expect him to act in certain ways but we can't always expect him to like it. He has a right to his feelings. We are not trying to regulate his feelings, only his behavior.

Suzanne Szasz

In good discipline, we are firm about what we say and do, and we are clear about what we expect.

Usually our uncertainty comes from feeling unsure about whether or not we should have asked this of him. That is a question we had better ask ourselves *first* whenever we can.

7. In good discipline *we are clear about what we expect.* We try to make it clear to the child. Then we stand our ground with sympathy for his feelings but no weakness.

8. *We leave the matter behind when it is over* without trying to rub it in. Rubbing things in may spoil the learning.

Discussions about the toddler and the three- and four-year-old child included other things which have to do with discipline. It is part of toilet training in the case of the toddler, for example. It is

Rubin

**Because of self-discipline, we are freer to en-
joy experiences and friends.**

Bakers of Wonder Bread

related to the development of the conscience in the case of the three-
and four-year-old.

Understanding about discipline is an important matter. We all
have a good deal to learn about it as we take over more and more
of the management of our own lives. Self-discipline is necessary for
this. With self-discipline we have a better chance to accomplish our
goals. Because of self-discipline we are freer to enjoy experiences
and to find satisfactions.

We continue to learn about discipline and authority all our
lives. We want the children we care for to get off to a good start as
they begin learning.

ACTIVITIES

TO DO AND DISCUSS

1. In your notebook, list ten examples of behavior which you would consider signs of a spoiled child. Beside each example, write the probable reason why that type of behavior developed. Can you draw any generalizations by analyzing your list?

2. Plan a role-playing session showing a mother and her spoiled child. Have the mother vary her reactions to the child's nagging by being strict, permissive, and attentive. See how the child might react to each of the mother's attitudes. Why might the child react in each of these ways?

3. Try to remember back to a temper tantrum you had as a child. Write an essay describing the cause and how you felt about it. What was the result of your tantrum?

4. Arrange a panel discussion on parents and their methods of punishing young children. Base the discussion on your own experiences or incidents which you have seen.

TO THINK AND WRITE ABOUT

1. In what ways is an overindulged child really a deprived child? Explain.

2. In what ways does giving a child attention prevent him from becoming spoiled?

3. How does self-discipline grow out of parental training? Why do you think some people lack self-control?

4. Think back to your own childhood. Can you recall ever having a feeling of resentment after being punished? Describe the incident.

5. How may a parent punish a child without having him develop resentful feelings? Give examples.

REFERENCES

PAMPHLETS AND PAPERBACKS

Auerback, Aline B.
The Why and How of Discipline
New York: Child Study Association of America, 1957

Baruch, Dorothy
How to Discipline Your Children
Public Affairs Pamphlet No. 154
New York: Public Affairs Committee, Inc.

Hymes, James L.
Discipline
New York: Bureau of Publications, Teachers College, Columbia University, 1949

Polier, Justine W.
Back to What Woodshed?
Public Affairs Pamphlet No. 232
New York: Public Affairs Committee, Inc.

Spock, Benjamin
Baby and Child Care, Revised Edition
New York: Pocket Books

Spock, Benjamin
Dr. Spock Talks with Mothers: Growth and Guidance
New York: Crest Books, 1961

Wolf, Katherine
The Controversial Problem of Discipline
New Haven: Child Study Center, Yale University, 1953

BOOKS

Baruch, Dorothy
New Ways in Discipline: You and Your Child Today
New York: Whittlesey House, 1949

Fraiberg, Selma
The Magic Years (Chapter 8)
New York: Charles Scribner's Sons, 1959

Read, Katherine H.
The Nursery School: A Human Relationships Laboratory, Fourth Edition (Chapter 9)
Philadelphia: W. B. Saunders Company, 1966

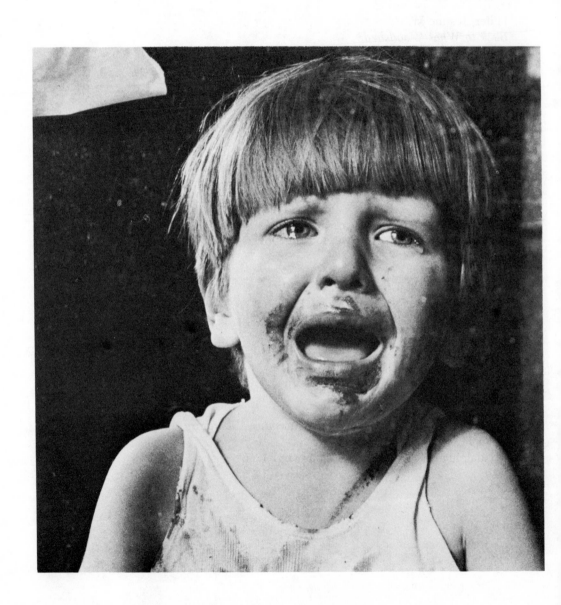

8 Stumbling Blocks in Growing

In this chapter we shall discuss three of the common stumbling blocks in growing. Everyone faces these stumbling blocks at times, and everyone must learn to cope with them to grow in a healthy way. The three stumbling blocks we will discuss are feelings of jealousy and rivalry, feelings of anger and resentment, and problems of authority.

Why are these such universal problems?

What are constructive ways of coping with these problems?

It is important to remember that healthy personality growth does not depend on the absence of problems and conflicts. It depends on how we solve the problem or how we manage to deal with the conflict. Growth comes from reaching solutions to a problem. Solving one problem successfully enables us to deal better with the next problem. Sometimes we try solutions which block our growth and make it more difficult to deal with the problems which follow. One person, for example, wants to make friends with someone else. If he is not immediately successful, he may be critical of the other person and blame him for acting as he does. This response is likely to block him in achieving the friendly relation he wants. Another person in the same circumstance may try a different approach and find it successful. It is easier for this person to make friends the next time. We grow as we overcome obstacles.

235

FEELINGS OF JEALOUSY AND RIVALRY

One of the stumbling blocks to healthy growth is the jealous feelings with which we all struggle. These feelings are natural because we love and care about other people and want them to care, too, and sometimes we are not sure of our place with them or of the meaning of what they do.

Beginnings of jealousy and rivalry. Feelings of jealousy and rivalry have their beginning in the early experiences of an individual in his family. Because of this, they are strong feelings. They continue with us through life, motivating much that we do.

As the baby becomes more aware of the world around him, he also becomes aware of the rivals he has for attention and affection. In the beginning as an infant he felt as though he were the center of the universe. But with time and experience there comes the awareness that attention has to be shared, that one must compete with

A baby is the center of her universe. Gradually she learns that she must share time, attention—and the cookie.

Carlos N. Crosbie

others for it, that others have important places, too. Perhaps we are never entirely sure of our place in any group. Relationships keep changing. It takes time to build enough assurance to be confident that we will have a place with which we will be satisfied. It often takes painful effort on our part to achieve this.

It is natural for the young child to be tremendously concerned about the place he holds in his mother's affections. He is sometimes resentful of the time and attention she gives to household tasks, the time she spends at the telephone, with a casual visitor, or, even more, with a good friend. Children often do not like their mother's best friends because of the struggle with jealous feelings which are aroused by seeing her with them.

But the most important rival at first is the father. The child becomes aware of how much of the mother's attention is given to the father. The child wants to hold on to the most important place himself, but he senses that the mother and father are interested in each other in ways which do not include him. He is confronted, too, with

Suzanne Szasz

The young child may feel the father is a rival and become jealous of him.

the fact that his feelings are mixed or ambivalent ones. He is jealous of his father, but he also wants attention from his father very much. He must struggle with this conflict. Slowly he must resign himself to knowing that he cannot have the most important place, that he must cope with his jealous feelings somehow and find a place for himself in the affections of both his mother and his father. The young child does not accomplish all this without great effort. He may be fussy and irritable and act unreasonably as a result of his struggles to cope with these feelings. His parents help him by not

American Telephone and Telegraph Company

**A child with brothers and sisters
has many opportunities to learn to
cope with jealousy and rivalry.**

provoking any unnecessary jealousy. They help him by being patient and kind and loving, but he will still have some unhappy moments.

Mothers and fathers help a child as they steadfastly maintain their love for him as well as their love for each other. The child is reassured by the fact that their love is not disturbed by his feelings. It is harder for a child if there is serious friction between parents. He does not find reassurance. His jealous feelings may frighten him and leave him tied to one parent. He is less able to find a healthy resolution of his conflicts. If he is fortunate, the child gradually manages to cope with his feelings and to become sure of his place as a child in the affections of both parents.

Another real occasion for jealousy, especially for the first child, is the coming of a new baby. The child's place in the family is changed. Attention necessarily centers on the new baby. We have begun to appreciate the strength of the jealous feelings which many children have. It takes time and patience and wisdom on the parents' part to help a child resolve the conflicts he feels. It is not wise to deny them. The readjustment is hard, but in making it in constructive ways the child gains strength and is better able to cope later with competitive situations he meets in life. It would be serious if the child showed no jealousy over a new baby's arrival. It would suggest that the child did not value his place in the family. The *way* he manages his feelings is important.

The child who lives with brothers and sisters has many opportunities to grow through coping constructively with feelings of jealousy and rivalry. In the family he has a chance to find ways of managing his love and hate feelings. The particular type of sibling rivalry he experiences will influence his adjustments in personal relations throughout his lifetime. He has gone through a training from which he should emerge better able to feel comfortable about rivals. The child who has no brothers and sisters has fewer chances to learn how to cope with feelings of rivalry and jealousy. He must learn to deal with these feelings in experiences with playmates.

In dealing wisely with the friction between siblings, parents make one of their most significant contributions to the personality growth of their children. If parents manage to deal with each child in individual ways, without favoritism, leaving each as free as possible to work out his problems but stepping in when the conflicts are too intense or one-sided, the children will have confidence that disagreements and conflicts with those they love can be managed. Good sibling relations are a source of great support to children. They are the result of the efforts of thoughtful parents and fortunate circumstances.

In coping successfully with feelings of jealousy and rivalry, the child faces these feelings and turns them into constructive channels, uses their energy to accomplish things in the world of work, to create, to be a person who does important things, and to care for and be concerned about others who need care. He does this when he uses the love side of his jealous feelings. He has harnessed the energy and drive of jealousy and channeled it to constructive uses.

This is a summary of the origins of jealousy and rivalry which arise out of our earliest and deepest relationships. Now let us look at ways in which we may recognize these feelings in children and help a child deal with them.

Sharing attention.   Many people have a good deal of trouble at times in sharing the attention of a person who is important to them, like a parent or a teacher or a best friend. They don't like it when a good friend spends time with someone else. It makes them uncomfortable and unhappy. It is likely that when these people were children they were not successful in resolving the conflicts which come with sharing attentions. They may not have had the kind of guidance then which would have helped them find a place for themselves even with rivals present. They feel resentful and hurt. Perhaps they may be the kind of individual who always seems to need a great deal of attention, more than is available. Some children want more attention than do others.

Paul is an example. He is very quiet and is just beginning to make friends at nursery school. He plays with Wendy one day and they have lots of fun. He is very happy. Later Paul sees Wendy playing with Helen, laughing and talking. He says to Wendy, "Are you her friend?" Wendy nods yes. Paul says sadly, "Then you aren't mine." He has not yet reached the point of feeling that one can be friends with more than one person. He has been very jealous of two older brothers who, in their turn, are very competitive. No one in his family feels sure of his place.

One needs to feel valued even when one is not the center of attention. It takes self-confidence to realize that one is still a person of value and worth even though one is not always chosen first or played with exclusively, even by a good friend. It takes confidence to realize that people are our friends even when they prefer someone else at the moment. Too often we turn away and act unfriendly when this happens, thus making other people less friendly to us.

Children may become jealous over sharing the attention of anyone who is important to them.

Carlos N. Crosbie

Every mother has had the experience of having a child climb all over her and demand things from her when she was talking on the telephone. She has had the child act naughty (and thus get attention) when there was an important visitor.

When the young child acts this way, he is trying to hold on to his place. It is easy to feel annoyed with him, but a mother needs to understand what a child is telling her by acting this way. She needs to take time for an explanation such as, "I will soon be through telephoning and then I'll come with you. You may play with your cars while you wait." He may feel more satisfied if she gives him a kiss or a loving pat as she says these words. His doubts are over then.

As long as he feels he is still important to his mother, he can be less demanding. He can share attention. Later when his mother has more time, she may make it clear to him how she would like him to behave while she is telephoning. She can prepare him ahead of time. It helps, too, to approve when he does behave well.

Children usually are jealous over sharing the attention of any person who is important to them. If you are caring for a child, you may find he dislikes having you give attention to any other person or thing. He may be concerned about his place with you. You can try to manage in a way which will help reassure him.

When a new baby arrives. A really critical time comes when a new baby arrives and the child's place changes. He can grow very anxious and may suffer a lot. He needs help in finding that he *has* a place even though it has changed. His mother needs to show him by really giving him some special attention or some time that belongs just to him, that she still cares just as much for him as before. She can help him learn to be comfortable and not feel less valued because he has to share attention. It takes time to learn this.

One mother kept a cookie in her pocket when she was nursing the baby at first, so that when the two-year-old came up she could give him something to eat and thus make it possible for him to feel less upset about seeing her feed the baby.

What the child needs is help in feeling satisfied. He can also begin to realize that he does not really have to depend as much on attention as he grows older. We can help by simple explanations such as, "The baby takes a lot of my time. You want me to play with you. I'd like to and there will be time later. You are my big boy now. I'm glad to have a big boy." The world does change as we get older. It holds new possibilities.

At this critical point fathers play a very important part. A father can give support to the child by spending time with him on excursions and by sharing work and play experiences with him. The child

When a new baby comes, the child's place in the family is changed. It is important that the father give the older child more time and share experiences with him.

finds he has a new and wonderful place with his father. Sharing experiences with a young child may be the start of a companionship which is rewarding to both father and child.

We can also put into words what we expect of him so that he is clear about this, too. "When we go into the bedroom where the baby is sleeping, we will both walk quietly and just whisper. I'm sure you can do it just the way I do."

It is important that we feel sure ourselves that jealous feelings are natural and that they can be managed. Then we can help the child by our confidence, or our casualness and our firmness. If we are not afraid of these kinds of feelings we are more likely to expect that the child, with time, can behave in acceptable ways.

A place in the group for everyone.   If you happen to be caring for a group of children, you need to be aware of the jealous feelings with which all children have to struggle at some times. When you hold one child in your lap, you may need to take care that the other children feel as sure as possible that you care about them, too.

Children are very sensitive to what is happening in situations like these. If a child is being held because he has been hurt and needs comfort, the other children will usually feel good about this. It is reassuring. It is what they would want to have happen to them, so they feel safer as they watch the child.

If the child is there just because the adult enjoys having him there and it makes her feel good, the other children feel left out. They may wonder, "Doesn't she like me?" They feel jealous, and no wise adult provokes jealous feelings. These are not good feelings to have. The children may act "naughty" to get attention, or they may retreat from trying to get attention. Any way it happens, there is trouble. We have to use our very best judgment and be aware of the feelings of all the children. They need to be sure of their place with us.

Every child needs to feel he has a place with other children as well as in his family.

James A. Say

Rivalry in groups.   When young children are together in nursery school groups or Sunday school, they are often concerned about their place with the teacher. They may want to sit next to her at story time or be first in doing what she asks. It is sometimes hard for the teacher to manage but it may be important to arrange the situation if possible so that there isn't a "first" or that no one is "next" to the teacher. She may sit facing them, for example. This reduces the occasion for rivalry. It is also important to find ways of showing each child that he or she is important in some way and has a place. Children need reassurance in their first group experiences that they are important as individuals. They need attention, even the quiet ones who never ask for attention. These may be children who are just too timid to demand it.

Observe a group of children with a teacher and see what you think they may be feeling about their place in the group. How sure are they that the teacher values them and thinks they are important? What did you observe?

Learning to share a place in the group is a very important learning for a child. A teacher needs to be aware of the way children are feeling, so that she can be careful to show that she likes them *all* even when she is doing something for an individual child. She needs to help them grow in their capacity to share attention with others without pushing them toward this goal.

Misbehaving to get attention.   Bobby, a three-year-old who was covered with mud from play outdoors, was being helped to clean up by his nursery-school teacher. Two children began to run noisily around the room; they tipped over the table on which there were some paint jars, making a mess. Why did this happen?

We might call them naughty, but if we are trying to understand them, we would suspect that they were jealous. They did not like seeing the teacher so busy with Bobby. They wanted a share of her attention. Here is what had happened earlier.

Experiments   **Flyer**

Everything is new and wonderful
to a young child. He finds pleasure and learning opportunities all
around him. On this and the following page you will find some
valuable learning experiences available to the child. (Chapter 6)

Role-playing   **Rubin**

Excursions   **Flyer**

Water play

Nova Scotia Information Service

Plants

Flyer

Animals

W. Miller

When Bobby came in covered with mud, they had noticed him and were interested. They asked questions of the teacher and wanted to go to the coatroom to watch him get cleaned up. Perhaps they wished they had had fun in the mud, too. But the teacher told them to go back to their play and went on to the coatroom with Bobby. They felt left out. So now Bobby had the teacher all to himself! By misbehaving they did something to get the teacher to pay attention to them.

In this case, the teacher might have prevented the naughtiness of these two children if she had included them and made cleaning up Bobby an experience in which they shared. She might have said, "Bobby certainly needs some washing up! My, how muddy. We'd better help him get washed. What were you doing, Bobby?" The two children could have gone to the coatroom with Bobby and the teacher. There they could have had a part in helping him wash, change his clothes, and get cleaned up. They would have been satisfied that the teacher was interested in them as well as in Bobby.

Children often misbehave to get our attention when they feel they have been left out, or that others are getting much more attention than they are. We should never scold a child for feeling jealous

Some children need attention so badly they will misbehave to get it.

V. La Rosa & Sons, Inc.

or try to make him feel ashamed. Feeling ashamed only makes matters worse. It is harder to like people when one is ashamed of oneself. A child is jealous because he cares and wants to feel that the adult cares.

FEELINGS OF ANGER AND RESENTMENT

Feelings of anger and resentment are also feelings which everyone has. The infant may cry in discomfort and rage when he wants feeding. The toddler may have a temper tantrum when we take something from him. Angry feelings are strong feelings. They may

Everyone has feelings of anger and resentment.

Chas. Pfizer & Company, Inc.

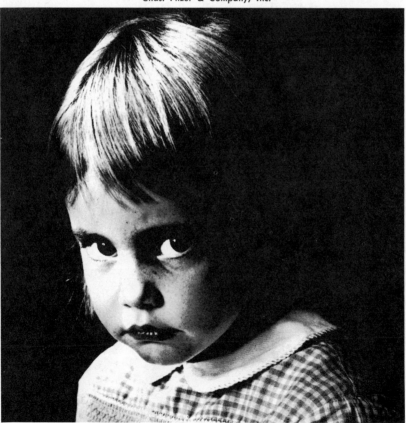

be a strong force in constructive efforts or in destructive ones, depending on how we manage them. They may be stumbling blocks
in growing unless we can accept them and then can deal with them
with understanding.

Everyone feels angry sometimes. Everyone knows what it is like
to feel angry. We have all felt angry and resentful at times, and these
feelings make us unhappy. Angry children are unhappy children.

Accepting feelings.   Many children, not all, who are quiet and
don't join in the play with others are really afraid of the bad feelings
they have inside them. They have become too afraid of these feelings to act at all. They feel it is very bad to be angry. They feel that
no one will like them. They are afraid to act for fear these feelings
will come out and other people will know about their anger and hate.

Tommy played by himself in nursery school, doing the same
thing over and over. He hardly ever spoke and always did what the
teacher asked. He wasn't any trouble but he was missing out on a
lot of fun in the group. One teacher made friends with him and
spent time with him. Soon he showed that he didn't want her to give
her attention to anyone else. This was a good sign. It showed that
he cared about her and that he was beginning to dare to demand
something. Whenever she had to leave, she was careful to explain
why she had to leave him. She tried to give him all the attention he
wanted.

One day when he was in the sandbox and she was near him, a
child came up to her and gave her a pan to hold. Tommy threw
some sand directly at the teacher. She was startled but took time to
think what it meant. He had been very afraid to express feeling in
the past. Because she felt it was good that at last he had been able
to show his displeasure directly, she did not reprove him at this
point. She only said quietly, "Next time throw it at my feet." He
played more freely after that.

The next day he tried to take a favorite tricycle from another
child who was using it. The teacher stopped him, saying, "No, she's
using it." He hit at the teacher's dress, not really touching her. She
said, "I know you really want it. You're mad at me because I won't

let you take it. But you can have it later." Then he ran to the jungle gym and climbed up on it, the first time he had done any climbing. He felt freer and better able to do things now because he had shown his teacher how he felt and she had not been angry with him.

Because he trusted himself to show how he really felt in a good relationship with a teacher who understood, he became less afraid of himself and his anger. He could play. He began to change into a more active child who could enjoy himself. He no longer did exactly what the teacher said but he began to live with the whole of himself and feel that he could be liked by others for what he was—a real person. He began to enjoy playing with other children. He got angry with them and was less upset when they got angry, too.

Paul, who was also quiet and passive, took this way of feeling freer. He began to call everyone, "Hi, rotten apple." After he had done this, he seemed able to play more actively. He dug in the sand, threw sand over a ball and covered it. Soon he shouted to everyone and anyone, "Hi, you *big* rotten apple." Then, no longer a passive child, he began making friends with people.

A child has to be sure that his aggressive feelings are all right, that the responsible adults will stop him without getting angry when he is aggressive in unacceptable ways. Then he can play freely. He can feel it is safe to make friends. He can be creative and make things.

Managing feelings.   The way in which we manage our feelings may be a big stumbling block in the healthy growth of personality. There are different ways to manage feelings. Perhaps the first step is to recognize that feelings can be managed.

We can try to hide our feelings or deny that we feel the way we do. We can express our feelings, bringing them out in words or in action, doing something about them or with them. What we do can be destructive or constructive, harmful, harmless, or helpful.

There are differences in patterns for expressing feeling. We can guide children in learning to manage feelings so that these feelings will not act as stumbling blocks.

We all develop patterns or ways of managing uncomfortable feelings. These patterns start when we are small children. Since these patterns influence the kind of living we do, it is important to understand how to manage difficult feelings in healthy ways. We can help children, and ourselves, manage feelings in ways that will help rather than hinder the process of growth.

One way to help a child manage feelings well is to make sure that he is not overwhelmed by having to face too many difficulties. He needs to be protected, not from all difficulties, but from too great a load of trouble. It is a matter again of being presented with the world in "small enough doses" so that he can master it. It is a matter involving some mutual regulation. We avoid doing things which make a child feel jealous. *We avoid teasing.* We avoid making a child feel angry needlessly. We avoid adding to the burden of uncomfortable feelings a child has to carry.

Another way to manage feelings in a constructive way is to be honest about the way we feel. When we are jealous, the worst thing to do is to pretend that the jealous feeling isn't there. To say, for example, "I don't care" (if we really *do* feel hurt), when we see a friend enjoying someone else will never solve the problem. It just piles up more bad feelings.

Since it is hard to be very clear about what happens with feelings, we may prefer to think that our unhappiness or resentment is actually *caused* by the other person rather than our own feelings of jealousy. We blame other people and we get very mixed up in our relationships with people. Of course, some of the trouble may lie with the other person who is thoughtless and inconsiderate or not loving. But the person who has denied to himself that he has certain feelings loses sight of the part his *own* feeling plays in his behavior. He hasn't much chance of changing his behavior and improving the situation when this happens.

It is very important to help children start out being honest about the way they feel. When they are jealous or mad, they need to say so. Later, they will learn that there are times when one doesn't tell others but is just clear about it with oneself.

We really need to stop and say to ourselves, "I don't like it a bit." Just doing this helps. We need to be honest with ourselves. It is all right to have all kinds of feelings. All people do. That is what

International Paper Company

Some children need help in recognizing their true feelings and time to accept them.

it is to be human! The thing we are concerned with is managing well the feelings we have, not just wishing them away, like magic. They exist and they are much more likely to be managed well if we look squarely at them.

If we say, "I don't like it a bit when Jane talks to Mary," we may be free to think about it and say, "Gosh! That's funny. I like to talk to Mary, and Jane shouldn't get mad at that, so I guess I really shouldn't get mad at Jane." It seems different then.

If Jane is mad, we may think about it and say, "Maybe I've done something she doesn't like and she's really mad at me." She may be behaving like the children who spilled the paint when they felt left out because Bobby was getting all the attention from the teacher.

In this case the thing to do would be to ask Jane, "What's happened? I felt badly when I saw you talking to Mary. Are you mad at me?" That's getting to the heart of the matter and things can get cleared up. It shows you trust yourself and your feelings and trust your friend and can be honest.

Because the things we do when we feel resentful, for example, often get us into trouble, we are likely to cover up the way we feel. We try to pretend even to ourselves that we don't have these feelings. If we have been scolded for being mean to a brother or sister, we hide the feelings even from our family.

The need to express feelings.   One of the most important things we have learned about feelings is that they need to be *expressed*. They need to be expressed, not blindly, but with awareness.

It is a long process to learn about ourselves, what we feel and how we can express feelings in satisfying and constructive ways. It is a process that should begin in the first years. A person is fortunate if he has been helped to be clear about his real feelings rather than to hide them and grow confused. He is fortunate if he has been helped to be clear about the feelings behind his actions.

Feelings can be expressed in actions. At first children are not able to put feelings into words. They may need to tell us how they feel through the way they act. We need to understand their language.

A baby cries when he is hungry, unhappy, or hurt. Crying is a way to express feelings. A child cries, too, and he isn't a "cry baby." He is telling us how he feels, trusting us enough to believe we care about knowing. Children who have not had parents to care for them sometimes do not cry much even when they are badly hurt. This is a poor sign. They have stopped feeling that someone cares.

Feelings are also expressed through vigorous activities like hitting, throwing, kicking, running. Children need plenty of chances to do all these things. Vigorous action drains off strong feelings that become too much to manage. Who hasn't felt better, less angry about something, after a good hard game outdoors? All of us need this kind of an outlet for our strong feelings.

We only need to keep the action safely "channeled" with children. The hitting should not be done at a person, only at an object such as a pillow or punching bag or a dummy figure. Throwing at a target, throwing a bean bag at a wall, banging something hard, pounding clay, all help drain off anger.

Children need plenty of chances to express feelings through vigorous action. Hitting should be done at an object rather than at a person.

Rubin

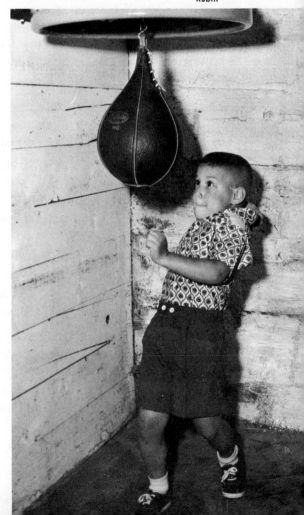

Encourage the child to express his feelings this way. You can say, "It feels good to do this when you are mad." If children feel free to hit objects and drain off their angry feelings, they can play with other children more peacefully.

Feelings can be expressed in words and also changed through words. As soon as a child learns to talk, he can put his feelings into words. Words are the most useful way to be clear about what is happening inside us and to let others know, too. We should be careful not to discourage a child from using words to express his feelings. He can't manage feelings well if he keeps them inside himself.

By the time he is five, a child should have developed both an awareness of social relations and an ability to manage his feelings in a variety of ways. "I hate you. You're mean," he says. We can say, "I know that's the way you feel. I guess you didn't like what I did." We never say to a young child, "Don't talk like that. It's bad to say such a thing." We let a child of five or six know how we feel about what he says. We let him know that we understand how he feels when he says it. If we need to, we direct him to other outlets for his feeling. We make sure that he realizes that he can be honest with us, but that people outside the family may resent open expression of feeling or the use of certain words.

We all know that no one is kind and loving all the time. We all get angry. We get tired and discouraged and we are impatient with other people. We are jealous or envious or selfish or cruel at times. Everyone is! People are hard to live with. Some are harder to live with than others. Sometimes the hardest person of all to live with is yourself.

We find it easier to live with ourselves if we *like* ourselves and are comfortable about all the feelings we have. We like ourselves better when we can accept *all* our feelings. We are helped in living with people if we are comfortable about all the kinds of feelings they may have.

If a mother is comfortable about the fact that her child gets angry with her sometimes or that brothers and sisters don't like each other all the time, she makes it easier for them to modify these feelings with time. She may not like the fact that the feelings are there, but she accepts them and doesn't make the children hide them from her.

Every little child will wish at times that his baby brother or sister had never been born. It's a pretty good thing if he can say it. It will make it easier for him to be glad about the baby at other times. It will make it easier if he knows his mother understands the way he really feels. It is no help if she says, "Don't feel like that." Then he can't share his thoughts with her.

Every child will be angry at times with a brother or sister. It helps if his mother says, "I know you are cross with him right now. It is hard to have him use your train without asking. I know how you feel. He made a mistake, and I hope he'll remember another time. We all make mistakes. Remember when I forgot to leave a piece of cake for you? I was sorry about that. Remember when you forgot and used my scissors and I got very cross?" A child can face a situation better with this kind of help.

Just talking can do a lot to help draw off angry feelings. It is a good pattern to use in learning to manage these feelings. They begin to disappear when we put them into words.

Feelings can be expressed creatively through music, art, poems, and stories. The child who goes to the easel and paints is expressing feeling. An angry child may cover the paper with black and only a bit of red or blue. At another time when he is happy, he may use mostly yellows or reds. The child who sings as he plays is usually expressing contented feeling. These are creative and constructive ways of expressing our feelings. Feelings expressed in these ways are no longer stumbling blocks to growth—our growth or the growth of others.

Feelings expressed creatively are no longer stumbling blocks.

Flyer

Creative people are people who can express *all* of themselves. They aren't afraid of the dark sides. It takes both the bright and the dark sides to make a whole person. Both sides are manageable, the good and the bad. We need to begin to learn as children what we are like and how to live with ourselves in ways which make use of all of our capacities. Feelings can provide energy for getting really difficult things done or for being creative, or they can keep us from accomplishing what we should.

Channeling anger constructively. When we try to hide our anger, we find it appears again in unexpected ways. We are familiar with the stories of the man who is angry with his boss and comes home and criticizes his wife's cooking–or of the man who gets mad

Children with strong feelings have a harder time learning to cope with them.

Marshall/dpi

with his wife and goes out and kicks the dog. We may have had an experience in which we were very patient through a difficult, trying day and then suddenly exploded with anger over a trivial incident, to our own surprise. All the anger we had piled up earlier and had not had a chance to express spilled out at this trivial incident.

It may be dangerous and it is always disturbing to have feelings spill out where they do not belong. We can give children no greater help in emotional growing than to help them learn to be aware of the feelings they have, to be aware of what is causing them, and to do something about them at the time they occur, even if the doing is no more than realizing that these feelings exist. Anger does not just disappear, but it can be drained off.

Guiding children so that anger does not remain a stumbling block means identifying anger whenever we are aware that the child feels angry. It also means putting the anger into words for him, "I think you are mad at someone because of something," and then helping him drain it off in ways that do no harm. Anger turned against oneself can be very damaging. Children often turn anger inward, feeling it is safer to feel angry at themselves than with their parents or other people. Children cripple their growth this way.

Anger is a strong feeling. It can be channeled into avenues which lead to constructive accomplishments which take energy and drive. If it is left to work out its course blindly, it destroys much that is of value.

Some children have stronger feelings and impulses than do others. They may have more of a struggle in learning to cope with these feelings. We have a greater challenge in guiding them wisely and with skill. The rewards may be great for they are likely to be people of energy and drive who will assert themselves as leaders wherever they are.

WE HAVE FEELINGS, TOO

While we can accept the fact that a child may feel angry at us or his friends and we can accept the fact that it is important for him to be honest about his feelings, we do not necessarily need to put up with what he may do. We have a right to our feelings, too.

If he keeps on telling us that he doesn't like us we may say, "I know how you feel now, but that's enough. Try telling me something else." Children learn from our responses to them. We can show them that we accept our feelings and do not deny the way we feel.

THE PROBLEMS OF AUTHORITY

Another stumbling block in growing lies in the problems having to do with authority or of bossing or being bossed. There are healthy ways and unhealthy ways of meeting these problems.

Bossing and being bossed. The healthy person needs and wants to be an individual, to assert himself, to do things in his own way and in his own time, and to work towards goals that are important to him. But he also needs and wants to be with other people and have them as companions and friends. He wants things which come only through working with other people.

When any of us live and work with people, we must take directions and follow some rules. We must fit into the group as well as be an individual. A successful balance in this is not easy to achieve. Often, the closer the relationship with people, the more difficult is the balance and the more important it becomes.

For a society to be a good one its members must come to terms with the matter of authority. They must not be afraid of it or feel resentful about it. They must understand its value. They must feel responsible for it, deciding when to lead or to follow, knowing what is involved when they make these choices. They may conform, or they may rebel, but they should not do it blindly. They must be able to live with satisfaction as individuals within the framework of a social order.

Learning about authority. The extent to which anyone finds a good balance in coping with matters of authority will depend partly on what he has learned about authority as a child. If children are bossed around a lot, they are likely to grow up disliking authority or trying to escape from it. They are likely to get into trouble when they themselves try to be a boss someday.

People in authority may be strict, or they may be indulgent. They may be arbitrary or reasonable. They may be concerned, or they may be busy or indifferent. They may explain things, or they may not. From the kinds of experiences the child has with people who are important to him he may learn to respect authority or to resent it. He is sure to develop ways of coping with it or living with it. His way may be by cheating and lying and fighting it in some way. It may be by taking it too hard, or it may be by facing it comfortably. Fortunately there are usually a good many people who are important in a child's life. His experiences are seldom all good or all bad. A child is fortunate when he has had most of his experiences with people who use authority in responsible ways.

All of us must learn to follow some rules and to come to terms with the matter of authority.

Because the child is dependent on other people when he is young, he has a difficult task in finding a balance between fitting into a group and asserting himself. He must depend on his parents and then on his older brothers and sisters and later on his teachers. He has to discover who he is and what he can do within the framework of what all these people will permit. He must do this while he is quite dependent on them and quite inexperienced. Is it surprising that people have trouble understanding the problems of authority?

The right kind of discipline will encourage a child to meet the problem of authority with a good balance of self-respect. If adults are sympathetic and loving as well as firm, they help a child. He sees adults being responsible for doing what needs to be done without making it seem harsh or frightening.

Even young children must learn that authority means responsibility, not free rein to punish someone else.

We have discussed other aspects of discipline in an earlier chapter. Children need wise discipline if they are to cope well with problems of authority.

A child is also helped to cope with the problem of authority by the way the adults around him make him feel about being little. If he feels of no value because he is little, he is helpless to defend himself. "You can't have this because you might break it," or, "You can't go because you're too little," or, "You do as I tell you. No questions!" He can only wish for the time when he will be big enough to push people around.

One of the important things anyone needs to learn is that authority means responsibility—not just control and pushing people around him. If we treat a child with respect even though he is little and dependent on us, we show him that we do not have to take advantage of size and strength. He can see authority used in fair and responsible ways which leave others with feelings of self-respect. He himself is free to grow more independent, too. Wise parents use authority in these ways.

Learning through playing with others.   As we watch them in their play, we can see the way children are working out the problem of achieving a good balance for themselves in giving and taking directions. Let us take as an example the behavior of two four-year-olds in a nursery school and see what a teacher does in helping them with this problem in their relationship.

Janice and Jerry play together constantly. Janice takes the lead, giving Jerry directions which he seems to enjoy following. She has good ideas, uses language well, and is skillful socially. Jerry is slower in speech and movement and depends on her. They play happily together day after day, paying very little attention to anyone else.

If one observes carefully, one notices that Janice is really pretty "bossy" and that Jerry occasionally resists in a mild way and even plays with another child. Janice gets upset when this happens.

Should they be separated? How would you feel if someone tried to separate you from your best friend?

We should remind ourselves that they are playing together because they *want* to. Being together really satisfies a need for them both. Jerry may still need to be dependent. He may have a lot of "unfinished business" left in this task of growing to be an independent person on his own. If we separate him from Janice, he may just find someone else to depend on. Janice needs to find out from Jerry, not us, about how people feel about being bossed. She may really need to do this bossing.

Jerry is the one who must assert himself in their relationship. When he is ready to try it, there will be opportunities to help him. For example, Janice was already there when he came to school one morning, playing in the housekeeping corner where the two usually played together. She called to him, but he answered, "I'm

As they play, children work out a balance of giving and taking directions.

going outside." Janice protested to the teacher, "Jerry shouldn't go out when I don't go out." Jerry said uncertainly, "But I want to go out. I'm going to play with Timmy."

The teacher encouraged Jerry to carry out his wish. "It's all right to go out, Jerry. It's a nice day. I'm glad you are going out. You can come in and play with Janice later." In this way she helped him stand up for himself.

Jerry did go out and joined Timmy at play. It was his own decision. He was ready to separate himself from Janice, and the teacher helped him. He might not have been able to do it by himself for Janice was his best friend. He liked her, but the teacher's support helped him feel more certain that it can be all right to pay attention to one's own wishes, to assert oneself and do what one likes. Acting this way does not need to mean that one is less friendly.

The child who is unsure of himself needs encouragement to make decisions for himself.

Lakeside Laboratories, Inc.

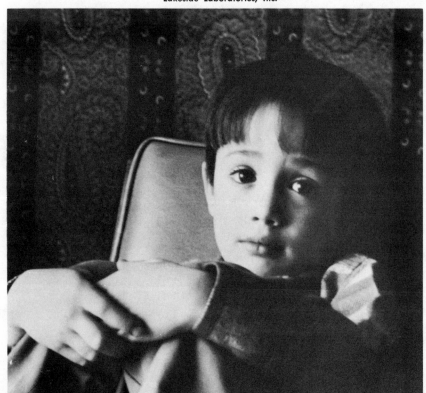

When Jerry was younger, at home, he may have been disapproved of when he began to show more independence. He may have gotten the idea that the only way to get along with people was to do what they wanted. But we know that this is not always a desirable way to get along. Now the teacher is helping him learn differently.

Janice, too, needs help. Perhaps she is unsure of herself with others unless she is "boss." She may only feel sure that people like her when they do what she wants them to do. Unless she can control matters, she may feel as though she is pretty helpless.

When she was younger, she may have been expected to be more competent and grown-up than she really felt. She may have felt that she should be able to make things happen. She may not have been accepted as she was, a little girl who was not yet big and able to manage everything. So, to make herself more acceptable, she tried to manage things and people and felt she was failing if she could not control them.

She needs help from the teacher in learning another point of view. In this case, the teacher said, "You like having Jerry with you, I know. But he's going out now. He'll be back later. You and he will play together again." She gave Janice something else to think about by adding, "I wonder what you are going to do with those dolls." Janice seemed satisfied and continued her play. She seemed to feel more comfortable alone, without someone to boss. Later the teacher helped Janice again by finding another child to join her.

It will take more than one time for these children to learn the lessons they need to learn: 1) that one can stand up for oneself and still be friendly, and 2) that one can feel comfortable and liked even when one is not controlling and bossing. These are good things to learn. They help in all relationships.

These are lessons which are part of learning to live with the realities of authority, with bosses and rules and restrictions. These lessons go along with learning that one can give in with no loss of self-respect and that at times one cannot. They go along with learning to decide wisely how to act independently and be responsible for one's own decisions.

People who have learned to feel responsible about matters of authority do not assume authority when it is unnecessary. They do not avoid assuming it when it is needed. They make the kind of citizens needed in a democracy.

ACTIVITIES   **TO DO AND DISCUSS**

1. a. Observe a child over a period of time and make notes of the situations in which:
      (1) He expresses anger or resentment.
      (2) He bosses others.
      (3) He accepts authority.
      (4) He tries to get attention from adults.
   b. In what ways did he handle these things? Which ways were constructive and effective? Which were not?

TO THINK AND WRITE ABOUT

1. How have you been influenced by the position you have in your family, such as being the oldest child, the middle child, or the youngest? In what ways can parents help in relations between siblings?

2. Why is it better for a child to express his feelings rather than hide them? Describe how a child's feelings might be expressed:
   a. When he has a great many difficulties.
   b. When he is jealous of someone.
   c. When he is really angry about something.
   What do *you* do when you have these feelings? How many different ways do you use to drain off such feelings?

3. How can you help a child who is too afraid of his feelings to play freely?

4. How can an adult use *words* or *ideas* to change a child's feelings in these situations?
   a. When the child says, "I hate you. You're mean!"
   b. When the child expresses antagonistic feelings about a new baby brother or sister.

5. How would you help young children find a balance in the following authority-dependency situations?

  a. William is continually being requested to do as he is told and ask no questions.

  b. John, a vigorous, energetic boy, feels he should be able to assert himself and do what he likes at all times.

  c. Helen feels that the only way to get along with people is to do what they want.

6. How do words like these affect a child's ideas and feelings about authority? "You come in when I tell you to. I don't care whether you are ready or not."

7. How do you feel about being bossed? Discuss this question in class and see how many different ways there are to feel about it. Which ways are most helpful, or lead to the best results?

8. How do you feel about doing the bossing yourself? Discuss this question as you did Number 7.

9. What are some examples of responsible attitudes and actions toward authority on the part of an adult?

PAMPHLETS AND PAPERBACKS   REFERENCES

Arnstein, Arlene, in cooperation with the Child Study Association of America
What to Tell Your Child
New York: Pocket Books, Inc., 1964

Baruch, Dorothy
Understanding Young Children
New York: Bureau of Publications, Teachers College, Columbia University, 1949

Cadden, Vivian
Crisis in the Family
Chicago: National Research Bureau, Inc.

Escalona, Sibylle
Understanding Hostility in Children
Chicago: Science Research Associates, 1954

Mayer, Greta and Mary Hoover
When Children Need Special Help with Emotional Problems
New York: Child Study Association of America

Neisser, Edith G.
How to Be a Good Mother-in-law and Grandmother
Public Affairs Pamphlet No. 174
New York: Public Affairs Committee, Inc.

Ogg, Elizabeth
When a Family Faces Stress
Public Affairs Pamphlet No. 341
New York: Public Affairs Committee, Inc.

Ridenour, Nina
Some Special Problems of Children Age 2 to 5 Years
National Mental Health Foundation, 1947

Ross, Helen
The Shy Child
Public Affairs Pamphlet No. 239
New York: Public Affairs Committee, Inc.

Rubin, Theodore I.
Jordi, and Lisa and David
New York: Ballantine Books, Inc., 1962

Thorman, George
Family Therapy—Help for Troubled Families
Public Affairs Pamphlet No. 356
New York: Public Affairs Committee, Inc.

Wexler, Susan
The Story of Sandy
New York: Signet Books, 1955

Wolf, Anna W. M.
Helping Your Child to Understand Death
New York: Child Study Association of America, 1958

BOOKS

Axline, Virginia
Dibs: in Search of Self: Personality Development in Play Therapy
Boston: Houghton Mifflin Company, 1964

Fraiberg, Selma
The Magic Years (Chapter 7)
New York: Charles Scribner's Sons, 1959

Frank, Mary, and Lawrence Frank
How to Help Your Child in School
New York: Viking Press, Inc., 1950

Hospitals and Children: A Parent's Eye View
Robertson, James, ed.
New York: International Universities Press, Inc., 1963

Read, Katherine H.
The Nursery School: A Human Relationships Laboratory, Fourth Edition (Chapter 8)
Philadelphia: W. B. Saunders Company, 1966

Scheinfeld, Aram
Twins and Super Twins
Philadelphia: J. B. Lippincott Co., 1967

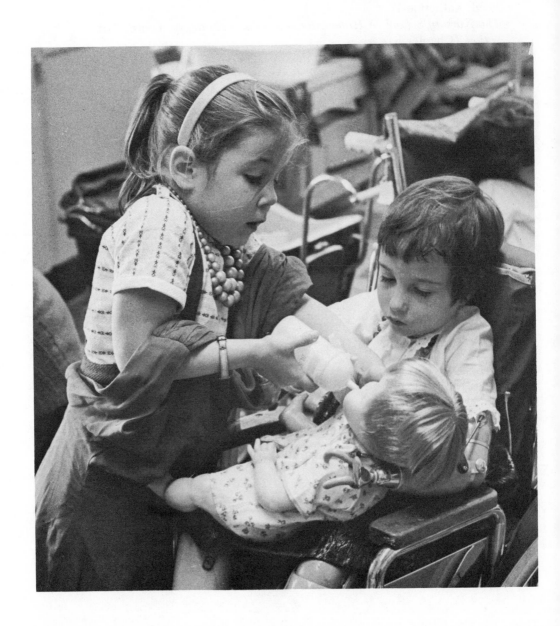

9 Handicaps and Crises

Everyone has some difficult situations to face in life. We may say, "If only I didn't have this problem or that problem." But problems keep popping up and we keep having to find ways of meeting them.

Children often have crises and handicaps to face. Some children we meet may have only one parent, because of either death or divorce. Their mothers may work outside the home, leaving the child with a succession of baby sitters. Or, their mothers may be ill and unable to give the kind of care which mothers usually give to children. The family may be of a different nationality, race, or religion from the neighboring families. The family may have more money or less money than other families around them. The child may be adopted and feel that he is different from others.

Many factors may be important in determining how a child feels or acts. Any one circumstance is only a factor among many others. But these make a real difference, depending on the circumstances and on what the individual child is like. Heredity and environment both influence a person's reactions to circumstances.

Some children we will meet are handicapped physically by injury or disease such as crippling polio or cerebral palsy. They may often be sick. Or, they may be handicapped by being blind or deaf. They may be mentally retarded and unable to learn at the same rate that most children of their age can learn. Some children may be brain damaged or they may be emotionally ill and unable to react the way most children do.

It is important for all these children that the people they meet avoid adding to their difficulties by lack of understanding and sympathy. Everyone has problems, but some children carry a heavier burden than others. They need more understanding. We can lighten the burden if we are more aware of what can be done to help them grow and develop.

Some children carry a heavy burden and need special understanding.

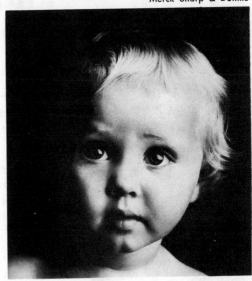

AN ONLY CHILD

Jane was an only child. Her parents loved her very much and she was a delightful child, friendly and intelligent. Her parents felt sorry that they could not have more children. They knew that only children have some problems, but they felt that the problems need not be greater than those of other children, just different.

They spent a lot of time with Jane because they enjoyed her, but they had time for their own friends, too. When they went out, they left Jane with a baby sitter whom she knew well. They sent her to nursery school when she was three. She was happy there for she liked people and entered into all activities easily. Jane's parents encouraged other children to play in their yard. When they went on drives or trips, they almost always took one of Jane's friends along. Jane did not feel different from other children. Her parents were firm in their discipline and expected her to take responsibility, but

Parents who are understanding can help an only child grow up into a happy adult.

American Telephone and Telegraph Company

they did not expect her to act like an adult as parents of only children sometimes do. They gave her time to be a child and did not push her into growing up.

Not all parents of only children are able to be this understanding. Some only children are pushed and indulged and do not grow up into happy people unless they receive a good deal of help from someone else.

ADOPTED CHILDREN

Peter and Steve were twin boys who had been adopted when they were infants. They were lively, healthy boys and their adoptive parents were very happy with them. When they were three years old, they went to nursery school. Here they made friends readily and fitted into the group well. They liked each other's company but they spent as much time playing with other children as with each other. They were sturdy and independent.

After they had entered public grade school the parents adopted a little girl of two named Helen. She was plump and moved slowly.

She seemed to find it hard to fit into this busy, active family. Her adoptive mother found Helen more difficult to manage than she did the boys. Perhaps she preferred boys to girls. Perhaps the mother and Helen did not "fit" well together as happens sometimes even with children born into a family. Their interests and their tempo of living differed.

Helen found it hard to play with other children when she went to nursery school. Her greatest joy came from pets, the rabbit and the chickens. She was resistant to routines, and no teacher ever got very close to her. At home she did not get much attention from the two boys. Her adoptive father enjoyed her more than the other members of the family did, but he was a busy man and was not at home a great deal. Helen went through school feeling lonely and apart from others and full of resentment. She felt people were against her. As soon as she was old enough, she left home and found a job in a distant city. Peter and Steve kept in close touch with the family.

Adopted children can become part of a happy family when parents and children have made the special adjustments necessary.

National Biscuit Company

The problems of adopted children are always somewhat special. Both parents and children have adjustments to face in their feelings about adoption and the reasons for it and other people's attitude toward it. When these are made well, the relationships of adoptive parents and their children are as close and warm as those of natural parents.

A CHILD WITH ONLY ONE PARENT

Bill was a bright, alert four-year-old. His mother had died the year before. There were no relatives nearby and his father was caring for him alone. During the day Bill was left with a woman in the neighborhood. His father picked him up on the way home from work and took him back to the trailer where they lived. Sometimes

Children with only one parent have special needs and special problems. The one parent and understanding friends are especially important.

Aetna Life and Casualty

they had supper in a restaurant on the way. Bill and his father were depending on each other. They both carried a heavy burden. Bill tried hard to do everything his father told him to do. His father tried hard, too, to be both mother and father to the little boy.

They managed this way for several years. Bill played with children in the neighborhood, but he had a feeling that he was different from the others somehow. When he entered school, he was much happier for he did well in school and a motherly, understanding teacher meant a great deal to him.

It is more common for a child to be brought up by a mother alone than by a father. The problems are similar, for boys and girls both need two parents if they are to understand the role of a man and of a woman. This was discussed earlier under identifying with one's sex role. A child brought up by a mother alone probably does not feel as different from others as the child brought up by a father only. The child may have less difficulty at first, but his problems may become greater at adolescence. Children such as these are helped by the fact that there are men interested in elementary education today as teachers and principals. The school, too, may be a help to these children, as it was to Bill.

Children with only one parent have special problems. They have a special need to share experiences with friends and teachers who are understanding. Much of their security must come from the one parent. Every child gets mad at a mother or father at times, but when he is mad at one parent, he can feel good about the other parent. The child with one parent is less free to feel this way and more likely to bury the feeling inside himself where it sometimes causes trouble. The parent, too, has no one to turn to in relieving his or her feelings. The relationship of the child and the parent has to bear strains which are "diluted" in the ordinary family by the variety of relationships possible for the members.

Some communities have an organization called "Parents Without Partners." Its members are parents, either mothers or fathers, who are bringing up a child or children alone. They meet to talk over their special problems and give help to one another in carrying the load of raising children without the help of a partner. Parents

Without Partners recognizes the need these parents have to share their problems with others who understand.

When there is a death in the family with children, or a parent is ill for a long time, an understanding "homemaker" provided by an agency in the community can often help keep the family together while the other parent has time to work out more permanent plans. In such a case children do not lose the secure feeling that there is a place for them where they can feel truly at home.

CHILDREN WHOSE MOTHERS WORK
OUTSIDE THE HOME

John and Betty are children who have been left with a succession of baby-sitters. John is two and a half, and Betty is only six months old. Their mother works as a secretary while their father has a job as a mechanic in a garage. His work is often irregular. When the father is home, he cares for them. When he has to go to work, he leaves them with a neighbor or gets a young girl down the street to come in. It is not easy for any member of the family.

Very young children need to be cared for by their mothers.

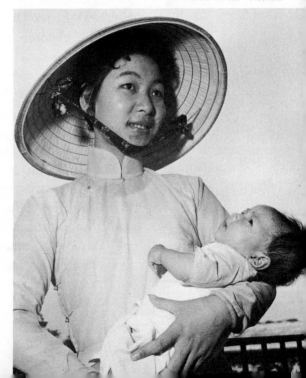

John cries a lot and finds it difficult to settle down to play. He seems always to be seeking someone or something. He runs out to the sidewalk and talks to people who are passing by. He gets into trouble because he takes small things he finds. He has no children of his own age to play with. It seems likely that John's problems will increase. His restlessness and irritability may make school difficult and he will not know much about making close friends.

Children need their mothers especially in the first two or three years of life. When mothers work outside the home while their

When mothers of young children must work outside the home,
the children should be cared for by a real mother-substitute.

children are young, the children should be cared for by someone
who can be a real mother-substitute. She should like children and
should care for them on a regular basis in either her home or the
children's home. Only if there is a real mother-substitute, liked by
both the children *and* the parents, can the children develop in
healthy ways.

Foster day care services and day care centers can meet these
children's needs if they are well-run places. Children under three
years of age are usually better cared for under a foster day care
plan. In this plan a social agency supervises foster day care homes
where a qualified woman cares for only two or three young children
in her own home. In most cases she is paid a regular salary by the
agency. The parents pay the agency an amount based on their ability to pay. The children are assured better care than if they are left
with a baby-sitter whom the parents do not really know well.

Day care centers usually care for children of three, four, and
five years. In a good day care center the groups are small, so the

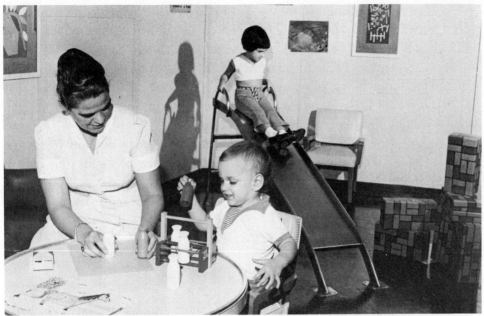

Well-run foster day care services and day care centers can meet the needs of children whose mothers work outside the home.

child can feel he has a place in it. There are perhaps 12 to 15 three-year-olds and 15 to 20 four-year-olds in a group. Sometimes the groups are of mixed ages. A large center may have several separate groups, each with a professionally trained director. There are two adults in every group. The child has a place for his own clothes, his own bed, and a nourishing hot meal is served at noon. The day is planned with periods of active play outdoors and with periods of rest. Good day care centers provide an educational program such as nursery schools offer. These centers give the child a chance to grow and learn in healthy ways as children do in homes.

The need for day care centers is much greater than the number of centers available. There are many places where children are cared for in groups which do not meet even the minimum standards for children's health and social and emotional welfare. Parents need to protect their children by a careful investigation before they leave a child in any center. They need to be informed themselves about what a good center is like and what they should expect.

Citizens should be aware of the kinds of group care for young children being provided in their community. Learning in the first years of life is so important that provisions for group care of children should be the concern of all citizens.

Not all children whose parents both work outside the home have the kind of care which adequately supplements the care a mother and father can give. As a result, these children will have behavior problems which can be met only by a good deal of understanding help.

THE NEGLECTED CHILD

Mary's mother had been very ill at home for many months. Mary was the youngest in a large family. Her sisters, who were much older, helped in nursing their mother. They took responsibility for managing the household duties. But Mary was only two. She was not allowed in the sickroom and played quietly by herself. She was a good child. She spent much of the time outdoors. Sometimes she would cry at the closed door of her mother's room. She could not understand what was happening. Everyone in the family gave her some attention but no one had much time for her. They all felt anxious themselves and were kept very busy.

Mary's mother died after nearly two years of illness. The family carried on as they had been doing. The father was often away and left things to his oldest daughter. Mary was looked after by a neighbor most of the time. She caused no special trouble except that she sometimes ran away.

But Mary had more and more trouble as she grew up. She had not been sure of her place in the family. She had felt pushed out when she was growing up. Her mother's closed door stood for rejection to her. She had misunderstood things that happened. She was never sure that anyone really liked her. In those beginning years,

When he left the hospital, his doctor wisely instructed the parents to let him be as active as he wished. He told them to trust the child to know when he needed to rest during the day. He said that anxious warnings about the danger of getting too tired would only result in his taking less responsibility for himself.

Bobby was able to make a remarkable recovery from what had been a serious illness. He had had reassurance and support from people he trusted when he was most in need of it. In the time following his illness, too, he was not over-protected or indulged. His parents trusted him to regulate his activity to his strength. In this they had the backing of understanding doctors.

Bobby entered school eager and interested in it. He was a leader among the children in his neighborhood, absorbed in the projects they all engaged in. He may have gained self-confidence through having mastered a serious crisis with the help of his parents.

A BLIND CHILD

Alice entered a nursery school at three and a half. She was blind. Her blindness was the result of time spent in an incubator as a premature infant. Fortunately we know enough today so that this type of blindness does not occur often. Alice's parents had help from a person on the staff of their state department of health, trained in work with blind children. She helped them make plans for Alice's future. She also helped them understand more about how they could encourage Alice to grow and develop, letting her do things for herself and play with other children.

Most important of all, she helped them talk about their feelings. It is hard for loving parents to face the fact that their child is different from others and must live with a handicap. Sometimes parents are not able to talk about these things. They keep their thoughts to themselves where their fears and anxieties multiply. But Alice's parents were helped to talk freely about how they felt. Because they did, they felt more comfortable about Alice and with Alice. They could help their friends feel more comfortable with her, too. They

The blind child enjoys many of the experiences the sighted child enjoys.

could explain to the other children in the neighborhood about blindness, how it was like having your eyes closed and how Alice depended on feeling with her hands and feet and on words for descriptions of what things were like.

With only a little extra supervision, Alice could play outdoors. She entered nursery school, eager for the new experience, and made a place for herself among the children. The teachers learned, through the help of the trained worker who visited the school and talked with them, to be careful not to do things for Alice that she could do for herself and to treat her as a person who was learning and growing and finding her way as the other children were doing.

Alice is now doing well in grade school, spending five days a week at the special school for the blind and returning to her home for the weekends. She travels by herself on the bus. She plans to attend the regular high school in her own home town when she is older. Alice has had understanding help and has made progress in mastering her tasks in growing.

A MENTALLY RETARDED CHILD

Philip had seemed like such a wonderful baby at first. He was placid and good and a lovely-looking infant. He seldom cried. He was nearly a year old when his parents were forced to admit to themselves that he had not developed as he should. He was making no effort to sit up or talk. Philip's family found it very hard to face the diagnosis that he was retarded mentally and would not grow like other children. Their dreams of what he might someday become would have to be changed.

They were very unhappy. His mother did not want to see her friends. It was painful to her to see their babies who were active and busy. She hardly wanted to see Philip at times. She took him to many different doctors. Some of them suggested remedies, but

The child whose mental progress is extremely slow can bring pleasure. When he is older he may be happier with other children like himself.

Shield of David Institute for Retarded Children, New York

there was no cure. Finally they talked with an understanding counselor. With his help, they began to think about how they might plan for Philip's future, and help him grow in his own way.

Fortunately there was a school not too far away which was for children who were too retarded mentally to enter the public school. When Philip finally learned to walk, his mother drove him back and forth to school each day. She met other mothers whose children were like hers. She then began to talk about her problems with the director. She watched the teachers work with the children with patience and kindness and firmness. The teachers expected things of these children. Philip seemed happier. She could see some changes in his behavior. He was slowly learning to do some things for himself.

His mother's feelings began to change. She could share the responsibility for his care. She was happier, too, as she watched him begin to learn. She loved him, and now she could face the future with some hope.

If Philip's parents had had other children to care for, they might have decided to place Philip in the state institution for mentally retarded children because they would not have had time to meet his special needs. They could have continued to see him regularly and bring him home for visits. He would have been with people who understood and accepted his rate of growth. He would have had a place with other children like himself just as he has in the special class at the school he attends.

COMMON PROBLEMS

We will meet children who have not faced any of the difficulties we have mentioned, but who still are having a difficult time in living with other people and liking themselves. They are in trouble even though the reasons are not clear to us.

When we are trying to understand children's behavior, we need to be aware that they may have had many kinds of experiences which have special meaning for them, either helpful or harmful.

**Some children are troubled for obvious reasons
and some for reasons we may not know about.**

Many seemingly unimportant experiences may cause real disturbance in people's lives. Moving to a new community is an example. It may be very hard to leave one's friends behind at certain points in one's life and go to live in a strange place and find new friends. It may be easier to do this when one is eight or nine than when one is thirteen or fourteen. It may be easier for some people than for others. It may be easier if one happens to find a new friend quickly or if people in the new school and community welcome strangers.

The "timing" of an experience is important. If a child has to adjust to a new house and yard just after he has had to accept a

North American Van Lines

A common experience such as moving can be upsetting to
some children.

A child's age may be important in
determining what an experience
means to him.

Julia Richman High School, New York

new baby in the family, for example, he may find the move more difficult than he might otherwise have found it. Mary, who was separated from her mother at two, might not have found it so difficult if this had occurred when she was six years old. The year-old child is more seriously disturbed by his mother's absence than the four-year-old is.

TO DO AND DISCUSS

ACTIVITIES

1. Read an article on homemaker services and report on it to class.

2. If there is a social agency in your community which offers a homemaker service, find out how the homemakers are selected and trained, how they are paid, what services are offered, and what types of families are served.

3. Report on one or more children who may be the victims of serious neglect. (a) What is the reason for the neglect in each case? (b) What personality weaknesses may a child have as a result of long and persistent neglect?

4. Contact a local social agency which places children for adoption and request information concerning the procedures to be followed and the criteria for selecting adoptive parents. Get a pamphlet or brochure, if possible.

TO THINK AND WRITE ABOUT

1. List several things that parents of an only child can do:
    a. To insure adequate socialization.
    b. To provide opportunities for play with other children.
    c. To prevent the child from becoming overindulged.

2. What type of arrangement is best for each group of very young children when mothers are forced to work outside the home?
    a. For children under three years of age.
    b. For children three, four, or five years of age.

3. In what way can each of the following assist a child with only one parent?

   a. Men teachers in the elementary schools.
   b. Sharing experiences with friends and teachers who are under-
      standing.
   c. The organization, Parents Without Partners.
   d. A homemaker provided by a community agency.
4. How can the relationships of adoptive parents and their children become as close and warm as those between natural parents and children?
5. What role must be played by parents when a child has a serious illness?
6. What is the best way to help a blind or otherwise handicapped child
   develop properly?
7. What are some typical symptoms which may lead parents to suspect
   that their child is mentally retarded?
8. What constructive steps should be taken by the parents of a retarded
   child?

REFERENCES   **PAMPHLETS AND PAPERBACKS**

Brumbaugh, Florence, and Bernard Rosche
Your Gifted Child: A Guide for Parents
New York: Collier, 1962

Burgess, Helen S.
Stepmothers Can Be Nice
Public Affairs Pamphlet No. 198
New York: Public Affairs Committee, Inc.

Carson, Ruth
So You Want to Adopt a Baby
Public Affairs Pamphlet No. 173
New York: Public Affairs Committee, Inc.

Dittman, Laura
The Mentally Retarded Child at Home
Children's Bureau Publication No. 374
U. S. Department of Health, Education, and Welfare

Freeman, Lucy
Children Who Never Had a Chance
Public Affairs Pamphlet No. 188
New York: Public Affairs Committee, Inc.

Hart, Evelyn
How Retarded Children Can Be Helped
Public Affairs Pamphlet No. 288
New York: Public Affairs Committee, Inc.

Hill, Margaret
The Retarded Child Gets Ready for School
Public Affairs Pamphlet No. 349
New York: Public Affairs Committee, Inc.

LeShan, Eda J.
The Only Child
Public Affairs Pamphlet No. 293
New York: Public Affairs Committee, Inc.

LeShan, Eda J.
You and Your Adopted Child
Public Affairs Pamphlet No. 274
New York: Public Affairs Committee, Inc.

Milt, Harry
Serious Mental Illness in Children
Public Affairs Pamphlet No. 352
New York: Public Affairs Committee, Inc.

Timberg, Eleanor Ernst and Kathryn Aring Gorhan
Selected Reading Suggestions for Parents of Retarded Children
Children's Bureau, U. S. Department of Health, Education, and Welfare, 1968

Weingarten, Violet
The Mother Who Works Outside the Home
New York: Child Study Association of America

Wolf, Anna W. M.
Helping Your Child to Understand Death
New York: Child Study Association of America, 1958

Wolf, Anna W. M., and Lucille Stein
The One-Parent Family
Public Affairs Pamphlet No. 287
New York: Public Affairs Committee, Inc.

Growing Up in School and Community

10

We are all influenced by the communities in which we live, even though the most significant influence is that of our homes. Relationships within the family lay the foundation for feelings of trust and confidence. We build on these foundations as we extend our world through experiences outside our homes. The patterns of thinking and feeling which we have established in the family will influence our responses to the outside world. As we grow, the community in which we live, the people we meet there, and the new situations we face will play an increasingly important part in shaping the kinds of persons we are. But each of us remains unique, the product of our individual heredity and environmental circumstances. The community is an important part of this environment.

Let us look briefly at what growing up in the community may mean to a child. We have been discussing the growth and development of young children in the first years which are years spent largely at home. But if we are interested in understanding and guiding children, we must also consider the kind of community in which they may live. As the child grows older, the school and, later, other aspects of community life play an increasingly important part in influencing the direction of his growth. As Walt Whitman has written, the child who goes forth becomes part of all he encounters and it becomes part of him. Every parent needs to be concerned with what his child may be absorbing from the community.

289

Some of us have grown up in large cities. Some of us have grown up in small towns or in the country. We may find it hard to imagine what it might be like to grow up in a place different from the one which we know. We are likely to prefer the city or the country, depending on which we know best. We have all been influenced by the place or places where we spent our childhood, just as we are now being influenced by the place in which we are living. We are not always aware of the ways in which our community may be influencing us.

There are all kinds of communities. One may be clean, neatly kept, and attractive. The neighborhood or the whole community gives the impression of being cared for by people who like living in it. The people there have created a good environment. Another place may give a very different impression. Paper, broken bottles, and all kinds of trash are scattered about. There are few trees and flowers. Sagging doors and broken screens have not been mended. Unkempt and uncared for, this neighborhood or community gives the impression that its people do not feel much respect for themselves or for their world. These people have not created a good environment for themselves.

No community offers an environment which is favorable in all respects or unfavorable in all respects. Some communities offer more than others. Much depends on the people living there. In addition, every individual is influenced by his community in different ways, and responds to it with his own unique patterns.

American Gas Association

Caterpillar Tractor Co.

What do you know about your community? What services does it offer? Who pays for these services? What advantages does this community have? What limitations? What can citizens do to improve the community?

Let us look briefly at some of the things which a community may offer which will affect the growth of children and the welfare of families living there.

GROWING UP IN THE SCHOOL

One of the most important resources in any community is the school system. Education today is playing a larger role than ever in the lives of people everywhere. More years are spent in school. More of a person's education takes place in the school. Adults are likely to return to school for vocational or personal improvement. Good schools are one of the greatest assets a community can have.

Entering School. Entering school is an important step for a child. It is a big step on the road toward independence. He will now spend more and more of his time with people outside his family. He will find friends of his own. He will learn more and more about the larger world. A successful school adjustment will depend to some extent on some mutual regulation between home and school. As with parents and children earlier, each must give some.

G. Belson

On his first day at school a shy child may prefer to play alone.

It is necessary for the child, the parents, and the school to work together to find a way to present school experience to the child so that he can be free to learn and grow in his individual way while also becoming a part of a group of other children.

How are children likely to deal with the new situation of entering school?

Some children will be cautious, waiting and watching, trying to see what it is all about and at last finding their places and taking part with confidence. Some of them may need special attention and others may not want much attention. They may like to depend on themselves and to proceed at their own rate in moving into the group. Others may hold back because they are really unhappy and afraid. They are bewildered by new experiences. They do not feel sure that there is any place for them. They need someone they can depend on for help.

Some children may need special attention when they start going to school.

San Diego City Schools

Some children plunge eagerly into the new activities of school.

In contrast, other children plunge eagerly into activities. They make mistakes and meet rebuffs, but these do not seem to bother them. They like doing things and soon find a place for themselves in the group. They express their ideas freely and may sometimes seem bossy, but this may be their characteristic way of dealing with experiences. Still others assert themselves in very demanding ways. They want to be "first" every time or to have the most of everything. Sometimes these children are unhappy and afraid, too, but their feelings are coming out in different ways than in the case of the timid children.

We see, too, many individual differences in the extent to which the children in a group seem to trust themselves and the teacher. We see differences in how sure they feel about themselves and in how independent they are. These differences will be there even though the children are quiet, active, slow, or quick to respond. An understanding teacher will perceive these differences and will adjust her expectations to them.

The developing sense of industry. For the school-age child the next task to master in personality growth is the development of feelings of satisfaction in accomplishment as opposed to the hopelessness which goes with feeling inferior. If the school situation is a favorable one, children of school age find increasing satisfaction in work and in achievement.

Children need a large measure of success at first in order to have faith in their own capacities. The confident child likes to work and accomplish things; the child who lacks confidence feels his efforts may be futile. With a belief in themselves, children enjoy working to achieve goals which are meaningful to them. They work with a sense of joy and do not waste their energies. The good school promotes healthy personality development as it encourages a child in his efforts to learn.

The end products or goals of activity are now more meaningful to children of school age than formerly. They are interested in both individual and group goals. As individuals they turn their efforts to learning to read and write, and to gaining skills in many areas. They also find satisfaction in group activities, such as games and projects. They like to work together and help each other. By the time children are six or seven, they usually prefer playing and working in groups to being alone. Group effort has become a real force in determining what they try to accomplish.

As children grow, their interest in accomplishment can be directed to individual or group goals. Some societies stress individual goals, others stress group goals. Where individual goals are stressed, each person competes against the others in working for his own ends. Little place is left for cooperative efforts. On the other hand, where group goals are stressed, individuals work to accomplish for the good of the group, with little opportunity for individual achievements.

The most lasting satisfactions come from environments in which both individual and group needs are served. In our society, it is possible for people to have freedom to develop their individual potentials and initiative. Opportunities are also available for individuals to find satisfaction in working together for things which are important, not just to the individual, but to everyone in the group. What we do in schools and in homes to help children establish patterns of work and accomplishment will determine the kind of balance our society attains in this respect.

A transition point. Each new experience throughout our lives presents a problem in adjustment. It is not always easy to move from the familiar to the new, especially when there is a great deal that is unfamiliar and little in our background to prepare us to cope with it. It is important to learn effective ways of coping with new situations for we keep facing them all through our lives. When we cope successfully with these transitions from the familiar to the new and strange, we grow in confidence.

The Soap and Detergent Association

Children need opportunities to feel competent and successful to help them develop faith in their own capacities.

Transition points are significant, and entering school is one of these important points for a child. Children who enter school are experiencing a separation from their familiar world. They are testing themselves out in a new environment and discovering things about themselves and others. They often need help in establishing successful patterns of coping with the new surroundings. When they succeed in doing this, they strengthen the trust they feel in themselves and in their own capacities for dealing with new and different experiences.

It is often easier to observe the characteristic patterns of a person as he faces new situations than it is at other times. By observing a child as he enters school, we may get a better idea of how far along he is with the developmental tasks he faces, with the forces of trust and confidence he has managed to build in himself. We may understand more about the kind of image he has of himself and of the world. We see some children who are already able to

Entering school is a transition point for children as they face a separation from their familiar world. The child who makes the adjustment well strengthens her feelings of trust in herself.

take the initiative in exploring and discovering things, trying themselves out in new roles, producing new combinations of ideas and finding a place for themselves in different groups. These children possess self-confidence. They are ready for school experience and need little help as they proceed with learning. They are using their capacities in creative ways.

Preschool experience.   Going to kindergarten or nursery school is usually a good first step in beginning school. Children leave their families for only part of a day, and are with children of their own age. They learn many of the things which will prepare them for learning to read, write, and use number concepts. Most of all, they learn ways of behaving in a group with a teacher. They learn what it is like to be in school. They learn more about themselves as they adjust to the expectations of other people.

For most children, experience in nursery school or kindergarten increases the likelihood of successful school experience. There is a tremendous amount for children to learn before they are ready to use symbols—that is, to learn that marks on a page stand not only for words and numbers, but also for ideas and concepts. Success in mastering symbolic learning depends to a great extent on the adequacy of the child's previous opportunities for learning. It depends on a variety of firsthand experiences where attention has been given to abstracting and associating elements in the experiences (identifying likenesses and differences, for example) and developing skill in formulating and communicating thoughts. Abstract learning is a very complicated matter, as we all know, and the foundations for it seem to be laid in experiences during the early years of a child's life.

In kindergarten, children learn to live in a group, adjusting their behavior to the needs of the group.

San Diego City Schools

The foundations for abstract learning have been laid in the experiences in the early years of a child's life.

Not all children have had sufficient richness and breadth of experience or have made enough use of language communication in these early years to lay a good foundation for school learning. Many children have had very limited experiences. They may never have been beyond a few city blocks. They may never have seen an open field, a barn, or a boat. Or they may have lived in an isolated valley and never have seen a tall building, a train, or a fire engine. Words relating to such things have little meaning to them. If, in addition, they have lived with people who do not use speech much, who talk only when necessary and seldom use words to describe or explain things, these children are handicapped when they enter school. Learning in school depends on the ability to use words, form concepts, correct misconceptions, and develop reasoning ability.

Most children will profit from the kinds of experiences offered in a good nursery school or kindergarten. These experiences will probably include a rich variety of firsthand activities, of exploring and combining things. Attention will be given to language communication—explaining and clarifying concepts. Experiences will be based on the child's level of readiness and will not consist of attempts to introduce first-grade learning to the child. For some children whose experiences have been quite limited, time spent in nursery school or kindergarten may be essential if they are to succeed in school. Academic success is important, not only in its own right, but also because of its effect on the child's belief in himself and in the value of his efforts.

Because we are becoming increasingly aware of the significance and extent of the learning which takes place in the preschool years, we now have Headstart programs under the Office of Economic Opportunity in the federal government. These programs serve the needs of children who have lacked adequate learning opportunities in these important years. The goal of Headstart programs is to make up as far as possible for these early disadvantages. The programs are set up to offer a wide variety of materials for play. There are experiences with art, music, and language, excursions into the community, and contacts with a variety of adults and other children. Improving the nutrition and health of the children is also a part of the program. Groups are small so that the children can profit from individual attention and guidance. There is evidence from extensive research studies that such programs can do much to overcome the handicaps of early disadvantages.

The Headstart program, of course, is similar to the one in a good kindergarten or nursery school. While most children will profit

The Soap and Detergent Association

Many children have very limited experiences. Nursery school and kindergarten will give them a better start in first grade.

Irvin Simon

Headstart programs provide learning experiences and play materials for children who did not have them in the early years.

from a year spent in kindergarten, those children whose early backgrounds have been limited may profit from more than one year in such a program before entering school. They are more likely to stay in school if they meet with success there. Making the best use of the capacities one has becomes increasingly important in the complex world in which we live today. People who drop out of school usually fail to share in the benefits of our rapidly expanding society as they otherwise might.

Today many of our public school systems have kindergartens. These are for five-year-old children and sometimes include the older four-year-olds. Nursery schools generally are not part of the public school system. The age range in nursery school is usually from three to five or through five.

Learning in school. In the first grade the child begins his more formal school learning. Experiences in the primary grades differ in different parts of the country. Since children grow and learn in different ways and at different rates, schools must plan for their needs. In one school a class may be divided into groups, with slower learners in one group and faster learners in another. In another school the class may be ungraded, in which each child proceeds at his own rate in learning the basic skill subjects. In this system, the group stays with the same teacher for more than one year and she guides their individual progress while they remain with their age group. There is a growing emphasis on looking at early childhood education as a unit comprised of nursery school, kindergarten, and the primary grades. A

In the first grade art and music experiences will continue and more formal learning will begin.

child should meet with as much success as possible in his early school years. There is general agreement that no child should be "failed" in his first year of school.

It is interesting to know how other countries meet the matter of individual difference. In some countries the school pays little attention to these differences. The child is expected to fit into the system with very little mutual regulation. Some countries give the child more time to mature before he starts school. The age of school entrance is set at seven. In England, for example, there is an "infant school" attended by children from five through seven. The work is equivalent to that done in our kindergarten and primary grades. Many European countries have nursery schools which prepare the

Hammid/Rapho-Guillumette

Nursery school provides opportunities not only for intellectual learning but also for social and emotional development.

children for school life. These nursery schools are attended by a larger proportion of children than are similar schools in our country.

School, of course, provides opportunities for intellectual learning. The child is fortunate when the experiences provided are broad and cover many areas. He is fortunate when they are suited to his level of readiness and his individual way of working. We continue to develop better methods of teaching so that children learn more with less effort. This is important for there is a great deal more to learn today.

In addition to intellectual learning the school makes possible a great deal of social and emotional learning for a child. At school he finds friends. Such friendships become especially important at the junior and senior high school levels, but the patterns for relationships are laid much earlier. At school the child must live and learn with others. He becomes aware of different points of view.

Tonka Toys

The child finds new friends and learns to share toys in nursery school.

He must begin to develop his own ideas about what things are important and right. He must decide in what things he will follow others and in what things he will go his own way. He must sometimes make compromises, but he must maintain his own separate identity while he fits into the social order and takes responsibility for it. All this is not easy. Much social and emotional learning takes place whether it is planned for in the school or not. We are beginning to give more attention to these areas of learning for they are personally significant to the child and influence the intellectual aspects of learning.

GROWING UP IN THE COMMUNITY

Every community has many types of services available to its citizens. The resources in any community will depend largely on the interest of its citizens and the effort they make to be informed and to play their part in the processes of government. To vote is not enough. It is important to understand the needs of the community and the issues involved in order to vote in an informed way. It is also important to do things for the best interests of the community if it is to be a good place in which to live.

Good communities strengthen good homes. In establishing a home each of us should be concerned about the conditions in the community where our children will be growing and learning. Let us look at some of the resources which are available in a good community.

Health services. A good community provides services which protect and promote the health of its citizens.

A hospital with good provisions for infant and maternal care is important to a community.

General Tire and Rubber Company

a. An adequate *public health department* will provide preventive services to help maintain high standards of health in the community. These services should include such things as inspections of the water supply and hygiene of food handlers and restaurants. They may include prenatal clinics, classes for expectant parents, well-baby clinics, school health services, and inoculations against public health risks such as smallpox and polio.

Federal grants are available through state departments of health to help maintain a full-time public health doctor working with public health nurses and sanitarians. Adequate standards for public health services are outlined under these grants.

b. A *hospital* is another important service. The Hill-Burton Act of 1946 makes federal funds available to help communities provide adequate hospital facilities.

Since most babies in the United States today are born in hospitals, a hospital with good provisions for maternal and infant care is important. Premature babies need special care and a good hospital will have the necessary facilities. If the hospital offers "rooming-in" arrangements (permitting the infant to be with the mother rather than in a hospital nursery), this is an indication that the hospital is giving attention to the emotional as well as the physical factors in maternity and newborn care.

c. *Guidance clinics* provide important services needed in a good community. Marriage counseling, family counseling, and child guidance counseling should be available. Well-staffed guidance clinics offer professional counseling to individuals or families who have problems which may interfere with satisfying and productive living. They help prevent delinquency and mental illness.

d. A safe *water supply* and adequate *sewage* and *garbage-disposal systems* are important to the health of a community. These services should be inspected carefully and frequently and maintained carefully.

Social services.   A good community provides social services for the welfare of its families.

Fisher-Price Toys, Inc.

A well equipped and well staffed day-care center for children whose mothers work is an asset to a community.

a. *Child care services* should include *day care centers* where young children may receive competent care when their mothers are at work outside the home or are unable to care for them for some other reason. The centers are usually supported by community funds. They may be operated by public or private agencies. The parents pay a fee, usually in proportion to their income. In 1958 there were more than two million children under six years of age whose mothers were working full time outside the home. The majority of children in most day care centers are children whose mothers are the sole support of the home. In many cases these children had no relative to care for them. It is often difficult for a working mother to find someone who can be counted on to give good care to a child on a regular basis. Well-staffed and well-equipped day care centers are urgently needed in most communities today. A good day care center returns manyfold the investment the community makes in it by protecting the welfare of children and giving support to the efforts of parents to maintain good homes.

Day care centers often provide *after school care* for children who would otherwise not be supervised in the time between the closing of school and their mother's return from work. They provide a place where the child can go after school, have a snack, play, and perhaps do his homework. He has responsible adult supervision in the center. His parent calls for him on the way home from work. This type of service helps prevent delinquent behavior and promotes healthy development in children who might otherwise feel neglected.

Some communities provide *home day care* for children under three years of age. An agency will investigate and supervise selected homes where a child under three may be left during the day. In most cases the federal Children's Bureau does not recommend group care of children under three years of age, for individual care is important to very young children. By the time a child is three, he should be ready to attend a day care center, where he can still receive individual care but share it as a member of a small group.

A community also needs *foster homes* for children who need to be cared for outside their own homes on a full-time basis. Caring for children under six in any type of institution on a twenty-four-hour basis is not considered desirable, and is not permitted in most states. Foster homes should be carefully selected and supervised to protect the child. Trained social case workers are needed for this.

b. A *homemaker service* is another community service which may be very important to young children as well as to older people. If a mother has an extended

Home day care for children under three is provided by some communities.

One-A-Day Brand Multiple Vitamins

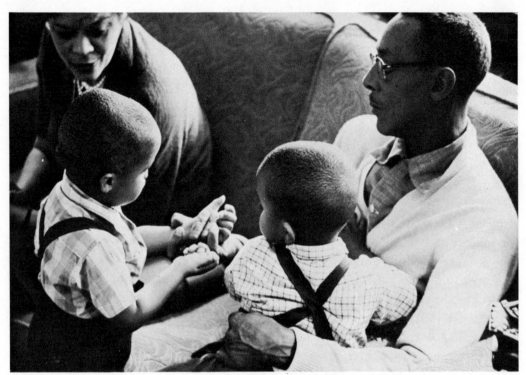

Children's Bureau Photograph by Burgess Howard

A community needs foster homes for children who must be cared for on a full-time basis.

illness and is unable to care for her family, the family may be able to remain together by using such a service. A homemaker is selected, trained, and paid by an agency, either public or private. She does the homemaking until the mother can care for the family herself. As in the case of the day care center, the family pays the agency according to their ability to pay. Homemaker services can be very useful in the case of older people. Old people may be able to continue living in their own homes if they have help for a few hours a day or once a week from a competent homemaker.

c. A *visiting nurse service* may be a great help to older people and families with young children. Many times a child, a mother, or

The mother who is overburdened with young children and illness in the family should request aid from the homemaker service.

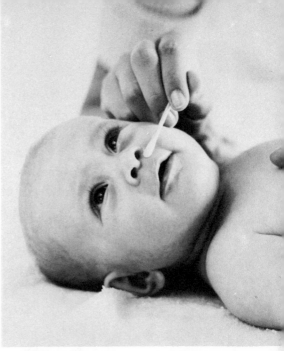

The visiting nurse may help the mother with the care of the young baby.

an older person can be cared for at home if there is some nursing service available. It is less expensive than hospital care and may be much better for the mental health of the patient and the family.

d. Both private and public agencies may offer *social case work services* to families. The nature of social case work has been changing through the past decades. The emphasis today is on helping people utilize their own resources to meet problems which arise. The professionally trained case worker discusses with a family the resources of the community and the role of agencies to which the family may turn. She helps them work out plans for the management of finances or solutions for problems of relationships. She tries to strengthen the family so that it can meet the strains which it faces. Good social case work is important for individuals and families having difficulties.

e. *Legal aid* service may be provided for families in need of such help. A well-staffed and well-administered *juvenile court* and perhaps a *court of domestic relations* provide important guidance in working out acceptable solutions for troubled families. These services seem to be especially needed in cities.

Recreation.   A good community makes provisions for the recreational needs of all the people living there.

a. There should be *playgrounds* and *park areas.* Some playgrounds may be on school grounds. Neighborhood parks should provide play equipment: slides, swings, a baseball diamond, and perhaps tennis courts. There may be a "tot lot" for the youngest children and their parents, with a sand area and a hard surface for wheel toys. Areas for picnics and for play should be available in the park.

b. A good *community center* offers recreational facilities to all members of the family—children, teen-agers, and adults. What the center is used for will depend on the interest and initiative of the

A good community provides parks and playgrounds.

National Association of Real Estate Boards

people in the community. There may be play readings or drama groups, craft groups, square dancing, and sports of all kinds. Scout groups or campfire groups may meet in the center. In the city such recreational centers are especially important.

c. A *swimming pool* and a summer *program of activities* are also important. The pool may be part of the community center. The summer recreational programs may be held on the school playgrounds. Opportunities for sports, music, drama, and craft activities make life in the community more enjoyable. Sometimes there are summer camps maintained by the recreation division of the local government. With more free time people need provisions for making wise use of their leisure.

d. Good *movie theaters* and an *auditorium* where concerts and lectures can be presented add to the recreational facilities of a community.

Education. Every community should offer opportunities, both formal and informal, for its citizens to continue their intellectual growth.

Education becomes increasingly important in today's world.

The Prudential Insurance Company of America

A good public school system is vital to a community.

a. As we mentioned earlier, a good *public school system* is one of the most important resources in any community. Schools can be centers of intellectual stimulation for adults as well as young people. Films, travelogues, lectures, and discussions on subjects of current interest all add to the life of the community. A strong parent-teacher organization can be an asset and should help citizens become better informed about educational questions and enable them to foster good educational practices in their schools. With active citizen support, school bonds will be passed when they are needed, and responsible, civic-minded people will serve as members of the board of education.

Adult education programs or programs for continuing education should be part of this kind of school system. Such programs may include Americanization classes for would-be citizens, classes in arts and crafts, woodworking, music, or sports, as well as in academic subjects and vocational education. These programs enrich the intellectual and recreational opportunities of a community.

b. Another important resource is a well-stocked *public library*. The library may have a children's reading room and story hours for children of different ages. It will have programs to encourage reading and will make its resources easily available for children and adults.

c. A good community may have *lecture* and *concert series* to bring the best in discussion and music to the people. There may be

A well-stocked public library is an important community resource.

A good community library has a separate section for children.

organized groups for the discussion of questions of local, national, and international interest.

Religion.   In a good community there should be a sufficient number of *places of worship* for the people living there. These places of worship will be well-attended and well-supported by the members. There will be services and programs to meet the spiritual needs of young people as well as older people.

Churches and synagogues which are actively interested in the welfare of the people and of the community are a source of great strength. They help give sound direction to the life of the community and to its growth.

Citizenship.   In a good community citizens will find ways to assume responsibility and to share effectively in the democratic processes of their community.

There may be service clubs of men and women who are alert to needs in the community. They give support in many types of projects. They may help a family which faces some crisis. They may purchase a piece of needed equipment for the local hospital, make a survey to determine some other community need, or perhaps arrange to provide a service such as sponsoring a day care center. These groups may also give leadership by taking a stand on issues such as the attitude toward minority groups in the community or toward providing better living conditions for disadvantaged families. During political campaigns, civic organizations may arrange for discussion and clarification of issues. They may gather information about candidates running for office and about issues to

Service clubs are alert to the needs of the community. One project may be to provide a nursing scholarship for a local girl.

Winthrop Laboratories

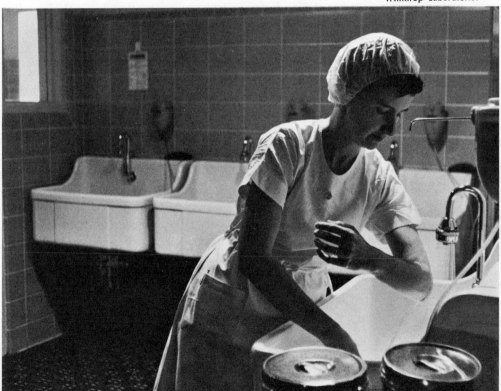

be voted on so that the voters may be informed. Other groups may
be active in arranging for exchange students from other countries
to come to the community, or for local students to study in other
countries and thus broaden the outlook of people in the community.
There are many ways in which citizen groups may contribute to
the enrichment of community life.

As it becomes necessary for governments to perform more and
more services, it is increasingly important for citizens to be informed
about the conduct of government and to feel responsible for having some share in the process. This is the essence of democracy.

Do citizens in your community take an active part in local government by informing themselves on issues, by voting, by being candidates for public office, and by supporting officials who are competent?

A good community is governed by responsible officials who
have the support of the citizens. Support is essential for a good police force. Adequate police and fire protection are likely to be found
in communities where citizens are interested and active in the affairs
of the community and support competent officials, including law
enforcement officers.

What is the attitude toward law enforcement in your community? What is
your own attitude?

In a good community zoning ordinances ensuring attractive and functional
expansion are passed and enforced. Growth

Community zoning ordinances regulate the lo-
cation of shopping centers.

B. Hamilton

You can contribute to your community by caring for children whose parents are voting.

Volunteer workers such as "candy-stripers" perform a great community service by helping to care for hospital patients.

is orderly and there is provision for such things as parking areas, shopping areas, and recreational areas. Plans take into consideration beauty as well as convenience. Sidewalks are in good repair; there are trees, open spaces, and benches in park areas. Streets are wide enough for the traffic, well-maintained, well-lighted, and free of litter. These things make a community a comfortable, pleasant place in which to live and bring up children. They happen because citizens are concerned about them and make an effort to achieve them through participation in responsible government.

What is the attitude toward city or area planning in the community in which you live?

We have talked about the services which we may expect from our community. We must remember that we ourselves owe something to the community. There are many small but important ways to give something back to the community in return for all that we receive. Children do something when they keep the school playground clean and the street free of litter. We all do something when we take care of public property and keep parks clean and in order. We help when we carry on our jobs in a responsible way. We also do our part by taking an active interest in the support of sound government and by giving some of our time to activities which help improve the life of our community—volunteering for youth programs or programs for handicapped people or old people, for example, or contributing to the cultural activities of the community.

In a democracy the government is the people. The responsibility for creating a good type of community for children to grow up in rests with us. Growing up in a good home, a good school, and a good community makes a difference in the lives of all of us. When the community is a good one, the child who goes forth will find what he needs to enrich his growing. Then he, in his turn, will be able to contribute someday to making this world a better place for living.

The Prudential Insurance Company of America

When the community is a good one, the child who goes forth will find what she needs to enrich her growing. Then, she in her turn, will be able to contribute some day to make this world a better place for living.

Dorsey Laboratories, Division of the Wander Company

ACTIVITIES

1. Learn as much as you can about a nearby Operation Headstart program. Try to arrange for one or two of your friends to go with you to see the activities and report back to your class about what you have seen.

2. Find out how many different opportunities for education are provided for both young people and adults in your community. Be prepared to discuss your findings in class and suggest changes in the educational system.

3. List the various recreational facilities available to the people of your town. What would you like to have added to those already available? Compare and discuss your list and those of your classmates. Perhaps your class could contact a representative of the local government and suggest some changes which would be beneficial to the entire community.

4. Prepare a report about one of the following topics. In each case, consider particularly provisions for individual differences.
   a. Early education in a foreign country.
   b. A comparison of primary education in two or more countries.
   c. A comparison between your parents' early education and your own experiences.

TO THINK AND WRITE ABOUT

1. Children react in various ways to the new situation of entering school. How would you help each of the following to adjust?
   a. The child who is cautious and trying to see what it is all about before participating freely.
   b. The child who plunges eagerly into activities and makes mistakes.
   c. The child who is unhappy and afraid, and bewildered by these new experiences.

2. In what ways does a child's entering school provide the following:
   a. A significant transitional step for him.
   b. An opportunity for his teacher to observe his progress with developmental tasks.

3. What can a teacher do to prevent a disadvantaged child from feeling hopelessly inferior in school achievement?

4. What types of learning experiences are provided in "Headstart" programs in order to help children from disadvantaged homes overcome their learning deficiencies?

5. How does the school aid the child in learning and adjustment by:
   a. Providing for individual differences.
   b. Providing opportunities for intellectual development.
   c. Providing opportunities for social and emotional development.

6. What types of physical and mental health services should be provided by a good community?

7. Give an example of the type of family situation in which each of the following social services would be helpful:
   a. Day Care Centers
   b. Homemaker Service
   c. Visiting Nurse Service
   d. Social Case Work service
   e. Legal services

8. If you were planning a recreational program for your community, what provisions would you make to meet the recreational needs of all the people?

9. What major function should be performed by each of the following in a community education program?
   a. Public schools
   b. Adult education programs
   c. Public libraries
   d. Lecture and concert series

10. What strengths may practicing religious groups add to a community? Are the various groups in your town adequately provided for?

11. How may community members assume civic responsibility and share in democratic processes through each of the following:
    a. Service clubs
    b. Civic organizations
    c. Becoming informed about local issues
    d. Strengthening law enforcement
    e. Favoring community planning
    f. Doing something to help the community

Applebaum, Stella
Your Family's Health
Public Affairs Pamphlet No. 261
New York: Public Affairs Committee, Inc.

Dach, E. M.
Your Community and Mental Health
Public Affairs Pamphlet
New York: Public Affairs Committee, Inc.

Day Care Services
Children's Bureau Folder No. 51
U. S. Department of Health, Education, and Welfare, 1960

Escalona, Sibylle
Children and the Threat of Nuclear War
New York: Child Study Association of America

Freud, Anna
Safeguarding the Emotional Health of Our Children
New York: Child Welfare League of America, 1962

Gruenberg, Sidonie M., and Hilda S. Krech
The Modern Mother's Dilemma
Public Affairs Pamphlet No. 247
New York: Public Affairs Committee, Inc.

Harrington, Michael
The Other America: Poverty in the United States
Middlesex, England: Penguin Books, Ltd., 1963

Home Maker Services in the United States—A Report
Public Health Services No. 746 (also 654)
U. S. Department of Health, Education, and Welfare

Ogg, Elizabeth
Your Nursing Services Today and Tomorrow
Public Affairs Pamphlet No. 307
New York: Public Affairs Committee, Inc.

Ogg, Elizabeth
When Parents Grow Old
Public Affairs Pamphlet No. 208
New York: Public Affairs Committee, Inc.

Ogg, Elizabeth
Psychotherapy—A Helping Process
Public Affairs Pamphlet No. 329
New York: Public Affairs Committee, Inc.

Osborne, Ernest G.
You and Your Child's School
Public Affairs Pamphlet No. 321
New York: Public Affairs Committee, Inc.

Stevenson, George S., and Harry Milt
Tensions—and How to Master Them
Public Affairs Pamphlet No. 305
New York: Public Affairs Committee, Inc.

Universal Opportunity for Early Childhood Education
Washington, D. C.: Educational Policies Commission, National Education Association, 1966

Weingarten, Violet
The Mother Who Works Outside the Home
New York: Child Study Association of America

BOOKS

Brim, Orville
Education for Child Rearing
New York: Russell Sage Foundation, 1959

Hymes, James L.
Effective Home-School Relations
Englewood Cliffs, New Jersey: Prentice-Hall, Inc., 1953

Read, Katherine H.
The Nursery School: A Human Relationships Laboratory, Fourth Edition (Chapters 14 and 15)
Philadelphia: W. B. Saunders Company, 1966

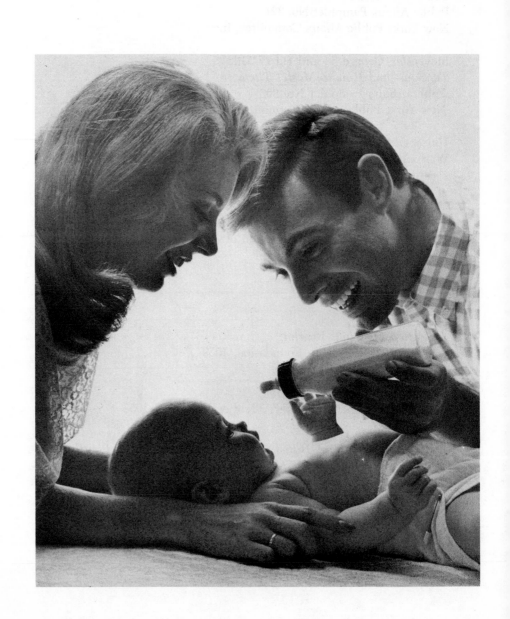

Children Are Members of Families

II

The children we meet come from many different kinds of families. They have already been influenced by their family experiences. The child's first understanding about what he is like, about what other people are like, about what it means to be a man or a woman, and about giving and receiving love grow out of his family experiences. From such experiences he learns, also, something about managing feelings of jealousy and rivalry. The child experiences his first close relationships with people within his family.

Family experience tends to be favorable for a child if he has parents who are happy together. When there are strong bonds of affection between the parents, they serve as good models for him. They give him the freedom and the discipline he needs. They answer his questions and give him opportunities to learn.

A favorable family experience means that the child is freer of needless fears and anxieties than one in a less fortunate family situation. Such a child can move more easily toward independence and a life of its own as a man or a woman, and is better able to take responsibility and to enjoy the experiences life brings.

As we care for and observe children, we learn to understand more about families and what they offer. We should try to help children whose family experiences have been less favorable by providing them with what they may have lacked.

THERE ARE MANY KINDS OF FAMILIES

All children are members of families. We each grew up in some kind of family through infancy and childhood. We therefore all know something about family life. We have all been influenced by our family experiences.

Some families are small. Some are large. Some have children spaced far apart in age. Others have children close together in age. Family patterns differ, also. Rural families are likely to have patterns of living that are somewhat different from those of city families.

A family changes. It varies at different times in its life history, as when the children are young and then when they are older. Circumstances change families, as when the father takes a new job, the family moves to another part of the country, or one parent dies.

Shafer/dpi

The children we meet will come from many different kinds of families.

Different cultures follow different patterns in family living. A Japanese family, a Mexican family, and an American family have different customs. But all over the world children are growing up in families.

The process of growing up is partly a process of separating oneself from one's family. It is a process of becoming increasingly independent and eventually taking responsibility for a family of one's own.

The bonds of affection among grown people are different from those among children. The ties between a husband and a wife in a good marriage are strong. It is the strength of these ties that helps the children to feel secure.

A man and woman who are happy and satisfied in their relationships with each other create a healthy climate for children to grow in. They show their children how a man and a woman can live together, enjoying each other and enjoying being parents.

The kind of family experience a child has known influences what he is. Walt Whitman put some of this idea into words when he wrote the poem "There Was a Child Went Forth," which appears in his collection of poetry, *Leaves of Grass*. He wrote this about the parents of a child:

". . . he that had father'd him and she that had conceiv'd him
        in her womb and birth'd him,
They gave this child more of themselves than that
They gave him afterward every day, they became
        part of him. . . ."

From the parents who become "part of us," we build our ideas about what we are like and our ideas about the relationships of husband and wife and parent and child. The standards and values of our parents become part of us just as much as the "family usages" and the language we speak.

If his family loves and values him, the child feels himself to be a valuable person. He builds confidence and self-respect. If the parents are pleased with what he does, he feels good and wants to accomplish more. If, on the other hand, the members of his family

Suzanne Szasz

If his family loves and values him, the child feels himself to be a valuable person.

are continually scolding or reproaching him, he comes to think of himself as a troublesome person, and he may continue to develop that way. The child tends to become the kind of person his family expects him to become. It helps us to understand the child if we know something about the way in which his family regards him.

FAMILY EXPERIENCES TEACH THE CHILD ABOUT LOVING

One of the most important things that a child learns from his early experiences in the family is about love and loving.

The basic learning about love begins for each of us when, as infants, we are cared for lovingly. Babies are easy to love —at least most of the time! Mothers want to care for them, love them, feed them, protect them, and give them what they need. Getting what one needs, feeling loved, feeling wanted and safe are good experiences for anyone to have. They lay a good foundation for relationships with people and make it possible to grow in healthy ways.

Having the experience of being loved by a mother and a father and perhaps by brothers and sisters makes it possible for a child himself to be loving. He can give love in return. There are things we learn from experience better than we can be taught about them.

The baby discovers his body. The infant starts early to discover himself and his body. He sticks a thumb or a finger into his mouth. He gets a different sensation from the feel of his own body than he does from the bottle or the rattle. There is a dawning realization that this is "me." He discovers his toes and examines his fingers and plays with them. He touches all the parts of his body. They feel different. When his mother washes his neck, his stomach, or his genitals, he gets different sensations. He is different in different parts of his body.

We let the baby explore and discover his body in his own way. We avoid overwhelming him with too many body sensations, such as tickling him too much or smothering him with kisses. He may get excited and overstimulated with more sensations than he can manage. This leaves him upset and confused and somehow out of touch with his own body. He needs time to come to know what his body is like and what he can do with it.

Young children often handle their genitals. This is part of the ordinary process of discovering themselves. Frequent handling of their genitals may mean that their clothes are too tight or that there

Experiences with grownups of both sexes are important to both boys and girls if they are to understand sex differences in a real way, not just words.

Suzanne Szasz   Max Tharpe from Monkmeyer

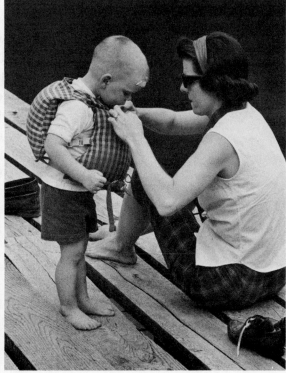

is some irritation. It may mean that they are seeking comfort. They may lack a feeling of being secure and loved. We simply add to a child's distress by reproving him. We need to help him feel better about himself and his world. He is not being "bad" by touching his genitals. As he grows and finds more activities that are satisfying to him, the child gradually stops touching his genitals.

The baby becomes aware of differences between the sexes. The infant soon discovers that there are differences among people. The way his father holds him is different from the way his mother does. His father's voice and the way he plays with the baby are different. From such experiences the baby begins to *know* about sex differences long before he understands the words *male* and *female*.

Every child needs to have experiences of being cared for by a father as well as a mother as a basis for understanding the meaning of *masculine* and *feminine*. He needs these experiences in his childhood so that he may in time come to know what it means to be a man or a woman. Sometimes children grow up in one-parent families. In such cases it is especially important that they have a chance to be with male and female relatives, such as uncles and aunts or friends of the family. Experiences with people of both sexes are important to both boys and girls if they are to understand sex differences in a real way, not just as words.

Later the child adds to his understanding of sex differences through experiences with a brother or a sister or with playmates outside the home. The older child may watch his mother caring for the new baby, bathing it or changing its diaper. He may help to care for the baby himself. He observes and asks questions, and his mother helps him to find answers to what he is wondering about.

Nursery schools or other group experiences are a help to children who do not have brothers or sisters. As they play together and use toilets together, they observe the differences between the sexes. They are free to ask questions and find answers. We help young children when we provide them with plenty of opportunities to learn more about what people of both sexes are like.

An older child may learn about sex differences by watching his mother bathe the baby.

Feeling comfortable about one's sex is important. Feeling comfortable about one's own sex is an important part of healthy growth and development. Accepting oneself as a boy or as a girl is not a matter of discovering that one has or has not a penis. It is a matter of the "models" one has to follow. A child tries to model himself after the people who are important to him. These people need to be people who accept themselves as male or female, as the case may be, and who accept the child as he is.

What are some experiences that help or hinder the child in accepting his or her sex? Here are some examples:

Parents who help a child to accept its sex are parents who like their little boy because he is a boy and like their little girl because she is a girl. They treat them as boys or girls, respecting their sex. Sometimes we see a father who wanted a son very much but has a daughter. The child finds that she must act like a boy to get his

Savings Banks Association of New York State

A little boy learns to identify with his father and see himself as a man.

approval. It becomes hard for her to feel good about enjoying feminine things. Sometimes we find a mother who does not really feel good about being a woman. She may have grown up in a family where girls were not valued. This made her wish that she were a boy rather than a girl. Her feelings are communicated later to her daughter, even though she does not put them into words. These feelings do not make it easy for the girl to want to be a woman. Sometimes we may see a mother who wanted a girl rather than a boy. She may dress her boy more like a girl and leave his curls long until he or his father protests. She is making it hard for her son to feel masculine. Fortunately, most parents who may have wanted a child of one sex or the other find that their feelings change when the baby is born. They like the baby and want it the way it is.

When we work with children, it is important that we like both boys and girls and accept them for what they are. We serve as "models" for them, and we need to feel comfortable about our own sex. We, too, need to like ourselves as we are.

Children learn from play. In their homemaking play, young children often try out different roles in the family. They pretend to be mothers or fathers, regardless of their sex. They want to understand more about what it is like to be a mother or a father. A boy may dress in women's clothes, or a girl may put on a man's hat and tie. This is natural and healthy. They are exploring and trying to understand roles. It is only if the boy continually dresses in girl's clothes, for example, or always wants to be the mother that we may suspect he is confused about his sex role. He may be having a hard time accepting himself as a boy. His parents need to think carefully about how they are treating him. They may need to consider how they have answered his questions about differences between boys and girls or where babies come from. In such a case we should make sure that we let him know how much we like little boys. We can encourage him when he takes the male role in play or does the kind of things boys usually enjoy, such as climbing up high, throwing balls, or building with blocks. But we will not make fun of him for dressing in girl's clothes. Feelings change from the inside, not the outside. He needs to have the chance to do his own changing and to discover satisfactions in being a boy.

The processes of elimination are important to a child. Urinating and having bowel movements are important matters in the life of a young child. It is disturbing to him if the adults around him feel disgust about these body processes, or if they try to make him feel ashamed of his behavior in connection with elimination. If this happens, the child may come to associate feelings of disgust or shame with other body processes. These feelings create problems later. They may, for example, make a child needlessly upset about certain medical treatments.

Learning to control elimination is a step in self-mastery and socialization for a child. He feels good about himself when he is successful. When he fails, he needs to be given confidence that he will succeed another time. We show him we are pleased when he stays dry. We let him help himself as much as possible. We want him to associate good feelings with his body processes.

We use the correct terms to refer to such parts of the body as penis and vagina. He should have such words in his vocabulary.

When a child is interested in watching other children use the toilet, we accept his interest as natural and acceptable. It is all right to want to know about everything. We need to feel comfortable ourselves. We may help him feel comfortable if we put things into words, commenting, "Boys stand up when urinating. Girls sit down." Such comments may help the child feel it is all right to comment and to ask questions about these matters.

CHILDREN ARE VERY MUCH INTERESTED IN
WHERE BABIES COME FROM

By the time a child is three, he is becoming interested in the question of where babies come from. It is important for him that we be ready with some answers. It may be helpful to read some of the good books on the subject that put explanations into words that young children can grasp, such as Karl De Schweinitz' *Growing Up: The Story of How We Become Alive, Are Born, and Grow Up;* or Marie Ets's *The Story of a Baby;* or Sidonie Gruenberg's *The Wonderful Story of How You Were Born.* There are also books to read to children about family experiences with a new baby.

The information that a child wants at first is simple. He is not interested in anatomy at this point. It is usually enough to say, "You grew inside your mother, under her stomach." Later he will want to know about the egg, or ovum, that was fertilized by a tiny sperm from the father and from which he started growing.

Most children imagine some fantastic things about prenatal life, in spite of all our efforts to make things clear to them. Selma Fraiberg, in her book, *The Magic Years,* points out that a large part of sex education is a matter of clearing up the child's misconceptions. Children have active imaginations at this age. They make up their own explanations and only slowly get things sorted out. It may be wise to ask, "What do *you* think?" when a child asks a question about babies. When we find out what he thinks, we are better able to clear up his misunderstandings. Also, we are less likely to give him information in which he is not much interested. It is also wise to avoid lengthy, detailed explanations with young children. When we tell a child more than he wants to know, he is likely to become confused. He is less likely to ask questions again. The important thing is to keep the conversational channels open. He needs to ask questions more than once before even the simplest facts of reproduction are clear to him.

Experiences that teach about growth and reproduction. There are many kinds of experiences that help extend the child's understanding of growth and reproduction. Children learn about growing things from experiences with animals—a cat with kittens, a rabbit with bunnies, a dog with puppies. As they watch animals caring for their babies and as they themselves share in the care of animals, they learn more about caring for young animals. With the arrival of a baby in his home or in the home of a neighbor, the child adds to what he knows about different kinds of care. A child can also discover that the egg may grow outside or inside a mother's body as he watches the hen sitting on the nest and the bird building a nest and sitting on it after the eggs are laid—in contrast to the rabbit who makes a soft nest for the babies just before they are born.

Watching baby chicks coming out of the eggs and observing a bowl of tadpoles slowly changing into frogs are further experiences that bring questions. The child slowly comes to understand more about growth changes and the time it takes for growth.

The way in which various baby animals are nourished is another fascinating subject. The child may observe a mother bird feeding her baby birds and a baby lamb suckling from its mother. He may watch a human baby nursing or taking milk from a bottle. These are absorbing experiences for him. He will have comments and questions.

Some children ask few questions. When this is the case, we may wonder whether the child feels that his question may be about a "forbidden" subject. We may need to raise some questions ourselves so that he can feel that it is all right to want to know about the subject in which he is sure to be interested. By the time a child is five years old, he should have a reasonably good understanding about how babies grow and are born.

Sometimes we meet a child who is incessantly asking, "Why?" without giving much attention to our answers. We may wonder whether he is afraid to ask the questions that are really on his mind. Such questions may be about reproduction. Instead of asking the real question, he keeps demanding "Why?" seeking and not finding out, because he has not asked the right question. It may be wise to offer some comments on the subject ourselves to help him.

Children love stories about what they were like and what they did when they were little or even what we did when we were little. Such stories help the child to learn something about the wonder of growth through time. He begins to realize that one has a past and can look forward to a future—a significant thing for us all. Grandmothers are usually good at telling such stories.

Sex experiences of the child.   Occasionally a child's interest in his body or in reproduction may lead him into explorations with other children, in sex play. It is probably important for us to be "preventers" of such sex play when possible. We should redirect children into other activities, but our redirection should be casual, without scolding or reproof. It is not "bad," for example, to try out taking a temperature rectally but it may do harm and it should be stopped with an explanation of why it should not be done. Children do not learn from unexplained prohibitions or disapproval. They may only become anxious or secretive. They need to understand reasons. Sex play is a natural outcome of an interest in finding out more about what people do. With more adequate supervision and explanation of what puzzles him, the child can become absorbed in exploring the vast range of experiences presently within his reach. Our part is to protect him from experiences which leave him anxious and guilty about what he may do with his body.

If he is unfortunate enough to have a sex experience with an adult, a young child will need to talk over the experience many times with someone whom he trusts. Talking about it reduces his anxiety and makes it seem less disturbing. Fear and anxiety are poor feelings to associate with sex. His parents can explain that some people are "sick" in the way they behave. They can help to reassure him that such things do not happen often.

A CHILD BEGINS LEARNING TO MANAGE FEELINGS OF JEALOUSY AND RIVALRY IN THE FAMILY

Members of a family love one another and help one another, but they also get angry with one another sometimes. They are jealous at times. Anger and jealousy are feelings that everyone has at times when he is living with others. A child must learn to manage such feelings. He begins in the family. The family is the "testing ground" for learning to deal with such feelings in constructive ways.

Personal relationships in a family are not simple. From the start the baby is involved in a triangle of mother, father, baby. He must share his mother's attention with his father. He becomes aware that he is *not* the *only* important member of the family.

If he is secure because he is having a generous amount of loving care, he can face sharing attention without feeling left out. He can even share attention with brothers and sisters. He may not like this sharing. He may sometimes resent it, but he can gradually accept it as he finds his own special place in the family.

There will still be times when every child will feel jealous. He will resent having to share attention. It is not easy to feel sure of one's place, especially when that place seems to keep changing. Parents help a child in this situation when they are happy in their relationship together, for then they do not need to compete for his affection.

The roles of mother and father.   The ordinary healthy baby starts with a strong attachment to the mother who cares for him. He is completely dependent on her, and he is concerned with only his own needs. He soon discovers and enjoys his father and others but continues to depend on his mother. He turns to her when he is hungry, tired, or hurt. At times, as he grows and develops, he feels some conflict in his relations with his father and his mother. He wants his mother all to himself. How many little boys have said that they are going to marry their mothers when they grow up! But in the end they must accept the fact that they are little boys, not yet men. They must move on to want to be like their fathers, not to take the place of their fathers.

A boy is helped toward this resolution of the conflict in his feelings if his mother is not too possessive and does not try to keep him too close to her for too long. He is also helped if his father is not too strict or harsh with him during this period. It is especially helpful if his father spends time with him. In a good family situation, the boy is able to move away from his dependence on his mother and his attachment to her and move toward his future role as a man.

When the family situation is not favorable because the father may be harsh or indifferent or the mother may be overly possessive, the boy may have a great deal of trouble managing his feelings. He may be very difficult, overly aggressive, or cruel with other children. He may, on the other hand, be overly passive and dependent. He may need a great deal of help if he is to grow, in healthy ways, out of his rivalry and dependency.

The conflict is usually most intense for the boy or girl around the ages of three or four. Even in a favorable family situation, the parents need to be especially patient and loving, but firm, with children at this time. When we take care of children at this age, we should avoid arousing jealousy and rivalry in them by such things as showing favoritism. We need to be sympathetic with the struggle they are having to manage the conflicts they feel.

For a girl the course of developing relationships through this period is different from that of the boy, but it is still difficult. She does not have to shift in her identifications in the same way. But she does want and need to have her father approve of her as a girl. She is in love with him in a sense, and her mother seems to be a rival. For her, too, as for the boy, help comes if the parents are secure in their love for each other so that there can be no real rivalry. The girl then begins to enjoy being like her mother rather than wanting to be her rival. She can enjoy doing the things her mother does and can look forward to her future as a woman. She finds increasing satisfactions with other children. She makes friends with them.

In the process of working through their feelings of rivalry and jealousy, children in a family sometimes quarrel with one another. But if the climate of the home is warm and friendly, and if the situations are handled reasonably by the parents, the children slowly learn how to manage their strong feelings. Through the quarrels and the reconciliations, they develop strong bonds of affection. They become able to differ, to compete, and to face failure without feeling upset, lonely, or helpless. They have battled successfully within the safe limits of the family. They have coped with feelings of resentment and jealousy. They are readier to turn the strength of such feelings into the service of real accomplishments.

The child's companionship and play with other children. Companionship with other children helps both boys and girls weather the storms of this period. The problems a child has in relationships with his peers are not so intense and full of conflict as the problems he has with adults. He lives in a real world with other children—one that seems more manageable and less full of fantasies. He can be successful in realistic ways. He learns with them and has fun doing things on his own level. He works and accomplishes his purposes. He explores and discovers and makes things.

In the family a child must learn to manage feelings of jealousy and rivalry.

It Takes a Lot of Growing—Carousel Films, Inc.

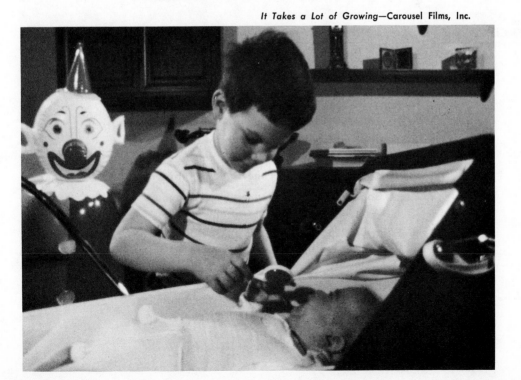

Group play in healthy neighborhood groups or in organized play groups (provided these offer plenty of opportunity for self-initiated play) gives the child a chance for relationships with children who are not his brothers or sisters. In group play the child can enjoy companionship with peers without the intensity of feeling that exists within the family. Feelings of jealousy and rivalry are easier to cope with at this age when they occur outside the family. The conflicts between friends are not as difficult to resolve as those between brothers and sisters. The child can learn to assert himself and yet remain friendly in the face of differences. All children need the chance to test themselves out in relationships with other children as they learn to deal with the feelings of jealousy and rivalry common to everyone.

In guiding children, we must be aware of all these feelings. We must be aware, for example, that a child will often be jealous when we give attention to another child. We must reassure him that we also value him and are concerned about him. We must avoid increasing needlessly the burden of jealous feelings. We must give instead the guidance that builds confidence, self-respect, and the capacity for close ties of affection and friendship.

ACTIVITIES   **TO DO AND DISCUSS**

1. **Observe and record an incident in which two or more children are playing "house" and pretending to be grown-up members of a family, such as a father or a mother.**
   a. **How do they portray their roles?**
   b. **What seems important to them in the roles?**
   c. **How does the observation help you to understand better the way a child may be seeing the roles of different family members?**

2. **Recall some situations in which you and your brother or sister or a friend quarreled. Describe the situation.**
   a. **What was the immediate cause of the quarrel?**
   b. **What other things do you think may have contributed to the quarrel?**
   c. **How did such quarrels usually end, and how did you feel afterward?**

3. a. Recall some misconceptions you may have had when you were young about where babies come from.

   b. How and when did you come to understand the facts about human reproduction?

TO THINK AND WRITE ABOUT

1. Discuss the possible ways in which a young child may add to his understanding about reproduction. How do you want your children to learn about sex matters? What reasons do you have?

2. Discuss the possible ways in which a young child adds to his understanding of the roles of a man and of a woman. What are some changes that have taken place in these roles in the last 25 years?

3. What are ways in which the community can be of help to parents in carrying out the role of a parent?

ARTICLES, PAMPHLETS, AND PAPERBACKS   REFERENCES

Eckert, Ralph
Sex Attitudes and the Home
New York: Popular Library, Inc., 1963

Hodges, Bruce
How Babies Are Born
New York: Simon & Schuster, Inc., 1966

Hymes, James L.
How To Tell Your Child About Sex
Public Affairs Pamphlet No. 149
New York: Public Affairs Committee, Inc.

Kirkendall, Lester
Helping Children Understand Sex
Chicago: Science Research Associates, Inc., 1952

Kirkendall, Lester A. and Elizabeth Ogg
Sex and Our Society
Public Affairs Pamphlet No. 366
New York: Public Affairs Committee, Inc.

Klemer, Richard H. and Margaret
The Early Years of Marriage
Public Affairs Pamphlet No. 424
New York: Public Affairs Committee, Inc.

Lerrigo, Marion and Helen Southard
Facts Aren't Enough
Chicago: American Medical Association, 1962

Lerrigo, Marion and Helen Southard
The Story About You
Chicago: American Medical Association, 1966

Levine, Milton
"Early Sex Education"
Young Children, October 1966

Levine, Milton
Helping Boys and Girls Understand Their Sex Roles
Chicago: Science Research Associates, 1953

Mace, David R.
What Is Marriage Counseling?
Public Affairs Pamphlet No. 250
New York: Public Affairs Committee, Inc.

Mace, David R.
What Makes a Marriage Happy?
Public Affairs Pamphlet No. 290
New York: Public Affairs Committee, Inc.

Milt, Harry
Young Adults and Their Parents
Public Affairs Pamphlet No. 355
New York: Public Affairs Committee, Inc.

Osborne, Ernest G.
Understanding Your Parents
New York: Association Press (Reflection Books), 1962

Sex Education and the New Morality
New York: Child Study Association of America, 1967

Wolf, Anna W. M.
Your Child's Emotional Health
Public Affairs Pamphlet No. 264
New York: Public Affairs Committee, Inc.

BOOKS

Arnstein, Helene, with staff of Child Study Association of America
Your Growing Child and Sex—A Parent's Guide
Indianapolis: Bobbs-Merrill Company, Inc., 1967

Baruch, Dorothy
New Ways in Sex Education
New York: McGraw-Hill Book Company, 1959

De Schweinitz, Karl
Growing Up: The Story of How We Become Alive, Are Born, and Grow Up
New York: The Macmillan Company, 1965

Ets, Marie
The Story of a Baby
New York: The Viking Press, Inc., 1939

Fraiberg, Selma
The Magic Years (Chapter 8, "Education for Love")
New York: Charles Scribner's Sons, 1959

Gruenberg, Benjamin and Sidonie Gruenberg
The Wonderful Story of You: Your Body, Your Mind, Your Feelings
New York: Garden City Books, 1960

Langstaff, Nancy, with photographs by Suzanne Szasz
A Tiny Baby for You
New York: Harcourt, Brace & World, Inc., 1955

Levine, Milton and J. Seligmann
The Wonder of Life
New York: Golden Press, 1952

Power, Jules
How Life Begins: The Exciting Story of Human and Animal Birth
New York: Simon & Schuster, Inc., 1966

Spock, Benjamin
Problems of Parents
Boston: Houghton Mifflin Company, 1962

Winnicott, D. W.
Mother and Child: A Primer of First Relationships
New York: Basic Books, Inc., 1957

Index